BAGHDAD or BUST

THE INSIDE STORY OF GULF WAR 2

BAGHDAD or BUST

THE INSIDE STORY OF GULF WAR 2

MIKE RYAN

LEO COOPER

First published in Great Britain in 2003 by
LEO COOPER
an imprint of
Pen & Sword Books Ltd,
47 Church Street, Barnsley,
South Yorkshire.
S70 2AS

Copyright © Mike Ryan 2003

A CIP record for this book is available from the British Library

ISBN: 1-84415-020-8
A catalogue record for this book is available from the British Library

Printed in Great Britain by
C P I UK

CONTENTS

PREFACE

On 20 March 2003, at approximately 05.30 local time (02.30 GMT), Cruise missiles fired from warships and submarines deployed in and around the Gulf region began impacting on central Baghdad the intention being to 'decapitate' President Saddam Hussein's military command structure with extreme prejudice- and to bring about the downfall of his evil regime, once and for all.

This book is a true account of the second Gulf War, as seen by the author and those that fought for the freedom of the Iraqi people.

DEDICATION

This book is dedicated both to the brave people of Iraq, who have endured so much for so long and are now free and their courageous liberators - the men and women of the British, American, Australian and Polish Armed Forces - many of whom gave their today for Iraq's tomorrow.

Their professionalism and selfless acts are an inspiration to us all.

ACKNOWLEDGEMENTS

I would like to thank the following individuals, organizations and companies for their kind help with this book: my good friend Faris, for his input on the current situation in Iraq; Dr Wafik for his opinions and political analysis on post-war Iraq; Saeed for his boundless enthusiasm and networking skills- you should be a diplomat; USAF PA, SOCOM, US DoD, 160th SOAR, 101st Airborne (Air Mobile), UK MOD, Australian DoD, 4 RAR, DVIC, NARA, USMC, RUSI, Irish Guards, RE, Royal Marines, RRF, Royal Artillery, RAF, RN, 16 Air Assault Brigade, ITN, and Avpro Aerospace.

All photographs unless stated otherwise are courtesy of the UK MOD, US DoD, Australian DoD and DVIC.

Special thanks to Brigadier Henry Wilson of Pen and Sword Books for believing in the project.

Finally, to my wife Fiona, and my daughters, Isabella and Angelina. Thanks for supporting me during the long months I spent researching and writing this book.

AUTHOR'S NOTE

In the interests of both British and American national security, certain technical, tactical, procedural or operational details have been either changed or omitted. This is for Operational Security (OPSEC) reasons, as there are still ongoing military operations taking place in this region.

BACKGROUND TO THE FIRST GULF WAR IN 1991

Operation 'Desert Storm' the 'Nintendo' war

On 2 August 1990, Iraq invaded its neighbour Kuwait, giving its leader Saddam Hussein control over a significant proportion of the worlds oil resources and it was feared that if the West did nothing, then Saudi Arabia, the key oil producer of the Middle East would suffer the same fate.

US President George Bush (Snr) realized that this situation was potentially extremely dangerous and initiated Operation 'Desert Shield' to prevent this from happening.

An international coalition force was put together under the flag of the UN with a mandate to retake Kuwait and this saw the largest concentration of special forces ever put together for a single conflict. In addition to the special forces and conventional coalition forces deployed for the ground invasion phase of the operation, the First Gulf War also featured the largest and most modern air-armada the world had ever seen.

On 17 January 1991, wave after wave of fighters, bombers and attack helicopters took to the skies for the commencement of Operation 'Desert Storm', the liberation of Kuwait. What then followed can only be described as systematic destruction on a scale never before seen.

For thirty-eight days, coalition aircraft attacked Iraqi military targets both in Kuwait and Iraq until there was virtually nothing left to hit. Every night our TV screens would be filled with multiple images of cruise missiles being launched from warships in the Gulf, followed by Patriot SAMs being launched to intercept Iraqs Scud missiles, followed by numerous video clips of precision guided bombs flying down air-shafts of command and control bunkers, making it all seem like a Nintendo computer game. This however was no game, as tens of thousands of Iraqi soldiers were being killed or wounded each week, and all because of one evil man, Saddam Hussein.

After the air campaign ended, the ground invasion phase commenced, but it was to be something of an anti-climax as it only lasted for 100 hours. It started off spectacularly enough with MLRS (Multiple Launch Rocket System) batteries firing salvo after salvo of rockets in support of advancing coalition armour and infantry- but ended quickly when the tired, hungry and war-weary Iraqi Army surrendered on mass, having endured weeks of relentless allied bombing that had quite literally decimated them.

Conclusion: The First Gulf War will probably be remembered in history as a war that was won by airpower alone, but that would be an inaccurate conclusion, as special forces also played a vital role in bringing about victory. Indeed, it can be strongly argued that had the coalition special forces failed in their operations to disrupt Iraqi Scud missile attacks against Israel, the outcome of the war might have been somewhat different.

As a point of interest, during Operation Desert Storm the coalition forces carried out a total of 109,876 sorties over the period of the forty-three day war, an average of 2,555 sorties per day. Of these, over 27,000 alone were targeted against Scuds, air defences, airfields, electrical power, headquarters, intelligence assets, biological and chemical weapons, communications, oil refining, and of the course the Iraqi Army. What makes this air-campaign unique in modern warfare, is not the amount of sorties flown or even the tonnage of bombs dropped; is the phenomenal accuracy and effectiveness of the precision-guided weapons used during this campaign, that is so impressive and unique.

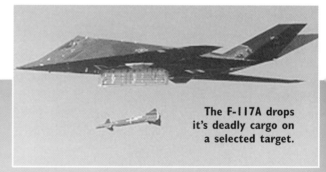

The F-117A drops it's deadly cargo on a selected target.

Cockpit imagery of selected targets from the Operation 'Desert Storm' campaign. These were familiar scenes for millions of TV viewers in the 1991 conflict.

The uniquely shaped F-117A Night Hawk in full flight, also known as 'The Black'.

INTRODUCTION

Since the end of the first Gulf War in 1991, a sense of unfinished business has prevailed throughout the United States Military and its masters in the White House- stemming from the regret of not taking out Saddam Hussein and his regime when they seemingly had the perfect opportunity to do so during Operation 'Desert Storm'. This issue has been debated over and over again on numerous occasions throughout the last twelve years in political circles, on miltary bases, in Congress and of course in the homes of Mr and Mrs Joe average in the good old US of A, without people fully understanding the rationale behind the decision to end the war when they did, without delivering the *coup de grâce* to Saddam when he was obviously on his knees - both militarily and politically. The truth of the matter is that during the latter stages of the war, both America and its coalition Allies were really pushing their luck, as they only had a UN mandate to remove Saddam from Kuwait and nothing more. For them to have pursued Saddam any further would have been illegal and downright dangerous as it would have caused further deep rifts to develop within the Middle-East possibly leading to conflict further a field.

One fact not fully appreciated at the time of the conflict, concerned the US Military's unease at the way in which the war was being portrayed by the media. This stemmed from the endless images of Iraqi ground forces being killed on masse by Coalition forces using precision guided munitions, making for shocking, yet compulsive viewing. The US top brass felt desperately uncomfortable with these images as they were portraying the war as a Turkey shoot and not a military conflict. The final straw, however, came when the horrific images of the Iraqi's fleeing Kuwait along the Basra highway were broadcast around the world as these showed graphic and deeply distressing scenes of utter carnage on a scale never before seen in a modern war.

The images showed decimated convoys of wrecked tanks, APCs, and vehicles both military and civilian, as well as the bodies of countless dead Iraqi soldiers. The scene stretched for literally miles and was the result of numerous air attacks prosecuted by American and coalition aircraft alike. At one stage in the air campaign, pilots refused to bomb or strafe any more Iraqi convoys as they felt that their actions bordered on cold blooded murder and not combat. In one case, RAF Jaguar pilots actually broke off an attack on the Kuwait to Basra road (nick-named the highway of death) as they felt that their mission was morally wrong as there clearly was no longer a threat to them or indeed the people of Kuwait.

Alarmed at the implications of such feelings, America's great and good

The most evil man in Iraq, Saddam Hussein, or is it?

amongst its military sought a ceasefire as soon as possible so as to limit any further political or military fallout thus Saddam surrendered. At this point in the procedings, America made a mistake that it would regret for twelve years. Instead of negotiating with Saddam directly, they dealt with his lieutenants leaving him free to go about his everyday evil business of killing, raping and torturing and this he pursued with a new and ever more determined vigour.

Not to be outdone by Saddam, America decided that if she could not beat Saddam by fair means, then she would achieve them by foul hence the Shia and Kurd insurrection in 1991. Exploiting Iraqs varied indigenous population, America encouraged an insurrection to overthrow Saddam-promising both military and intelligence support to those that subscribed to the cause- but when push came to shove it never materialized. To say that the Kurds and Shias were shafted, big time by the US intelligence agencies would be the under-statement of the year, but never the less it happened. America basically viewed the Kurds and Shias as a proxy force as they were to do all the dirty work against Saddam. They called the shots waiting in the wings to move right on in as soon as the situation allowed. However this was not to be, as America got cold feet about the insurrection and let Saddam and the remnants of his Army massacre the Shias and the Kurds on a massive scale the Kurds fairing somewhat better than their fellow revolutionaries in the south. Estimates put the Shia losses alone at hundreds of thousands, but we shall probably never know the real total, as entire families were brutally murdered and disposed of as if they were garbage thanks to America.

Iraq essentially has three main ethnic tribal sects, the Sunni, who primarily support Saddam, the Kurds, who detest Saddam and are based mainly in the north of Iraq, and the Shi'ite minority in the south, who absolutely abhor Saddam, and paid dearly for their hatred during the 1991 insurrection.

THE LEGACY OF THE FIRST GULF WAR

Following Iraq's humiliating defeat in the first Gulf War, and the failure of the insurrection against Saddam, Iraq reluctantly signed up to a series of UN National Security Council requirements. Among the many conditions imposed on Iraq, was the demand that Saddam agreed to the unmasking, verification and destruction of his Weapons of Mass Destruction (WMD). This demand included all apparatus for research and production and a list of all WMD programmes carried out prior to 1991.

In April 1991, the UN Security Council passed a series of resolutions establishing the authority of the UN Special Commission (UNSCOM) and the International Atomic Energy Agency (IAEA), entitling it to carry out the work of dismantling Iraq's arsenal of chemical, biological and nuclear weapons programmes as well as its Scud-type ballistic missiles.

The resolutions, resulted in the mass deployment of UN inspection teams to Iraq, but their work was hampered and frustrated at every opportunity by the Iraqis, leading to their withdrawal in 1998. Although their work was far from finished when they left, they did accomplish much during their tenure, to the frustration of Saddam Hussein.

Another major source of irritation for Saddam, were the 'no- fly' zones. These were set up after the first Gulf War to curb his internal repression of the Kurds and the Shia, and proved very successful. They were policed by both US and UK aircraft, who were engaged by the Iraqis on numerous occasions between the first Gulf War in 1991 and the second in 2003. The Iraqis, generally identified the British and American aircraft with their air-defence radar and then fired on them with AAA (anti-aircraft artillery) or SAMs. However, these aircraft were allowed to retaliate, and this they did on every occasion possible but not necessarily against the weapon system that had originally targeted them. Thus they were able to degrade Saddam's air-defence capability to such a degree, that when Operation Iraqi Freedom was launched, the resistance experienced by coalition aircrews from sophisticated integrated air defence systems was minimal, and largely ineffective compared to that of the first Gulf War.

The first humiliation, 1991. Iraqi POWs are stripped and bound.

In essence, the UN weapons inspection programme and the no-fly zone policy were a means of keeping Saddam in check until America had a legal and valid reason for terminating both him and his regime. However, on 11 September 2001, the status quo changed, and so did America. The gloves of patience were now firmly off for Saddam Hussein.

Liberation. A Kuwaiti citizen celebrates as troops rid his country of Iraqi invaders.

CHAPTER ONE

THE CASE FOR WAR

‘ **T**he time for denying, deceiving, and delaying has come to an end. Saddam Hussein must disarm himself, for the sake of peace, we will lead a coalition to disarm him.’

President George W. Bush, October 2 2002.

As the remains of the once tall and proud twin towers smouldered away in the bright sunshine of New York, only days after the terrible events of 11 September 2001, a man walked out in front of the large army of rescue workers as they paused briefly from their grim task of looking for survivors, and spoke. The man was America's President, George W. Bush, and as he stood on a pile of debris at Ground Zero on 14 September 2001 and addressed them, this is what he had to say when some of the rescuers in the crowd shouted over that they couldn't hear him; *'I can hear you. The rest of the world hears you.'* He then vowed, *'The people who knocked these buildings down will hear all of us soon.'* He was referring of course to those he really thought were behind the attacks on that fateful day: *'Saddam aids and protects terrorists, including members of Al-Qaeda,'* he later declared.

His rationale for such a statement lay in the fact that on 11 September 2001, as the world watched America burn, his arch enemy Saddam Hussein was sitting in a bunker in Baghdad, awaiting a US retaliation. But this was before the attacks had even begun!

Saddam Hussein and his evil regime had been linked to terrorism once before, when one of his intelligence officers, Ramzi Yousef, masterminded the first attack on the World Trade Centre in 1993 but the Iraqi connection at the time was never really taken seriously by the US Intelligence Services, as they were still gloating over their victory in the Gulf War in 1991. This was to be a catastrophic mistake-as Yousef had made detailed plans for a further attack on New York, where he indicated the use of aircraft in such an operation. But their significance and indeed their role was never understood. However, his maternal uncle, Khalid Sheikh Mohammed, did take the plans seriously-as he both masterminded and implemented the 9-11 attacks. Amazingly, there was another Iraqi connection in Mohammed Atta, the ringleader of the 11 September attacks, as he frequently met with Iraqi officials in Prague, prior to the attack.

THE EVENTS OF 11 SEPTEMBER 2001

11 September 2001, a date that will be etched in the minds of everyone around the world forever, as it marks the day that Terrorism Inc. perpetrated its biggest and most spectacular attack on the world's most powerful nation, the United States of America.

The attack commenced at 8.45a.m. US Eastern Standard Time, when a Boeing 767 of American Airlines crashed into the giant North Tower of the World Trade Center in New York. At first it was assumed that it was just a dreadful accident. However when eleven minutes later another Boeing 767 belonging to United Airlines hit the South Tower, it was clear that something very sinister was going on. As millions of people around the world watched the scene of carnage unfold on live television the first of the two towers started to collapse in a horrific and violent way, then barely twenty minutes later the second tower imploded in a similar manner. As the giant clouds of grey dust filled New York's spectacular skyline, a cold reality dawned on the world that it had just witnessed the worst terrorist atrocity in history, where thousands of innocent people, from all walks of life and from many nations, had been murdered in cold blood before their eyes.

It was a sickening scene but more was yet to come. News was now coming in of a further two incidents, involving airliners. It was confirmed that a Boeing 757 of American Airlines had crashed at 9.38 a.m. into the symbol of America's military power, the Pentagon. All fifty-eight passengers and six crew members were killed along with 190 people on the ground. It was later announced that a fourth aircraft had also crashed near Pittsburgh, in suspicious circumstances. Fearing that more attacks were still to come, President George W. Bush was advised to take to the air in his personal aircraft Airforce One, the theory being that while he was airborne he was safe from attack.

During the following days and weeks after the attack, it was revealed that the aircraft had all been hijacked by Arab terrorists under the alleged leadership of America's arch enemy, Osama bin Laden. The attacks had been meticulously planned and executed by a very sophisticated and well connected terrorist network which caused great embarrasment to the American Intelligence Agencies, as they had failed to stop them despite growing evidence of an intended attack on the American mainland.

The political and emotional fallout began to mount over who was to blame for the events on 11 September 2001, which was now being referred to as nine-eleven. There was just one question to answer. What was America and her allies going to do about it? Despite strong fears of a rash reaction from America's

The moment the South Tower was hit. The second impact proved that this was no accident.

President George W. Bush, bows his head in silence, after addressing the nation, in respect for those killed in the Twin Towers disaster.

President George W. Bush, he remained remarkably composed and rational in what was a highly charged and emotional period in America's history.

The following remarks were made in a CIA statement dated 7 October 2002:

> 'Our understanding of the relationship between Iraq and Al-Qa'ida is evolving and is based on sources of varying reliability. Some of the information we have received comes from detainees, including some of high rank. We have solid reporting of senior level contacts between Iraq and Al-Qa'ida going back a decade.
>
> 'Credible information indicates that Iraq and Al-Qa'ida have discussed safe haven and reciprocal non aggression. Since Operation Enduring Freedom, we have solid evidence of the presence in Iraq of Al-Qa'ida members, including some that have been in Baghdad.
>
> 'We have credible reporting that Al-Qa'ida leaders sought contacts in Iraq who could help them acquire WMD capabilities. The report-

ing also stated that Iraq has provided training to Al-Qa'ida members in the areas of poisons and gases and making conventional bombs.

'Iraq's increasing support to extremist Palestinians coupled with growing indications of a relationship with Al-Qa'ida, suggest that Baghdad's links to terrorists will increase.'

THE CASE FOR WAR

President Bush was also advised that Saddam's regime was at the centre of Osama bin Laden's terrorrist network and that his operation was purely an elaborate smokescreen. Essentially, Osama bin Laden provided the ideology, and recruited the foot soldiers, while Saddam Hussein provided the operational direction and terrorist training facilities. As one advisor said when referring to the 9-11 attacks, *'Only a state has the resources to carry out the most massive, stupendous attack in human history.'*

There is much to support this theory, as US forces discovered several terrorist training camps in Iraq, during Operation Iraqi Freedom and indeed fought with many foreign terrorists that were defending them.

After one counter-terrorist operation in north-eastern Iraq on 30 March 2003, a US Special Forces soldier remarked, *'There's plenty demonstrating Al Qaeda's presence.'* As credible as this information was at the time, it simply wasn't

The face of a terrorist. Osama bin Laden.

enough to justify an all-out war with Iraq, as ongoing military operations were already taking place against Terrorism Worldwide Inc. in places such as Afghanistan, Yemen and the Philippines under the banner of Operation 'Enduring Freedom'.

When America and its coalition allies first went to war with Iraq in 1991, they had a UN mandate to do so, but getting another one was going to be no easy task, as they were soon to find out.

And the justification for this new war was Saddam's weapons of mass destruction (WMD).

'America must not ignore the threat gathering against us. Facing clear evidence of peril, we cannot wait for the final proof- the smoking gun- that could come in the form of a mushroom cloud.'

President George W. Bush, 7 October 2002.

SADDAMS WEAPONS OF MASS DESTRUCTION

Under the leadership of President Saddam Hussein, Iraq had both developed and used weapons of mass destruction on a scale that is without parallel in modern history. For him, weapons of mass destruction were there to be used, be it against an enemy or indeed his own people. This threat was not an idle one either, as he had used chemical weapons on many occasions, as shown in the table below.

However, for reasons unknown he shied away from the operational use of biological agents.

DATE	AGENT	TARGET	CASUALTIES (Approx)
Aug 1983	Mustard	Iranians/Kurds	less than 100
Oct-Nov 1983	Mustard	Iranians/Kurds	3,000
Feb-Mar 1984	Mustard	Iranians	2,500
Mar 1984	Tabun *	Iranians	less than 100
Mar 1985	Mustard/Tabun*	Iranians	3,000
Feb 1986	Mustard/Tabun*	Iranians	8-10,000
Dec 1986	Mustard	Iranians	thousands
Apr 1987	Mustard/Tabun*	Iranians	5,000
Oct 1987	Mustard/Nerve agents*	Iranians	3,000
Mar 1988	Mustard/Nerve agents*	Iranians/Kurds	Hundreds

Known documented occasions where Iraqi forces have used chemical agents (Nerve agents are marked *)

The following chemical and biological agents are known to have been possessed (and even used) by Iraqi forces.

WEAPONS OF MASS DESTRUCTION
CHEMICAL AGENTS

MUSTARD: First used in the First World War in the form of a gas, it was one of the earliest chemical warfare weapons to be used in combat and created great suffering for all its victims. Mustard gas is a burning agent, and is usually delivered by means of a shell or a rocket warhead. It is a liquid, which gives off a vapour causing severe burns to exposed skin and eyes and, if inhaled, damages the respiratory tract, mucous membranes and lungs. If ingested, it causes vomiting and diarrhoea.

TABUN: Also known as 'GA', was one of the earliest nerve agents to be developed, and was originally used as an insecticide in Germany. It is a clear, colourless and tasteless liquid with a fruit like odour, and its primary effect is an unremitting attack upon the body's nervous system. The effects are extremely rapid, and involve tightness of the chest, vomiting, cramps, involuntary defecation, the collapse of the respiratory system and ultimately, death. A lethal dose of Tabun to the respiratory system, will kill within one to ten minutes, while from skin absorption, it can take between one to two hours.

SARIN: Also known as 'GB', is a nerve agent, and like Tabun, originated in Germany as a pesticide. It is a colourless, non-persistent liquid with a vapour that is slightly heavier than air so, therefore, it tends to hover just above the ground. When subjected to wet or humid conditions Sarin degrades swiftly, but with greater temperatures its lethality endures.

Initial symptoms are a headache and runny nose, followed by vomiting and diarrhoea, leading to convulsions and finally death. Only minute quantities of Sarin are required for an attack as was demonstrated in Japan on 20 March 1995, when a lethal dose was released in the Tokyo subway system-resulting in twelve deaths and fifty-four severe injuries.

VX: is the third of Iraq's nerve agents, VX (V= venomous) and was discovered by British scientists in the 1950s while developing an insecticide. After further research in both the United States, and Britain, it became a chemical weapon. It is a persistent and highly toxic nerve agent, which in its normal state is a clear, odourless and tasteless liquid. Symptoms may occur within minutes or hours, and are similar to those of Sarin.

BACTERIAL AGENTS

BACILLUS ANTHRASIS: This is a bacterium and causes anthrax infections through cuts in the skin (cutaneous), breathing (inhalation) or swallowing (ingestion). This is not the most effective weapon in Saddam's arsenal, as vitually all cutaneous cases can be cured with proper medical treatment-and if none is available, some eighty percent of victims will recover naturally without any form of professional medical help. However, in the case of inhalation, the outcome is far more serious as it resembles a common cold initially, then progresses to severe breathing problems and nrevous shock, culminating in death. If ingested, by means of liquid or contaminated foods, the result is intestinal anthrax, which is characterized by acute inflammation of the intestinal tract leading to symptoms such as vomiting, fever, vomiting blood and severe diarrhoea. In this form of the disease, the results will be fatal in some twenty-five to sixty percent of victims.

AFLATOXIN: These are fungal toxins that act as a highly potent carcinogen often killing the victim years later rather than instantly by way of destroying the liver. In the case of pregnant women, the effects can be horrific as they may result in babies that are either stillborn or have severe mutations at birth.

BOTULINUM TOXIN: Probably among the most toxic substances ever discovered, its effects lead to paralysis of the nervous system and result in death by suffocation. Initial symptoms usually start to appear within one hour of contact but can take up to eight days in some cases.

RICIN: A very potent toxin, that is a by-product of the castor plant bean (Ricinus communis), and one that has deadly effects. It is generally dispersed in an aerosol form and produces a pathologic change within a victim in eight hours of contamination and severe respiratory failure and death within thirty-six to seventy-two hours.

METHODS OF DELIVERY FOR CHEMICAL AND BIOLOGICAL AGENTS

Although Iraq has tried and employed many different methods of delivery for its weapons of mass destruction, the preferred method is by means of shell or rocket warhead.

The original method of delivery for their CW/BW agents in the early 1980s was by way of 155 mm artillery shells, which could carry three litres of agent and 122 mm rockets which could carry as much as eight litres. Both systems proved very accurate in operation, but required many rounds to be fired before an effective agent blanket could be laid over a designated target area. There was also of course the issue of limited range.

To overcome these problems, the Iraqis developed a series of aircraft bombs that had the capability to carry anything from sixty-five to eighty-five litres of agent, which was considerably more than the artillery based systems-but yet still not enough for the Iraqis. As a solution to their problem, they modified an aircraft drop-tank-normally used for fuel carriage-but now capable of delivering 2,200 litres of CW/BW agent. However, there was a problem in that Iraq, could never hope to match coalition air superiority, so therefore would find it extremely difficult, if not impossible, to deliver such a weapon accurately-unless it was on a one-way suicide mission.

Other methods were also tried by the Iraqis, including the use of modified helicopters and unmanned aircraft-but both methods proved unreliable and tactically unsound. That said, some aspects of the research was fed into other key programmes, such as the CW/BW warhead delivery system that was tried and tested on both the Scod-B and al-Hussein missile systems. However they were only launched with conventional warheads during the first Gulf War in 1991.

DELIVERY	MUNITION	AGENT	QUANTITY (Litres)	DATE
Artillery	122mm rocket	Botulinum Toxin	8	Nov 89
	122mm rocket	Botulinum Toxin	8	Nov 89
	122mm rocket	Aflatoxin	8	Nov 89
	155mm shell	Ricin	3	Sep 89
Helicopter	aerosol spray	Bacillus Subtilis	8	Aug 88
Aircraft	bomb	Bacillus Subtilis	65	Mar 88
	bomb	Botulinum toxin	65	Mar 88
	bomb	Bacillus Subtilis	85	Dec 89
	bomb	Botulinum toxin	85	Nov 89
	drop tank	Bacillus Subtilis/Glycerine	2,200	Jan 91
	drop tank	Simulation-water	2,200	Dec 90
	drop tank	Simulation-water/Potassium Permanganate	2,200	Dec 90
	drop tank	Simulation-water/Glycerine	2,200	Jan 91

Known documented occasions where Iraqi forces have tested biological weapons or simulated their use.

NUCLEAR WEAPONS

Although Iraq never possessed nuclear weapons, it certainly tried to develop them. Iraq, first started nuclear research in the 1950s, and had progressed to such a level by the 1980s, that it threatened the security of Israel. The Israeli's however, were not prepared to wait and see, and launched an air strike on 7 June 1981 against Iraqs nuclear reactor and research facilities at Osirak.

The mission was a complete success and set Iraq's nuclear weapons research back to such a degree that the Iraqis turned their attention to chemical and biological agents instead. However, during the Iran /Iraq War of the 1980s, they returned to their nuclear program and set themselves an objective of developing and producing a twenty Kiloton (KT) nuclear weapon which would be comparable in power with the American bombs dropped on Hiroshima and Nagasaki in 1945.

After the first Gulf War in 1991, the Iraqi nuclear program was set back yet again, on account of the activities of UNSCOM, who discovered large quantities of nuclear related material during their many searches-much of which was later destroyed or confiscated. As successful as these operations were, they were never enough to put paid to Iraq's nuclear ambitions, and indeed, on several occasions, Iraq was caught red-handed trying to buy forbidden items such as aluminium tubing.

THE THREAT

'Baghdad for now appears to be drawing a line short of conducting terrorist attacks with conventional or C B W (chemical and biological weapons) against the United States. Should Saddam conclude that a US-led attack could no longer be deterred, he probably would become much less constrained in adopting terrorist actions. Such terrorism might involve conventional means, as with Iraq's unsuccessful attempt at a terrorist offensive in 1991, or C B W Saddam might decide that the extreme step of assisting Islamic terrorists in conducting a W M D (weapons of mass destruction) attack against the United States would be his last chance to exact vengeance by taking a large number of victims with him.'

From a CIA letter to the Senate, dated 7 October 2002.

Armed with new intelligence on Iraq's WMD capability and indeed more importantly, its intent to use it, America set to work on planning a military campaign to remove it.

From a legal standpoint, America took the view that it already had UN resolutions in place that backed them for such a campaign. They included, resolutions 678 , 687 and 1441 that were adopted under Chapter VII of the UN Charter, which allows for the use of force for the express purpose of restoring international peace and security. UN Resolution 678, sanctioned in 1990, stated that 'all UN members are to use all necessary means to secure the removal of Iraq from Kuwait while Resolution 697, sanctioned in 1991 declared a ceasefire with Iraq provided 'IT SURRENDERED ITS WEAPONS OF MASS DESTRUCTION.' As for UN Resolution 1441, sanctioned in 2003,- this simply reinforced what had already been stated in previous Resolutions such as in 697.

The UN however, did not agree with America's legal viewpoint, and demanded the return of the weapons inspectors - thus starting a battle of wills between the Council of the United Nations and the President of the United States, George W. Bush.

By November 2002, America had an Operational Plan (OPLAN) in place for Iraq, but needed to deploy more forces to the region for what was to come. It therefore suited them to be seen to comply with the UN's wishes for more time to be given to Saddam to disarm rather than agree to the return of the UN weapons inspectors.

George W. also faced another problem, that being the issue of proof. No one in the UN doubted for one minute that Saddam was a tyrant or indeed that he had used weapons of mass of destruction in the past, as this was already an accepted and proven fact. However, what they didn't have, was cast iron proof that Saddam was still involved in the research and development of such weapons, and that he still possessed some-having hidden them from the weapons inspectors. What America needed now, was a 'smoking gun'; some piece of damning evidence that would convict Saddam once and for all before the eyes of both the UN Council and those at home in Capitol Hill who still doubted the legality of a war with Iraq on account of UN Resolution 1441, they felt it was little more than a legal fig leaf, designed to protect the UN from critiscism, rather than a ringing endorsement for US action.

THE CASE

To say that President Bush was frustrated with the UN, would be a gross understatement, as he felt that America had every right to go to war with Iraq, especially after the events of 9-11. There was also America's closest ally, Britain, to think of as the justification for a war with Iraq had yet to be accepted by both the British Parliament and the public at large. This was indeed a very serious issue, as the British Prime Minister, Tony Blair was getting a hard time from his political colleagues, ironically more so, from his own political party rather than those of the opposite house- with some of his most trusted and loyal government ministers eventually resigning as a matter of principle as they simply did not like, or agree with, what Britain and America were doing.

President Bush, not wanting to appear unsympathetic to Prime Minister

Blair's plight agreed to delay his plans for a short period, while the UN weapons inspectors went about their business in Iraq- the theory being that this would help Blair, and at the same time convince the UN Council members that this was a just war, and one that should be supported. However, Bush,s efforts with the UN were not going well as virtually every permanent member of the United Nations Security Council wanted to give the weapons inspection teams more time, as they seemed to be making good progress despite Saddam's best efforts to hinder them.

As America, tried yet again to persuade the UN to come around to their way of thinking by passing a resolution on Iraq, France dropped a political bomb shell on them, stating that no matter what happened, she would veto. For President Bush, this was the final straw, as there was no way that a Resolution could be passed now, and with his political patience now at an end, he gave the United Nations, what amounted to an ultimatum as they could not agree on a way forward, or indeed how to deal with Saddam Hussein and his weapons of mass destruction.

'The United Nations Security Council has not lived up to its respon-sibilities so we will rise up to ours' said Mr Bush.

Within days of Mr Bush's ultimatum, a summit was held on 16 March, at the US air base at Lajes on the island of Terceira in the Azores its purpose being to discuss the disarmament of Iraq. However, after only ninety minutes of talking between US President George Bush, British Prime Minister Tony Blair, Spanish Prime Minister Jose Maria Aznar and Portugese Prime Minister Jose Durao Barroso, it became obvious to all concerned that their was little left to discuss that had not been covered already on numerous occasions prior to this. With that in mind, the meeting ended with this statement by President Bush,

'Tomorrow is a moment of truth for the world. Many nations have voiced a commitment to peace and security and now they must demon-strate that commitment in the only effective way, by supporting the immediate and unconditional disarmament of Saddam Hussein.'

President Bush, then set a one-day deadline for the United Nations in which they were to demand the immediate disarmament of Iraq or for it to be disarmed by force.

However, before they could issue such a statement, President Bush gave Saddam Hussein and his sons a final ultimatum: leave Iraq within forty-eight hours or face war. In response, a defiant Saddam Hussein, stated that if Iraq were to be attacked, he would take the war to anywhere in the world, *'wherever there is sky, land or water,'* he said.

With war now looking imminent, the UN ordered the withdrawal of its weapons inspectors on 18 March - as there was a serious risk of them of being taken hostage if they remained in situ. It was now not a question of if there was going to be a war, but when and only one man had the answer to that question.

GOOD, BAD AND DODGY INTELLIGENCE

One of the most bizarre, and as yet unexplained aspects of the war with Iraq, relates to the case made before the United Nations by Colin Powell, when he tried to solicit their support by means of a document, that is now ridiculed throughout the world the so called 'smoking gun' dossier. This document was supposed to be the damning proof that would convince everybody that the war was just and right, and most important of all, neccessary. However, within minutes of the presentation commencing, it fell flat as all it basically consisted of was muffled taped telephone calls and non-substantiated allegations, that were long on assertion but short on fact.

The American's however, were not the only ones to make mistakes in the intelligence war, as Britain also dropped a political clanger in September 2002, when the British Foreign Minister, Jack Straw presented what he believed to be the British equivilent of the 'smoking gun' dossier.

The only parallel between the two, being the fact that they both ended up being discredited and ridiculed- so much so that the British document is now known as the 'dodgy dossier' and is the subject of much heated debate in Britain. This stems from the fact, that much of the document had been plagiarised from existing open source reports and documents, and an article by an Oxford PhD student, Ibrahim al-Marash. But the most damning part, concerned the claim that Iraq could launch a WMD attack within forty-five minutes by means of its surface-to-surface missile capability, a fact now hotly disputed by many. In his presentation to the Foreign Affairs Committee, Mr Straw described Iraq as 'uniquely dangerous' and a serious threat to the UK, by asserting that Iraq's 'illegal al-Samoud missiles' had a range of some 650 kilometres and were capable of attacking British military assets on Cyprus. However, this fact was proven wrong by the UN weapons inspectors, who found that it was only capable of a maximum range of 183km, and not 650 km as alleged. This figure however, was still beyond the UN imposed limit of 150 km, but even allowing for this, still fell way short of Mr Straw's claim. The revelation of such damning information is extremely serious for the British government, as it suggests that they led the British people into a war under false pretences; a very serious allegation indeed, as this is tantamount to treason.

CHAPTER TWO

THE INTELLIGENCE WAR

Military Intelligence is not discovered, it is produced by soldiers with special technical training. First they determine which things about the enemy and the environment are the most important to mission success. Then they determine the scope and parameters of these unknowns, develop theories about what they might be, and determine where and how they might look to discover the answers.

They and others then systematically search for the bits of information from across the battlefield that can confirm or deny their theories. As this information streams in, they confirm its reliability, analyze it for meaning, try to fit it into everything else they know, and attempt to synthesize it into a unified understanding of the situation. Finally, when this has been accomplished, they deliver the resulting Military Intelligence to those responsible for creating the plan and executing the operation to destroy the enemy.

MILITARY INTELLIGENCE

In order to defeat an enemy in combat you must first know something about him. How he prefers to fight, what weapons he has available, his numbers, his doctrine and how much he follows it, his current locations, his mission, and so on. You must also be able to take his information and combine it with the constraints imposed by the battlefield (weather, terrain, light and the socio-political situation) in order to formulate a prediction about what he can do and is likely to do. Only then can you create a battle plan that ensures his defeat. These things that you must know about the enemy are called Military Intelligence.

Mention modern warfare, and the chances are that you will discuss weapons such as the Stealth bomber and the Cruise missile. But how often will the subject of Intelligence be raised? Probably not much I suspect is the answer, and that's a pity because Intelligence plays a vital part in modern warfare.

In the days of the eighteenth century, intelligence gathering consisted of little more than spies and paid informants being sent overseas to monitor the movement of troops and ships in or around port areas. Although a crude and unsophisticated system by modern day standards, it was nevertheless in its day an effective one, simply because troops and their equipment could only travel overseas by means of ships or barges.

Today, the word 'intelligence' covers a plethora of different capabilities ranging from soldiers on the ground picking up local information, to satellites whizzing around the world that are capable of identifying an individual footprint.

Essentially, intelligence falls into four categories;

Space Based
Air Based
Sea Based
Land Based.

SPACE BASED: is defined as satellites or other vehicles that fly above the earth's atmosphere either in low or high orbit. Satellites effectively act as roving patrols over the earth, and generally operate in relatively predictable orbits. They can either perform as reconnaissance platforms or communication nodes, and in some cases both.

AIR BASED: is basically anything that flies, from hand held UAVs to high-flying strategic reconnaissance platforms and everything else in between. Air based reconnaissance is generally divided into two categories, tactical and strategic. Tactical covers the local battlespace, and involves small and medium size UAVs, such as the Gnat and Predator, as well combat aircraft such as the F-18 and Tornado, while strategic reconnaissance involves large UAVs such as the Global Hawk and high-flying platforms such as the U-2s.

SEA BASED: is defined as anything that operates on, above or under the sea. This includes conventional assets such as ships, aircraft, UAVs, helicopters and submarines, and unconventional assets such as those of underwater sensors, spy ships and special forces.

LAND BASED: is defined as all intelligence gathered on the ground. This term generally encompasses the activities of both military and government personnel, as well as those of informers and spies, etc.

Satellite based intelligence or SIGINT (Signal intelligence), as it is known within the military, is designed to detect transmissions from broadcast communications systems such as radios, radars and other electronic systems. The timely interception of such transmissions can be vital in modern warfare, as it provides valuable information to military planners on which to base decisions.

Take the Iraqi invasion of Kuwait for example. SIGINT provided one of the first warnings that an invasion was likely, when a Soviet built 350 mile range Tall King radar resumed operation on 29 July 1990 after being out of service for several months prior to the invasion. This small incident alone served as a trip wire and was enough to trigger intense US intelligence interest. From then on, all military activities and communications were monitored except for those using underground land-lines to communicate, as these, and indeed those of under-sea fiber optic cables cannot be intercepted by SIGINT. Contrary to popular belief, SIGINT also cannot detect non- electronic communications, i.e. those spoken by mouth.

SIGINT consists of several categories:

COMMUNICATIONS INTELLIGENCE (COMINT): is directed at the analysis of message traffic content and in its source. This particular work is extremely important as most military traffic is encrypted, and therefore requires computer processing to decode it. Also additional intelligence can be derived from analysis of the patterns of transmissions over time.

ELECTRONIC INTELLIGENCE (ELINT): This is devoted to the analysis of non-communication electronic transmissions, and includes radar transmitters (RADINT) and telemetry from missile tests (TELINT).

The United States operates four constellations of signals intelligence satellites in geostationary, elliptical and low earth orbits.

The current geostationary SIGINT constellation consists of three satellites. The first generation of these satellites was known as Rhyolite and had a ten metre wide receiving antenna, while the next generation known as Chalet, had an antenna width of tens of metres. The significance of the antennas width being, that the larger it is, the better it is at detecting lower power transmissions more precisely. Although the exact size of the latest generation of satellites is highly classified, what is known is that the last model, Magnum, which was launched in the mid-1980s had a deployable antennae of some 100 metres.

In addition to these geostationary SIGINT satellites, two others were launched in 1985 and 1987, to provide specialized coverage of the northern regions of the Soviet Union and, no doubt, others have been launched since to cover other potential threats.

In light of recent developments in both hypersonics and UAVs, it is highly likely that within the next decade there will be dramatic changes in the way that we carry out strategic reconnaissance and intelligence gathering. With new sensors and systems such as SAR (Synthetic Aperture Radar), we can now view radar imagery just like a photograph and can even see where enemy forces are hiding their troops and equipment, no matter how well camouflaged they are. This revolution in intelligence gathering has clear implications for ground forces, as they are now quite literally under surveillance twenty-four hours a day, which means that they are targets twenty-four hours a day.

Long gone are the days when photo-reconnaissance aircraft took photos of suspected enemy positions, and then raced back to their base to process them, while impatient photographic interpreters paced up and down waiting to pore over them. Now instead we have real-time imagery, so whatever the camera sees, we see, and all from the comfort of a remote viewing facility miles from the battlefield. This quantum leap in capability, has meant a seismic shift in tactics, techniques and procedures for operational and tactical planning, as we can now prosecute a war in real-time. For instance if a UAV (unmanned aerial vehicle) overflies a target and it is deemed high value, its operator can either engage it directly or data-link the details to other assets such as strike aircraft on combat air patrol (CAP). This capability minimizes the chances of a mobile target disappearing without being engaged and ensures an efficient and effective use of tactical assets.

In the case of air combat planners, they will in future warfare have the ability to use sophisticated software tools that will help compress the so-called 'kill chain' i.e. the time it takes to find, identify and destroy a target. Some of these technologies and concepts were operationally tested both in Afghanistan and Iraq and proved highly successful, especially in the anti-personnel role.

One initiative under investigation at present is the notion of a 'global strike task force', which would be made up of fighter and bomber aircraft on permanent short notice to deploy. Its role being to attack an enemy,s key command and control infrastructure, thus clearing the way for follow on forces, such as ground support troops. For such a concept to be successful, an unprecedented amount of battlespace information would be needed, and this would require an almost continual flow of intelligence, surveillance and reconnaissance (ISR) data. Infact twenty-four hour ISR capability is a prerequisite requirement of the global strike task force.

In one particular simulation exercise carried out at Nellis Air Force Base, Nevada, a global strike task force made up of F-22 fighters and B-2 bombers under the 24-7 ISR umbrella carried out a 'breaking down the door' attack against a foreign aggressor and rendered its force combat ineffective in a matter of hours.

Amongst the most interesting and useful technologies tried out during this simulation was a software program that collects and combines data from multiple stove-piped systems, and facilitates machine-to-machine talk for air-planning. So as to enable the global strike task force to become a reality, a totally new MC2A-X (multi-sensor command and control aircraft) was needed, and an experimental aircraft known as the Paul Revere is now under development.

The Paul Revere is a Boeing 707 flying information hub, equipped with communications links and workstations that receive sensor information feeds from the AWACS air-traffic control aircraft, the Joint STARS ground surveillance radar aircraft, the Rivet Joint signals intelligence aircraft and the

Airborne Battlefield Command and Control Center.

The Paul Revere has a crew of twenty-two, whose job it is to sort out intelligence information and data relating to 'Time critical targets', and then prosecute them right away with whatever strike assets are available. Should the Air Force decide to build an operational MC2A, its host platform will be a 767, as it is deemed the most suitable aircraft for the job. The long-term plan is to field the MC2A as part of a constellation of UAVs, space-based radar, space-based infrared sensors and ground stations.

In addition to the global strike task force concept, the USAF is also testing a new piece of software called the Master Air Attack Planning (MAAP) tool-kit, which is designed to retrieve and display all the intelligence information and data needed to build an air attack plan.

At present, battle planners currently spend as much as twelve hours trying to figure out what weapon to use against a designated target, as prescribed in the campaign blueprint, called the ATO (the air tasking order issued by the theater commander). The current procedure is to plot the air strike plan on a wall chart usually forty-eight to seventy-two hours before mission deployment commences, and then add post-it notes with target information as and when it comes in.

During a recent exercise, it took three people eight hours to plot their information on a wall chart, however when they switched to the MAAP tool-kit it with its on-line database and interactive capabilities, it only took a mere thirty seconds. Essentially the system is interactive with the target information displayed, and all actions are 'drag and drop', making it extremely easy to use. Air- Planners now, literally only have to grab aircraft icons on their computer screens and drag them on to a target location; once there a pop-up window allows them to specify their weapon of choice based upon the tactical information available. Because it is so effective and efficient, a typical ATO cell can now be reduced from nineteen to five people.

Also under development in the United States, at present is a new web-based software system that consolidates all battlespace intelligence received from ISR (intelligence, reconnaissance and surveillance) sensors such as those used on the U-2, the Global Hawk, the Predator, the Joint STARS, River Joint, AWACS, the Navy's EP-3 electronic warfare aircraft, as well as other US

Inset: The RQ-4A Global Hawk (Tier II+ HAE UAV). It can operate at ranges of up to 3000 nautical miles.

Below: The Predator UAV in flight.

national sensors. The rationale behind this complex programme, stems from the fact that today, each ISR platform has its own independent processing and control system. This, of course, means that the correlation of intelligence information takes too much time, and therefore delays decision timelines.

In effect the new system creates an overall picture of the theatre battlespace from a detached point of view, rather than a specific one. Should the tactical commander require more information on a subject, he simply clicks the icon on the screen and it will reveal the source of the intelligence as well as its location and current operational status; i.e. in the case of a UAV how much fuel it has left and how long it can remain on station.

As you can imagine such intelligence would be of immense value to an adversary, so stringent controls are in place to protect both its security and integrity. This is extremely important because the idea behind the web-system is that its contents can be accessed easily, but only by designated personnel. In theory, it is possible for an operator based thousands of miles away to re-task an ISR platform, but this in reality would only happen with the endorsement of a senior officer, as these are highly valuable assets. Indeed, some elements of these programmes have been tried out operationally, both in Afghanistan during Operation 'Enduring Freedom', and in Iraq, during Operation 'Iraqi Freedom', where they played a key role in de-conflicting the air space over the battlefield.

Currently within the military, there is a major drive to create a seamless 'Network Centric Warfare' capability that combines all elements of Command, Control, Communications, Computer, and Intelligence systems, or(C4I) as it is more commonly known.

Although this vision has not been fully realized as yet, work is well in hand to bring it about. Perhaps within the next decade or so, this integrated capability will be commonplace in our armed forces, but for now it is only an aspiration, albeit a very good one. Creating an integrated common C4I capability throughout our Allies is not as easy as it sounds, simply because everyone's systems architecture is different.

In addition to this problem, there is also the issue of language and protocol. For example the Americans use the term Intelligence, Surveillance and Reconnaissance (ISR), while in the UK the term ISTAR (Intelligence, Surveilance, Targeting and Reconnaissance) is used. In an attempt to avoid this confusion, the broader term C4ISTAR is used wherever possible as this is an internationally recognized term.

In a bid to overcome this problem once and for all, the US in November 2001, published an information guide called the ISR Integrated Capstone Strategic Plan (ICSP). This document stated that all ISR collection platforms and their sensors are to be interoperable with a commonly defined infrastructure. A commonly defined infrastructure is the focal point for integrating joint (multiple military services of one nation) and coalition (military services of more than one nation) interoperability. This common infrastructure requires a coalition to follow mutually agreed standards but does not require specific systems.

What may surprise you is the fact that the technology needed to achieve both joint and coalition interoperability is readily available now amongst NATO members, and has been for quite some time. In essence what is required for interoperability to be successful is a Common Operational Picture (COP) and a Common Tactical Picture (CTP) so that all forces engaged in a conflict fight as one cohesive unit. Also hindering interoperability is the issue of ever changing technology. For example if a unit knows that it will be upgrading its system capability in six months, will it correct a known fault before the upgrade? Probably not. Compounding this problem is the fact that while in a system of systems a weakness in one system is a weakness for all; a strength in one system may not necessarily result in strength for all.

New systems regardless of their sophistication and capabilities must be able to talk to older ones or they are useless, so it is imperative that system users follow the recognized IP (information protocol) or chaos will reign. This brings on the issue of system security. Information interoperability and assurance are actually two sides of the same coin. Yes, it is possible to develop a system with perfect interoperability, and yes it is possible to develop a system with perfect information assurance. However, it is not possible to develop a system with both perfect interoperability and perfect information assurance. In future operational planning, resource sponsors who develop requirements for new systems must take the time to define the tradeoff between information assurance and interoperability. While many of the tradeoffs between information assurance and interoperability become apparent after some serious reflection and evaluation of future operational trends, there is one area that remains somewhat insidious. There is a major difference between having all components of a network adhere to common standards, and having all components in a network identical. If all of the routers, servers, firewalls and operating systems in a network are identical down to model and version number, interoperability is certainly much easier. However, information assurance becomes a nightmare, because a security hole in one portion of the architecture can be exploited across all networks i.e. if networks are too closely 'inbred' a single virus infection can destroy them all.

CYBER WARFARE

The subject of network virus infection is an interesting one, as so-called cyber wars are now a significant part of modern warfare. We only have to look at Operation 'Iraqi Freedom', to see how a country's entire military combat effectiveness was substantially reduced, just by attacking its computer systems alone. Cyber-warfare is a serious weapon, and we ignore it at our peril. In the case of the Iraqi military, who ignored it totally, they found themselves under constant attack from infectious viruses, false orders and even pyschological warfare.

It is somewhat bizarre, that most of us will accept the realities of commercial computer cyber espionage, yet fail to accept and understand the realities of military and government espionage. Cyber espionage poses a very real threat, both to the military and to us as civilians, and in the next few years thanks to a US national policy for combating it, we may one day fully appreciate the seriousness of its effects.

Only recently a major cyber skirmish took place between China and Taiwan, resulting in the defacements and alterations of a number of each governments official web-sites. This however was not the first attack. In 1999, Taiwan experienced a nationwide blackout, followed a week later by a crash in the nations banking ATM systems, all results of a computer virus infection sent by China.

In a recent exercise, a reformed computer hacker stated that with twelve hand-picked computer technicians, he could do more damage to an adversary,s infrastructure than a B-1 bomber, and in a series of subsequent simulations carried out by US Intelligence, he was proven right. To counter this threat, at the Air Force Research Laboratory in Rome, N.Y, scientists are developing techniques and technologies for protecting data against cyber attack, as well as countermeasures to monitor and trace their source. This research is part of a vanguard of emerging fields known as cyberpathology, information resiliency, computer forensics and trans-attack analysis, all of which aim to assess damage, track, recover data and produce evidence for a counter attack or criminal prosecution if applicable.

Other counter cyber-warfare products include an electronic document tag that is planted or stored on a server, floppy disk or hard drive. The idea being that if an intruder connects to the tagged document by means of the Internet, a message is automatically sent back to a command centre for follow up action or monitoring. The tag can even be programmed to create a virus that will suck out all information contained within a targets computer, even if it is networked.

Cyber hackers are by nature devious and cunning, and play on the fact that most people within the military are computer security conscious while at work, but not while at home, and are therefore far more likely to succumb to an innocent looking e-mail on their home PC.

So next time you receive a dubious e-mail at home or at work, just beware because you never know.

ELECTRONIC WARFARE

In modern warfare as each side tries to gain as much intelligence as possible about their adversary, there is another war taken place in parallel that seldom gets a mention. They call it Electronic-Warfare (EW).

We all understand how intelligence warfare works in a conflict and more importantly why each side needs to learn as much as possible about their enemies tactics, strategy, location and leadership, but what we often fail to understand or indeed even appreciate is the importance of Electronic-Warfare.

The desire to gain superior awareness or 'knowledge dominance' in warfare is as old as combat itself. But in an era of multispectral sensors, instant communications and precision weapons, dominant knowledge may mean rapid and decisive victory, while inferior awareness may lead to rapid defeat. For an outcome of a conflict to be positive, it is simply not enough just to know your enemy, you must also ensure that your enemy does not get to know you. These twin imperatives of modern warfare are the rationale for the burgeoning mission of Electronic-Warfare.

Electronic-Warfare is classified under the umbrella of 'Information operations', and has been waged in one form or other for some sixty years now. Its introduction can be traced back to the advent of radar, when military forces around the world played a cat-and-mouse game with each other, that involved countermeasures and indeed counter-countermeasures. For a number of bureaucratic and doctrinal reasons, armed forces today prefer to differentiate between information and electronic warfare. However, for all practical purposes they are a common means to the same end, that being the goal of knowing your enemy better than he knows you.

In 1921, the Italian air-power theorist Guilio Douhet wrote in his highly influential treatise, *The Command of the Air*, that a prime reason why he believed offensive aircraft would revolutionize warfare was the impossibility of knowing all the possible routes they might use to approach intended targets. During the inter-war years, Douhet's argument became the accepted wisdom for fighting an air campaign, which probably explains why British Prime Minister Stanley Baldwin warned his countrymen in 1932 that 'the bomber will always get through.' Fortunately for the British they had radar, so any chance of the Germans being able to carry out large-scale surprise attacks against them was avoided, and when they did attack they were met by the relatively small but effective RAF, who ultimately prevailed. Since then, it has become apparent to military planners that the success of a modern day air-campaign is dependent on both the ability to suppress an enemy's defensive sensors, while at the same time having the ability to exploit them for offensive purposes.

In the early years of air-warfare, foiling enemy defences involved little more than flying under radar horizons or dropping reflective chaff. However, during the Cold War it was a different matter as Electronic Warfare became a far more complex and sophisticated affair. Part of the reason why Electronic Warfare became so complicated was simply down to the fact that; Defenders learned how to adapt to various strategies. Radars became more powerful, more discriminating, more agile and more effective. Command and control networks became more resilient and responsive and Surface-to-Air missiles (SAMs) became more numerous and smarter

In the case of the United States, things reached crisis point during the Cold

War when potential adversaries learned new and highly innovative ways both lethal and non-lethal of countering US Electronic-Warfare methods. As a result, the Pentagon embarked on a series of programmes that would give them back their edge, one of these was Low Observable (LO) technology, or stealth capability as we now know it.

As good as stealth was, it also brought problems, one of them being gross over confidence. This in part was down to the fact that in the early days of stealth it was oversold to the military as a revolutionary alternative to Electronic-Warfare. The sales pitch went along the lines, that stealth makes you invisable, so if you are invisable you cannot get shot down as your enemy cannot see you. That was the theory anyway, however the reality was somewhat different, as an F-117A pilot found out in Kosovo, when he was shot down by a SAM during Operation 'Allied Force' in 1999. Stealth does not make you invisable, it does however make your radar return appear much smaller then would be the case with a non-stealth aircraft of the same size. This of course means that a good radar operator will be able to spot stealth aircraft by virtue of their radar return alone, which is what happened in Kosovo.

By now the damage had been done within the US military, as they had neglected Electronic-Warfare to such an extent that it was now costing them aircraft in combat. In the 1990s the USAF withdrew its only two Electronic Warfare platforms, the EF-111 Raven and the F-4G Wild Weasel without replacing them. Instead the EW mission migrated to the US Navy's EA-6B Prowlers. This decision has created a problem for the United States military, as they now have a very serious shortage of EW aircraft, with only 120 Prowlers available.

To bridge this capability shortfall until the arrival of a new purpose built EW platform, the US military, is as a stop gap measure, currently investigating the feasibility of converting a number of surplus US Navy F-18 Hornet fighters into EW aircraft. This is actually a very good idea, since the F-18 has both the speed and range capability to keep up with modern strike packages, which is not always the case with the Prowler.

Ironically, as the United States has slipped behind in its EW capability, Europe has forged ahead, and in many cases now actually outperforms it, especially in the case of the SEAD (Suppression of Enemy Air Defences) mission, when performed by the Tornado multi-role aircraft.

In future conflicts, the role of Electronic Warfare (EW) may well be performed by unmanned platforms such as those of UAVs and UCAVs, as these systems are now deemed mature enough to undertake this vital and essential role.

THE DIGITIZED BATTLESPACE

By its sheer nature, warfare is inherently dangerous,confusing, unpredictable and difficult to control, where even the best planned operations can be thwarted by an adversary's refusal to concede defeat.

In the old days of linear warfare, a commander could see for himself what was happening on the battlefield and give orders accordingly. However, with the turn of the century when weapons technology and mass armies extended the scale of the battlefield this was no longer possible, as communications simply could not keep up. Thus, 'the fog of war' was born.

The First World War was probably the tactical commanders worst nightmare as communication consisted of little more than carrier pigeons, Morse shutters, semaphore flags and vulnerable telephone landlines that could easily be cut. As a consequence of this wars total mismatch between highly effective killing systems on the one hand and poor communication systems on the other, Generals felt powerless to intervene in a battle once events had begun.

Since then, of course there has been something of a revolution in communications, especially since the introduction of the radio. Now, the challenge is to sort out and manage the exchange of information so that it can be used in a form of tactical intelligence for both the benefit of the tactical commander and the soldier on the ground. Thanks to modern technology, we can now turn information into a digital form that can be used for the purpose of transmission, organisation, computation and display. In essence, Digitization gives us a birds-eye view of the battlespace as seen from all aspects, and not since the days of linear warfare has a general had such a good view.

Digitization gives a commander an instantly readable form of real-time tactical intelligence and information about the disposition and state of his forces, and with such information available a commander can direct operations with pin-point accuracy.

It is important to understand that digitization, in itself, is not a weapon, but it does however enable the better use of weapons. For example, if an infantry unit comes under effective enemy fire, the commander on the ground can instantly send back a contact report that will automatically generate support for him such as reinforcements, artillery, strike aircraft or attack helicopters.

In pure and simple terms, digitization is a military Internet that gives forces such as armour, artillery infantry and aircraft, a common tactical picture, so that everyone in the loop knows what's going on and more importantly where everyone is. It is basically the same technology that a taxi dispatcher uses to track the location of a cab, so that he can send the nearest one to the person requesting it.

There will effectively be two levels of digitization a lower tactical Internet primarily composed of voice and data radios connected to each other, and an upper tactical Internet for the use of voice, video and data exchange. This dual banding is essential as communications become fractured in urban areas and mountains, unless of course you have total cover; i.e. relay points on high buildings, unmanned aircraft flying twenty-four hours a day and satellites on permanent orbit over a designated area.

Having a seamless Digital communication system in future warfare will be essential, as modern day forces are considerably smaller than before, and yet have far more territorial responsibility. For example, an Army division today is responsible for an operational area of 120 x 200km, while by comparison, during the American Civil War, a brigade would occupy an area on the battlefield 200 metres long.

This tremendous growth in operational responsibility is only made possible by the use of digitization which effectively gives tactical commanders on the ground a force multiplication capability.

Coping with the demands of digitization requires a seismic shift in attitudes throughout the military, as many things need to change before its immense benefits can be felt by all. These changes range from new hardware to new software, such as the US Army's Battle Command Systems (ABCS) programme which has been designed to assist military planners in gaining access to sources of battlefield information, that includes logistics, maneuver, fire support, combat services support, air defence, intelligence, electronic warfare, terrain and even weather.

In recent years ABCS has moved from heavy workstations to light workstations, to small commercial notebook computers, and will no doubt move to even smaller systems in due course. There is no doubt that digitization will revolutionize the battlespace of the future, as every soldier is technically a reconnaissance platform and an information provider. However, we should not lose sight of the fact that technology supports the human on the battlefield, and not the other way around.

CHAPTER THREE

SHOCK AND AWE

With the storm clouds of war now gathering over Iraq, and a peaceful solution to this crisis now looking increasingly remote, America announced that it was going to mount a 'Shock and Awe' campaign against Iraq within days, and that the war would be a mere 'cake walk' for them.

In part their arrogant attitude was understandable, as they boasted the world's most powerful armed forces-bar none- with awesome destructive power to match. Their rationale was simple-they were going to overwhelm the Iraqis in days by means of a massive firepower demonstration that involved both cruise missiles and precision strike weapons in the first phase, followed by a massive ground invasion in the second phase. The architects of the 'Shock and Awe' strategy claimed that nothing could survive such a ferocious onslaught and that victory would be achieved by shocking the Iraqis into defeat, rather than killing or maiming them indiscriminately.

According to Harlan Ullman, a former US Navy pilot who co-wrote the book *Shock and Awe*, it would be nothing like the last Gulf War, when reporters in Baghdad watched Cruise missiles skim along above the city's streets.

'I don't think that anyone will be venturing outside during this attack,' Ullman suggested.

'During the last Gulf War the Allies launched 325 cruise and precision-guided bombs on the first day of a 40-day air campaign- now they are talking about 3,000 in 48 hours.'

The aim of the onslaught is to achieve "rapid dominance" both psychologically and militarily.

Ulman added:

'The idea is to replicate the shock and awe created by a nuclear bomb, but using conventional weapons.'

In essence, 'Shock and Awe' is the modern day equivalent of the highly effective

German Blitzkrieg strategy used during the Second World War - only brought up to date, and featuring more lethal weapon components in its orchestration of tactical and strategic assets.

US AIR WARFARE STRATEGY

The aircraft has evolved as an instrument of military and national power, Today, air space power is essential for success on and over the modern battlefield. In many instances it will be the most useful form of military power, the military power of choice, or both. Future advances in stealth, precision and lethality will make air space power increasingly more effective in all theatres of operations and at all levels of warfare across the range of military operations. Operation 'Desert Storm' (1991) validated the concept of a campaign in which air space power, applied simultaneously against strategic and operational centres of gravity (COGs), rendered opposing military forces virtually ineffective. Aerospace power emerged as a dominant form of military might. It was decisive primarily because it achieved paralysis of the enemy at all levels of war with minimal casualties to friendly forces.

A conscious decision to prioritize objectives may drive the phasing of the air campaign plan by dictating a specific mission flow based on strategic and operational considerations. This will translate into assignment of relative values for specific target sets and individual targets. Attacks on target sets may take place in series or in parallel. The priorities may force the selection of either one of these schemes or some combination of the two. Attack in series generally refers to attacking targets in the highest priority target set sequentially, beginning with the highest priority target and continuing to the lowest priority, before initiating attack on the next target set. Attack in series may also refer to a sequential attack based primarily on geographical considerations. Attack in parallel refers to attacking targets across several or more geographically dispersed target sets at the same time.

Most campaign plans are built in phases. A phase represents a period during which a large portion of the forces are involved in similar or mutually supporting activities (deployment for example). A transition to another phase such as a shift from deployment to defensive operations-indicates a shift in emphasis. Phasing may be sequential or concurrent. Phases may overlap. The point where one phase stops and another begins is often difficult to define in absolute terms. During planning, commanders establish conditions for transistioning from one phase to another. The completion of the phases is determined by accomplishing measures of merit based upon the enemy threat after thorough analysis. Measures of merit help the commander determine when the next phase of a campaign should commence. A measure of merit is usually an objective measure that is subjectively determined to help indicate how well a campaign is progressing. The commander adjusts the phases to exploit opportunities presented by the enemy or to react to unforseen situations. The prudent commander will do what is necessary to become superior in the air. The effort to achieve air superiority (a means to an end) should not be waged with air assets alone. Naval and ground forces should play a role whenever possible.

AIR SUPREMACY: is defined as the condition when the enemy air force is incapable of effective interference. Through the complete destruction of the enemy air forces, this condition is the ultimate goal of an air campaign. Yet, this condition may be difficult or even impossible to achieve. It may occur however, through the establishment of a diplomatic 'no-fly zone'. Under the condition of air supremacy, the air commander employs all of his aircraft at will.

AIR SUPERIORITY: is defined as the condition when the conduct of operations is possible at a given time and place without prohibitive interference by the enemy. This is a necessary and obligatory condition to attain success in combat and overall victory in a war. The most efficient method of attaining air superiority is to attack enemy aviation assets close to their source at maintenance and launch facilities, early warning and C2 sites, and ground based air defence sites.

LOCAL AIR SUPERIORITY: which is purely geographic in nature, is characterized by well timed air attacks to coincide with enemy aircraft downtime, returning sorties, aircraft rearming, or gaps in air defence coverage. This condition may also occur in sectors across the theatre of military operations where the enemy may not have adequate assets available to ensure air superiority. In certain situations or against certain enemies, local air superiority for a specified period of time may be a more realistic goal.

AIR PARITY: is defined as the functional equivalency between enemy and friendly air forces in strength and capability to attack and destroy targets. Under the condition of air parity, where neither side has gained superiority, some enemy capabilities affect friendly ground forces at times and places on the battlefield. Air parity manifests itself to the commander primarily in the amount of fixed-wing aircraft used for direct support of ground forces. More aircraft are dedicated to interdiction and strike missions to gain air superiority.

Targeting priorities can be gauged by understanding enemy centres of gravity. The centre of gravity is a label that planners and strategists find useful for devising maximum payoff courses of action. Some military theorists hold that any function of vital importance to the enemy is a center of gravity, whether or not it is vulnerable. Those things that are both critical and vulnerable are normally the best candidates for direct attack. Key features of a centre of gravity are its importance to the enemy's ability to wage war, its importance to the enemy's motivation and willingness to wage war, its importance to the enemy political body, population, and armed forces, and the enemy's consciousness of these factors.

The Daily Air Tasking Order (ATO) is the published order which directs all the air missions. The joint air tasking cycle provides a repetitive process for the planning, coordination, allocation, and tasking of joint air missions/sorties and accomodates changing tactical situations or joint force commander (JFC) guidance as well as requests for support from other component commanders. The joint ATO matches specific targets compiled by the joint force air component commander (JFACC)/JFC staff with the capabilities/forces made available to the JFACC for the given joint ATO day. The full joint air tasking order (ATO) cycle from JFC guidance to the start of ATO execution is dependent on the JFC's procedures, but each ATO period usually covers a twenty-four hour period. At any given time there will be three ATOs in the works. The ATO in progress, ATO nearing completion and the ATO that's just beginning. The battle rhythm depends on a number of factors, and will probably be different for each exercise and contingency.

The master air attack plan (MAAP) assigns available weapons, delivery platforms to targets. A target is a geographical area, complex, or installation planned for capture or destruction by military forces. Targets include the wide array of mobile and stationary forces, equipment, capabilities and functions that an enemy commander can use to conduct operations at any level-strategic, operational or tactical. Targeting is the process of selecting targets and matching the appropriate response to them taking into account operational requirements and capabilities. The targeting process has six basic phases/functions:

1. Commander's objectives and guidance
2. Target development
3. Weaponeering assessment
4. Force application
5. Execution planning/force execution
6. Combat assessment.

Although commonly referred to as a 'cycle', the joint targeting process is really a continuous process of overlapping functions independent of a particular sequence.

Battle damage assessment (BDA) is one of the principal subordinate elements of combat assessment (CA). At the joint force commander (JFC) level, the CA effort should be a joint programme, supported at all levels, designed to determine if the required effects on the adversary envisioned in the campaign or operation plan are being achieved by the joint force components to meet the JFC's overall concept. The intent is to analyse what is known about the damage inflicted on the adversary with sound military judgement to try to determine what physical attrition the adversary has suffered; what effect the efforts have on the adversary's plans or capabilities and what, if any, changes or additional efforts need to take place to meet the objectives of the current major operations or phase of the campaign.

BDA is used to update the enemy order of battle. Accurate BDA is critical to determine if the target should be reattacked. BDA should include information

Pre-strike and battle damage imagery of a facility that was used to jam radio broadcasts of foreign news services and internal groups that tried to disseminate news and ideas contrary to the regime's viewpoint. The red arrows in the image below, indicate structural damage to two sides of the building, indicating a clean and successful strike.

relating BDA to a specific target (e.g., target coordinates, target number, mission number, munitions expended, target description); time of attack; damage actually seen (e.g., secondary explosions or fires, enemy casualties, number and type of vehicles/structures damaged or destroyed) and mission accomplishment (desired effects achieved).

US LAND WARFARE STRATEGY

For any war to be decisive, its outcome must be conclusive. The threat or use of army forces is the ultimate means of imposing a nation's will and achieving a lasting outcome.

Land operations seize the enemy's territory and resources, destroy his armed forces and eliminate his means of controlling his population. Only land forces can exercise direct, continuing, discriminate, and comprehensive control over land, people, and resources.

Land combat continues to be the salient feature of conflict. It usually involves destroying or defeating enemy forces or taking land objectives that reduce the enemy's effectiveness or will to fight. Four characteristics distinguish land combat:

SCOPE - Land combat involves contact with an enemy throughout the depth of an operational area. Forces conduct simultaneous and sequential operations in contiguous and noncontiguous AOs. Commanders manoeuver forces to seize and retain key and decisive terrain. They use manoeuvre, fires and other elements of combat power to defeat or destroy enemy forces. Land combat normally entails close and continuous contact with noncombatants. Rules of engagement reflect this.

DURATION - Land combat is repetitave and continuous. It involves rendering an enemy incapable or unwilling to conduct further action. It may require destroying him.

TERRAIN - Land combat takes place among a complex variety of natural and manmade features. The complexity of the ground environment contrasts significantly with the relative transparency of air, sea and space. Plans for land combat must account for the visibility and clutter of the terrain and the effects of weather and climate.

PERMANENCE - Land combat frequency requires seizing or securing ground. With control of the ground comes control of populations and productive capacity. Thus, land combat makes permanent the temporary effects of other operations.

Ultimately, it is the ability of Army forces to close with and destroy the enemy that allows an army to dominate land operations. Army forces close with and destroy enemy forces through manoeuvre and precision direct and indirect fires. An adaptive enemy attempts to lessen the effects of operational fires. However, with their inherent qualities of on-the-ground presence and situational understanding, army forces make permanent the otherwise temporary effects of fires alone. Domination extends from the certainty in the minds of enemy commanders that close combat with army forces, backed by superlative air and naval forces, will have two outcomes - destruction or surrender.

An Army contributes forces to combatant commands to conduct prompt and sustained combat operations on land. The objective of Army forces is land force dominance-defeating adversary's land forces, seizing and controlling terrain, and destroying the adversary's will to resist. An Army, supported by an Air Force and Navy, has a forcible entry capability that allows it to conduct land operations anywhere in the world. An army can also achieve prompt and sustained land dominance across the spectrum of conflict. It concludes conflict decisively to achieve national and military objectives.

An Army conducts four types of operations-offensive, defensive, stability, and support - to accomplish missions in support of the joint force commanders objectives. Offensive operations aim at destroying or defeating an enemy. Their purpose is to impose the commander's will on the enemy and achieve decisive victory. Defensive operations defeat an enemy attack, buy time, economize forces, or develop conditions favorable for offensive operations. Defensive operations alone normally cannot achieve a decision. Stability operations promote and protect US national interests through a combination of peacetime developmental, cooperative activities and coercive actions in response to crises.

US LAND POWER STRATEGY

Support operations employ army forces to assist civil authorities, foreign or domestic, as they prepare for, and respond to, crises and relieve suffering. Commanders synchronize offensive, defensive, stability and support operations to defeat any enemy or dominate any environment anywhere, anytime.

Combat power is the ability to fight. It is the total means of destructive or disruptive force, or both, that a military unit or formation can apply against the adversary at a given time. Commanders combine the elements of combat power, manoeuvre, firepower, leadership, protection, and information - to meet constantly changing requirements and defeat an enemy. Defeating an enemy requires increasing the disparity between friendly and enemy forces by reducing enemy combat power. Commanders do this by synchronizing the elements of friendly force combat power to create overwhelming effects at the decisive time and place. Focused combat power ensures success and denies an enemy any chance to maintain coherent resistance. Massed effects created by synchronizing the elements of combat power are the surest means of limiting friendly casualties and swiftly ending a campaign or operation.

Manoeuvre is the employment of forces through movement combined with fire or fire potential, to achieve a position of advantages with respect to the enemy to accomplish the mission. Manoeuvre is the means by which commanders concentrate combat power to achieve surprise, shock, momentum, and dominance. Operational manoeuvre involves placing Army forces and resources at the critical place in time to achieve an operational advantage. It is complex and often requires joint and multinational support. Development and intra-theatre movements are operational manoeuvre if they achieve a positional advantage and influence the outcome of a campaign or battle. Tactical manoeuvre wins battles and engagements. By keeping the enemy off balance, it also protects the force. In both the offense and defense, it positions forces to close with and destroy the enemy. Effective tactical manoeuvre continually poses new problems for the enemy. It renders his reactions ineffective and eventually drives him to defeat.

Close combat is inherent in manoeuvre and has one purpose, to decide the outcome of battles and engagements. Close combat is combat carried out with direct fire weapons, supported by indirect fire, air-delivered fire, and non-lethal engagements. Close combat defeats or destroys enemy forces or seizes and retains ground. The range between combatants may vary from several thousand metres to hand-to-hand combat. All tactical actions inevitably require seizing or securing terrain as a means to an end or an end in itself. Close combat is necessary if the enemy is skilled and resolute; fires alone will neither drive him from his position nor convince him to abandon his cause. Ultimately, the outcome of battles, major operations, and campaigns depends on the ability of army forces to close with and destroy the enemy. During offensive and defensive operations, the certainty of destruction may persuade the enemy to yield.

Firepower provides the destructive force essential to overcoming the enemy's ability and will to fight. Firepower and manoeuvre complement each other. Firepower magnifies the effects of manoeuvre by destroying enemy forces and restricting his ability to counter friendly actions while manoeuvre creates the conditions for the effective use of firepower. Although one element might dominate a phase of an action, the synchronized effects of both are present in all operations. The threat of one in the presence of the other magnifies the impact of both. One without the other makes neither decisive. Combined, they make destroying larger enemy forces feasible and enhance protection of friendly forces. Because it deals directly with soldiers, leadership is the most dynamic element of combat power.

Confident, audacious and competent leadership focuses the other elements of combat power and serves as the catalyst that creates conditions for success. Leaders who embody the warrior ethos inspire soldiers to succeed. They provide purpose, direction and motivation in all operations. Leadership is key, and the actions of leaders often make the difference between success and failure, particularly in small units.

Doctrine is the concise expression of how army forces contribute to unified action in campaigns, major operations, battles, and engagements. While it complements joint doctrine, army doctrine also describes an Army's approach and contributions to full spectrum operations on land. Army doctrine is authoritative but not prescriptive. Where conflicts between Army and joint doctrine arise, joint doctrine takes precedence.

Doctrine touches all aspects of an army. It facilitates communication among soldiers no matter where they serve, contributes to a shared professional culture, and serves as the basis for curricula in an army Education System. army doctrine provides a common language and a common understanding of how army forces conduct operations. It is rooted in time-tested principles but is forward-looking and adaptable to changing technologies, threats and missions. Army doctrine is detailed enough to guide operations, yet flexible enough to allow commanders to exercise initiative when dealing with specific tactical and operational situations. To be useful, doctrine must be well known and commonly understood.

Multidimensional army forces provide a forcible entry capability to access contested areas worldwide. They can be ready to fight immediately and prepare for the arrival of follow-on forces. This capability is essential to reduce predictability, dominate a situation, deny an adversary his objectives, contain a conflict, conduct decisive operations, deter protracted conflict and terminate conflict on our terms.

Army forces are uniquely capable of decisive land warfare. The ability to close with and destroy enemy forces, occupy territory, and control populations achieves moral dominance over enemy will and destroys means to resist. Army forces close with and destroy the enemy to terminate conflict on our terms. Ultimately, this capability, coupled with strategic responsiveness, provides the foundation of conventional deterrence.

An army is capable of attacking an enemy, directly or indirectly, with lethal and non-lethal means, through the synergistic application of precision fires and manoeuvre. An army is organized and equipped to conduct combined arms operations, which include integrating joint capabilities and operations. Precision manoeuvre coupled with precision army and joint fires, gives the joint force commanders operationally decisive land power capabilities.

Conflict normally requires control of people and land to establish the conditions for self-sustaining peace. An army has a unique capability to dominate a situation and set those conditions, especially when this control requires a sustained commitment.

US SEA WARFARE STRATEGY

Naval forces are among the most useful of diplomatic tools. Policy makers can send them to over two-thirds of the world's surface at any time without having to obtain advance basing rights or prior permission to conduct naval movements. Having a sound capability for deploying military forces to almost any coastal (littoral) area makes it possible for the United States to provide the tangible leadership that is necessary to facilitate the assembley of coalition forces, or negotiate forward basing rights should the circumstances so require.

While US maritime forces may not be immediately visable offshore, they are a potent deterrent to potential adversaries since such forces can arrive quickly and remain indefinitely. Routine forward deployment provides the President of the United States with on-call military presence almost anywhere in the world and furnishes the capability to project military power and show credible resolve without provoking war. This presence also reminds potential adversaries of US military capability and resolve to enforce international law. In this regard, the oceans and US naval forces provide the United States with unparalleled peacemaking capability and promote the rule of law.

SEA DENIAL AND OPERATIONS OTHER THAN WAR

As world attention turns from the old ideological east-west confrontation of the Cold War to the economic disparity between developed free market societies and developing nations, there has been a re-emergence of maritime interception operations in situations short of hostilities. There has been no decrease in crises that require military operations other than war. Transoceanic operating and logistic capability permit the United States to take a lead in such operations, often as a member of a multinational coalition.

Since 1989, several multilateral embargoes have been enforced by coalition naval forces. These have been supported by the consensus of the international community and conducted under international law. Such embargoes are best understood as attempts to maintain world order, peace, and human rights rather than as acts of war. Modern maritime interception operations are typically mandated by resolutions of the United Nations Security Council, and normally allow humanitarian shipments of food and medicine to the civilian population. Naval visit and search operations are conducted with respect to international law and custom.

Examples of maritime interception operations include the multinational maritime interdiction operations against Haiti, Serbia/Montenegro and Iraq. These operations are less than airtight and require time to take effect. However, they are part of the foreign policy process which led to the implementation of democracy in Haiti, motivated Serbia to accept the Dayton Accord and reduced Iraq's capability for military aggression both before and after the Gulf War. The United States has been at the forefront of this emerging area of modern peacekeeping.

In the realm of military operations other than war, naval forces also contribute presence and amphibious capability, along with the ability to apply power at varying levels of intensity in smaller scale contingencies. Maritime forces seek to ensure continued, unhindered and unrestricted use of the sea to further national or shared interests and objectives. The following paragraphs discuss the nature of maritime force employment in peace and war. It must be remembered, however, that the distinctions drawn between peacetime and wartime operations are not clear cut in many instances.

Maritime forces lend themselves well to various peacetime operations, which differ from war time operations in some respects. Although in some situations peacetime operations are designed to influence governments and military forces (presence and deterrence) they are increasingly designed to influence non-national entities, such as criminal organizations and transnational groups. Non-governmental and non-military organizations often have the expertise and the finances to conduct certain operations and may be involved in peacetime operations to varying degrees.

Maritime forces should be prepared to deal with these other organizations and recognize the contributions they can bring to an operation. In some contingencies, maritime forces may operate more in a supporting or enabling role, contributing a supply of well-trained and equipped personnel who can adapt and sustain themselves. Peace time operations will normally have a varying mix of security, humanitarian and environmental components, and may be grouped under the following broad headings.

PRESENCE AND DETERRENCE: The presence of maritime forces can avoid confrontation and support political aims without necessarily violating national sovereignty. Maritime forces may strengthen diplomatic efforts by showing the flag (presence) in a benign fashion as a general indicator of interest and latent capability, thereby helping to prevent emerging conflicts. Alternatively, maritime forces can be deployed as a deterrent against specific actions. Maritime forces can also shield states at their request by establishing an at-sea presence within territorial seas, thus providing a trip wire function in threatened areas. These operations are, however fraught with danger because not all parties may cooperate with or refrain from challenging such deployments. Nevertheless, the use of maritime forces is less intrusive than the use of land based forces.

PEACE OPERATIONS: This term is used in a generic sense to cover a range of activities, including conflict prevention, peace making, peace keeping, peace enforcement, and peace building. The use of maritime forces in peace operations will usually complement land forces and may involve a considerable range of tasks. These tasks may include monitoring/observing ceasefires, interposition between the maritime forces of belligerents and establishing disengagement zones, providing a neutral venue for supervised negotiations, and preventing forces of the belligerent parties from violating agreements.

HUMANITARIAN OPERATIONS: Maritime forces are well suited to support humanitarian aid efforts that relieve or reduce the suffering, loss of life and damage to property caused by natural or man-made disasters. In particular, military forces are useful to provide a secure environment to allow the humanitarian relief efforts of other organizations to progress as directed by cognizant legal authority. Short notice readiness, flexibility and mobility allow maritime forces to respond quickly to a disaster, particularly if they have

45

Marines or other troops embarked. Maritime forces can be tailored to supplement or complement the efforts of the host nation, civil authorities, or non-governmental organizations. Maritime forces may provide personnel, equipment, supplies, medical and dental care, limited construction and engineering, communication, and transportation support.

PROTECTION OF SHIPPING AND FREEDOM OF NAVIGATION: When nations make claims over waters that are contested, challenges to freedom may arise. In such instances maritime forces can exercise freedom of navigation by transversing or exercising in the contested waters (in accordance with recognized international law). Maritime forces may also protect merchant shipping with flag state consent that could otherwise be threatened.

MARITIME CONSTABULARY TASKS: In the last three decades developments in international maritime law, particularly the extension of national authority further from shore, has resulted in a variety of low intensity constabulary functions. These functions are likely to involve naval forces as well as coast guards and/or civilian maritime agencies. Specific functions may include:
1 Enforcement of fisheries regulations and EEZ arrangements.
2 Operations against piracy.
3 Counter-terrorism.
4 Interdiction of drugs and other contraband trade.
5 Interdiction of the slave trade or illegal migration.
6 Enforcement of environmental regulations.
7 Control of traffic separation schemes and other maritime traffic management tasks.

ENVIRONMENTAL OPERATIONS: Maritime forces may also be tasked to respond to oil spills and other environmental disasters. In these cases, maritime forces can be a valuable source of trained and disciplined personnel as well as equipment. Often these operations will be conducted in concert with or in support of other governmental, international, or private agencies whose specific missions include disaster response.

EMBARGOES/MARITIME INTERDICTION OPERATIONS (MIO): Maritime forces may be tasked to enforce internationally imposed sanctions. Effective enforcements of sanctions may require sophisticated coordination of military operations at sea and in the air. This is especially true in areas of armed conflict or high tension, where the absence of commonly understood and accepted rules of engagement can greatly increase the risks to enforcement units. Assigned tasks may include stopping, inspecting, seizing and diverting suspect ships and aircraft establishing and enforcing a maritime exclusion zone for the maritime vessels of one or more parties to a conflict.

NONCOMBATANT EVACUATION OPERATIONS (NEO): Noncombatant evacuation operations are conducted to move personnel out of an area where deteriorating security conditions place lives at risk. This type of operation is similar to an amphibious raid, involving swift incursion, temporary occupation of an objective, and fast withdrawal after the mission is complete. During a NEO rules of engagement usually limit the use of force to that required to protect the evacuees and the evacuation force. Maritime forces may have an integral capability to accomplish a NEO without assistance from other forces. If not, ships stationed at sea may provide lift capability and the close, secure staging areas for other forces. By evacuating directly from a secure site to ships outside territorial seas a very low political profile can be maintained. The evacuation force commander must be prepared to deal with the political sensitivity of the situation that will be monitored, if not controlled, from the highest level.

OPERATIONS IN WARTIME: In wartime the activities of the maritime force are normally aimed at achieving sea control and projecting power ashore.

SEA CONTROL: Use of the sea requires a degree of control. Total sea control is rarely possible as long as an adversary continues to threaten forces in the area. Therefore, a degree of sea control is normally established within a designated area for a defined period of time. Sea control must provide security for forces, facilities, and sea lines of communications. Large maritime forces using an area for their own purposes can usually achieve and maintain sufficient sea control, but smaller specialist forces and civilian shipping require sea control to be established by other forces or escorts. Sea denial is a subset of sea control. Sea denial is achieved when maritime forces prevent an opposing force from using the sea for its own purposes. Sea denial is normally exercised in a given area and for a limited time.

POWER PROJECTION: Conflicts at sea rarely exist in isolation from a land campaign or the pursuit of territorial objectives. Even when the maritime component is operationally dominant, the ultimate outcome in the theatre is likely to depend on success ashore. Maritime forces often must be prepared to operate in the littoral environment to project force ashore as part of joint operations involving naval, air and land forces. Naval forces are normally the first forces into a crisis area and may comprise the enabling force that allows a joint force access to the region. Naval forces then contribute to operations ashore by conducting operations in direct or indirect support of those land operations. It is important to note that a maritime commander responsible for sea control may find it necessary to plan and execute power projection actions in order to achieve and/or maintain sea control.

TASKS FOR MARITIME OPERATIONS: Although the following tasks are primarily applicable to wartime operations, some, or all, may apply to any maritime operation. All require an on going surveillance effort, using both force and external sensors and good intelligence to create a common tactical picture on which the force can base decisions.

ANTI-AIR WARFARE (AAW): AAW encompasses the threat from all aircraft and airborne weapons, whether launched from air, surface, or sub-surface platforms. Denial of intelligence to the enemy and achieving adequate attack warning are crucial to the AAW battle. AAW is based on the principle of layered defense; defeating air raids using sea and shore based aircraft, long and medium range surface to air missile systems, point defense missile systems, guns, close in weapons systems, electronic decoys, jammers, and chaff. These layers are necessary to gain early warning, counter the enemy surveillance and targeting effort, destroy attacking aircraft before they can release their weapons, and finally, to destroy or decoy missiles before they can hit friendly forces.

ANTI-SUBMARINE WARFARE (ASW): The ASW protection of a force depends on defense-in-depth and close coordination between maritime patrol aircraft, helicopters, surface ships, and friendly submarines. The complexeity of such coordination, and the special environmental factors involved makes the submarine threat one of the most difficult to counter.

ANTI-SURFACE WARFARE (ASUW): Action against enemy surface forces may seek to achieve either sea control or denial. Long range warning from intelligence sources is valuable prior to detection by shore or ship based fixed wing aircraft, ship borne helicopters, or ships sensors. Once a threatening force is detected its composition and disposition must be ascertained before an attack can effectively be pressed home.

STRIKE WARFARE (STW): Maritime forces contribute to strikes against targets ashore using carrier-based strike aircraft, sea launched Cruise missiles, naval guns, and special operations forces. In maritime air operations, particularly in the littoral environment, air forces work in close cooperation with naval forces to ensure the most effective use of available air assets in strike roles.

AMPHIBIOUS WARFARE (AMW): An amphibious operation is an operation launched from the sea by naval and landing forces against a hostile or potentially hostile shore. Amphibious operations integrate virtually all types of ships, aircraft, weapons, special operations forces, and landing forces in a concerted joint military effort. Amphibious operations are probably the most complex of all joint operations; detailed, specialized knowledge and a high degree of coordination and cooperation in planning, training and execution are essential for success.

Maritime forces will be responsible for: the safe and timely arrival of seaborne forces at an amphibious objective, landing of a force in good order at the right place and time, defense of shipping, and control of ship-to-objective movement. An amphibious force can poise at sea, raiding or landing at politically decided time and place independent of shore infrastructure.

Command and Control Warfare (C^2W). Supported by intelligence, C^2W integrates the use of operational security (OPSEC), operational deception (OPDEC), physchological operations (PSYOP), electronic warfare (EW), and pysical destruction to deny information to, influence, degrade, or destroy an adversary's C^2 capabilities and to protect friendly C^2 against such actions.

SPECIAL OPERATIONS: Maritime Special Operations Forces (SOF) contribute direct and indirect support to sea control and power projection missions. Capable of operating clandestinely, SOF can provide advance force operations, hydrographic and near-shore reconnaissance in advance of a landing, direct action missions, combat search and rescue missions and the ability to degrade enemy lines of communications.

MINE WARFARE (MW). Mine warfare can involve both the offensive use of mines and defensive MINE COUNTER MEASURES (MCM). Offensive minelaying operations aim to dislocate enemy war efforts and improve the security of own sea lines of communications by destroying, or threatening to destroy enemy seaborne forces. MCM includes active measures (to locate and clear mined areas), passive measures (routing shipping around high threat areas) and self protective measures (ship signature reduction).

NAVAL CONTROL OF SHIPPING (NCS). A multinational maritime mission may require some form of control and coordination of shipping within a given region. The control and coordination of shipping aids the force commander by reducing the surveillance and reconnaissance effort and managing confrontation between shipping and an adversary. NCS is implemented by advising ship owners and operators of the situation, the region(s) affected, and the measures being implemented. Shipping authorities accepting NCS agree to provide position, movement and communication information to naval authorities and, subject to the master's discretion, comply with any routing information and direction given by naval authorities.

INFORMATION WARFARE: The ocean environment enhances military command, control, and communications. Ocean- borne platforms can provide military units deployed overseas with constant, secure, real-time communication with tactical and strategic leadership in the United States. Information superiority has several components: gathering, processing, and disseminating information; information operations to defend against attack; and information operations directed against an adversary's information. Information warfare is

The aircraft carrier USS *Nimitz* (CVN 68), guided missile cruiser USS *Princeton* (CG 59), and fast combat support ship USS *Bridge* (AOE 10) participate in an underway replenishment (UNREP) while deployed in support of Operation 'Iraqi Freedom'.

A US submarine on patrol.

A CH-46 Sea Knight flies toward USS *Kitty Hawk* during a replenishment at sea.

in its infancy but holds forth the hope of military dominance without the use of physical force or loss of life.

INTELLIGENCE, SURVEILLANCE AND RECONNAISSANCE (IS&R) The forward presence of ocean-based military forces enable the United States to gain a better understanding of developing political military situations. Developing better intelligence, surveillance, and reconnaissance are key ways to improve awareness of the battlespace, to track the disposition of enemy forces, to enhance transparency among nations (for example, reducing the risk of accidental war), and to monitor US allied and neutral warfighting assets. Better IS&R technology permits more precise tracking of enemy assets, allowing for more effective disabling of opponents with less use of firepower, less brute force, and less chance of collateral damage to noncombatants. It also promises the potential for improved tactical and strategic awareness, enabling forces to fight smarter. Thus, the use of up-to-date information technology and modern sensors can help reduce battlespace confusion, often referred to as the 'Fog of War.'

US AMPHIBIOUS WARFARE STRATEGY FOR THE UNITED STATES MARINE CORP

The US Navy and Marine Corps have put in place a well-crafted transformation strategy to ensure the nation has the Naval expeditionary forces, ships, aircraft, weapons, and systems-to carry out the full spectrum of roles, missions, and tasks in the new century. Expeditionary Warfare is the foundation for twenty-first century peacetime forward deployments, response to crises world wide, and warfighting to protect America's citizens and friends and vital US interests wherever and whenever they might be at risk. It is the essence of naval operations from the sea anytime, anywhere.

Current and programmed amphibious assets predominantly fall into four branches of the Expeditionary Warfare Division (N75): Special Operations (N751), Mine Warfare (N752), Amphibious Warfare (N753), and Explosive Ordnance Disposal (N757). All of these programmes are essential to, and support, the Navy and Marine Corps fundamental and enduring roles: sea control and maritime supremacy, power projection, strategic deterrence, forward naval presence and strategic sealift.

At the most basic level, an amphibious force consists of a navy element- a group of ships known as an amphibious task force (ATF)-and a landing force (LF) of US Marines (and occasionally, US Army troops). Together, these elements-and supporting units are trained, organized and equipped to perform amphibious operations. Now and in the future, commanders will have the ability to size and task-organize amphibious forces to accomplish a wide range of specific missions.

The resulting forces may range from a single Amphibious Ready Group/Marie Expeditionary Unit (Special Operations Capable) (ARG/MEA

SOC), to a larger organization capable of employing a Marine Expeditionary Brigade (MEB) or even a Marine Expeditionary Force (MEF).

Amphibious forces must be capable of performing missions ranging from humanitarian assistance and disaster relief to major theatre war (MTW). Additionally, they can be configured and deployed to operate at various levels of conflict and in multiple theaters simultaneously. They can provide a presence that may preclude adventurous actions by a potential belligerent. Because they are seabased and because the decision to position and engage amphibious forces will always be easily reversible, amphibious forces greatly expand the repertoire of available response options. Among other national resources, they are particularly well placed to provide a demonstration of US commitment and resolve to friends and allies as well as adversaries. Normally two to three ARGs are forward deployed: one in the Mediterranean/ Arabian Gulf-Indian Ocean area, and one or two in the Western Pacific area. The other ships of the ARG are either working up to deploy, in transit, or in overhaul. One ARG/MEU is forward based in Sasebo and Okinawa Japan.

In most cases, the ATF will be deployed under the protective umbrella of an aircraft carrier battle group (CVBG), which provides cover for the ATF and combat support to operations ashore. Ships of the ATF are capable of embarking and supporting other forces when the mission requires, including US Army, Special Operations Forces (SOF), or other joint and combined forces. The ATF will be sized and organized to support landing forces ranging from the smallest to the largest. It will consist of a mix of amphibious ships, support ships, and perhaps Maritime Prepositioning Force (MPF) assets, which carry equipment and sustainment for Marine forces.

A forward-deployed MEU (SOC) is the standard task-organized force used for most peacetime presence and smaller-scale, crisis-response missions. These smaller Marine Corps units can be mixed and matched to create larger and more capable MAGTFs.

The MEU (SOC) deploys onboard amphibious warships-three-ship amphibious ready groups- which carry the helicopters and amphibious assault vehicles that transport Marine combat and support elements ashore, as well as the vertical/short take-off and landing (V/STOL) aircraft- both fixed and rotary-wing - that provide integrated air support.

The Navy's 21st century amphibious fleet will eventually include thirty-six ships, intended to form 12 ARGs. Each ARG will normally consist of a large-deck amphibious assault ship, an LHA, LHA(R) or an LHD; an amphibious transport dock of the LPD-17 class; and a dock-landing ship of the LSD-41 or LSD-49 classes.

The OPERATIONAL MANOEUVRE from the SEA concept was published on 4 January 1996 by the 31st commandant, General Charles C. Krulak. Like its predecesser - the approach to amphibious warfare developed at Quantico during the 1930s - OMFTS was a response to both danger and opportunity in a fluid strategic environment. The danger, summarized by the phrase 'chaos in the littorals', originated with the myriad forces of national aspiration, religious intolerance, and ethnic hatred that marked the post-Cold War world. The opportunity came from significant enhancements in information management, battlefield mobility, and the lethality of conventional weapons.

OMFTS forsaw that a new series of threats and enhanced tactical capabilities would produce significant changes in the Marine Corps operational environment. The nature of war remained the same, and the Corps fundamental doctrine of manoeuvre warfare remained as valid as ever before, but chaos and technology would inevitably affect where we fought, whom we fought, and how we fought. OMFTS understood the need for military innovation; it encouraged debate and experimentation and provided a framework for Marines, Sailors, civilian emplyees and contractors within which to turn concept into reality.

OMFTS fuses amphibious ship and landing force manoeuvre to create and exploit opportunities in time and space to project amphibious power ashore as seamlessly as possible. The impact of this kind of manoeuvre warfare was foreshadowed in Operation 'Enduring Freedom', when Marines seized a forward operating base in Afghanistan, approximately 400 miles inland from their seabase in the Arabian Sea. However, though the Marines successfully demonstrated the viability of these new warfighting concepts with current platforms, they will not be truly realized until they are married with the future elements of the mobility triad The Advanced Amphibious Assault Vehicle (AAAV), the MV-22 Osprey tilt-rotor aircraft, and the Landing Craft, Air Cushion (LCAC).

URBAN WARFARE

All types of land warfare pose some degree of danger, some more so than others. But there is however one element that is feared more than most, and that is urban warfare.

Urban warfare goes under many names; in the American military they call it Military Operations on Urban Terrain (MOUT), while the British call it Operations in Built Up Areas OBUA). Regardless of the names it goes under, it is a bloody business and although every army trains for it, most try to avoid it.

Military Operations in urban terrain are nothing new, indeed the only thing that has changed about them is the scale. It is estimated that by the year 2010, that over seventy-five per cent of the world's population will live either in or around urban areas. This massive increase in urban growth has prompted an urgent need for forces to be both trained and equipped for fighting in built-up areas, as they are deemed the battlefields of the future. MOUT is defined as all military actions that are planned and conducted on a terrain complex where man-made construction affects the tactical options available to the commander.

In essence, urban combat operations may be conducted in order to capitalize on the strategic or tactical advantages which possession or control of a

Two soldiers of the 402nd Civil Affairs Battalion, train for urban warfare at Camp Doha, Kuwait.
US Army Photo by SPC Tyler Long

particular urban area gives or to deny these advantages to the enemy. Major urban areas such as towns and cities represent the power and wealth of a country, and are as such key targets in a war. The ability to either capture or deny a major cultural centre from its indigenous population can yield a decisive psychological advantage during a conflict, hence its importance.

Other urban areas that may be effected during a war include small towns or villages located in close proximity to lines of communication, or strategic assets such as airports, harbours and key bridges. Urban terrain operations are extremely difficult to mount in highly populated areas, as there is always a high risk of civilian casualties, and it is for this reason that soldiers rules of engagement (ROE) are far more restrictive than in any other combat environment.

In the last decade alone, there have been numerous examples throughout the world of urban conflicts that have challenged even the best of forces. One only has to look at the American experience in Mogadishu, Somalia to see an example of what happens when a modern well trained and equipped army is forced to fight its way through a densely populated urban area.

During this brief action which lasted for less than a day, crack Ranger and

55

Delta special forces supported by helicopters, fought a series of running battles against Somali militiamen that left eighteen Americans dead and over seventy wounded, while the Somalis, sustained some 500 killed and over 1,200 wounded.

However, the largest urban action in recent years prior to Operation Iraqi Freedom was in the city of Grozny, during the Russian intervention in the Republic of Chechnya. This action was characterized by a large, technologically sophisticated Russian force, engaging and being defeated by a small Chechen guerilla force. Grozny provides an insight into future large-scale urban operations, and has highlighted a number of shortcomings and deficiencies in both military training and equipment orientated towards urban warfare. During the first phase of the Grozny operation, the Chechens negated Russian firepower by virtue of operating in close proximity to their ground forces. This tactic caused considerable confusion in the Russian ranks and led to them sustaining heavy casualties. It was only when the Russians retaliated with excessive and unrestrained firepower and a complete disregard for collateral damage that they regained control of Grozny.

Although most western forces train in modern camera-equipped, purpose built urban villages, these are far too small to realistically represent and prepare future soldiers for combat in large metropolitan areas. There is also the issue of equipment. Urban Warfare requires copious amounts of ammunition, bandages and of course soldiers. One recent report on US forces stated that all units, except for special forces were under-prepared for urban warfare in respect of communications, combined arms tactics, techniques and procedures for armour, aviation, and close air support. It also stated that uncoordinated manoeuvre and over-watch are more common in urban operations and that general marksmanship standards were poor.

Other problems identified include poor allocation of resources and positioning of fire support assets, a complete lack of understanding and awareness of the restrictive rules of urban engagement as well as the need to minimise collateral damage, poor use of counter-battery fire and air defence artillery and a serious lack of operational focus.

The report also states that the US forces currently do not effectively locate their command and control nodes. Leaders at all levels have problems with rules of engagement and proportionally. Sniper teams are not properly planned for or considered eyes on the objective. Wargaming and course of action development for urban combat needs work; this must be more precise. The intelligence preparation of the battlefield (IPB) is not specific enough for the urban battle. The use of psychological operations and civil affairs operations are not planned well enough. Identification of decision points and setting conditions for success are not emphasized. Little thought is given to intelligence collection or care of civilians on the battlefield. The operations order does not properly allocate engineer resources for urban fighting. Units are not effective in suppress, obscure, secure, and reduce (SOSR) at all levels.

Engineers are attrited prior to the objective. Lack of eyes on the objective prevent obstacle identification. Re-supply and casualty evacuation are not conducted well. Urban specific supply items; Ladders, knee and elbow pads, ropes with grappling hooks, as well as specialty weapons and ammunition need to be made available. Speed, not haste, should be the norm in urban operations.

Due to political change, advances in technology and the army's role in maintaining world order, MOUT now takes on new dimensions that previously did not exist. Friendly and enemy doctrine reflect the fact that more attention must be given to urban combat. Expanding urban development affects military operations as the terrain is altered. The makeup and distribution of smaller built-up areas as part of an urban complex make the isolation of enemy fires occupying one or more of these smaller enclaves increasingly difficult.

Although the current doctrine still applies, the increasing focus on operations short of war, urban terrorism, and civil disorder emphasizes that combat in built-up areas is unavoidable. These new conditions affect how units will fight or accomplish their assigned missions. MOUT is expected to be the future battlefield in Europe and Asia with brigade and higher-level commanders focusing on these operations.

Tactical doctrine stresses that urban combat operations are conducted only when required and that built-up areas are isolated and bypassed rather than risking a costly, time-consuming operation in this difficult environment. Adherence to these precepts, though valid, is becoming increasingly difficult as urban sprawl changes the faces of the battlefield.

Commanders must treat the elements of urban sprawl as terrain and know how this terrain affects the capabilities of their units and weapons. They must understand the advantages and disadvantages urbanization offers and its effects on tactical operations. The brigade will be the primary headquarters around which units will be task-organized to perform urban operations. Companies, platoons and squads will seldom conduct urban operations independently, but will most probably conduct assigned missions as part of a battalion task force urban operation.

In future large-scale urban operations, soldiers will make extensive use of ground robots for roles such as intelligence gathering, sniping, walking point, mine-detection and anti-personnel roles. In the anti-personnel role, robots equipped with thermal imagers and body-heat sensors will have the ability to home in on enemy forces, no matter how well hidden.

HELL FROM ABOVE

In modern warfare, the general strategy employed to defeat an adversary is to bomb them-Period. This is done to reduce and neutralize the enemy's war potential by means of destructive explosion and fire. To accomplish this feat requires the use of both air dropped and air inserted munitions, targeted

The mighty B-52 Stratofortress of the 40th Expeditionary Bomb Squadron, displays the Stars and Stripes as it makes its way towards an unknown target.

strategically against installations, armament, and personal, and tactically in direct support of land,sea and air forces engaged in offensive or defensive operations. Bombing alone however, rarely brings about total victory, as you still at some point have to put 'boots' on the ground- both to seize the territory that you have just bombed, and to secure it- or else you run the risk of enemy reoccupation.

At the very least, a well planned and well executed bombing campaign will reduce an enemy,s capacity to fight, his ability to fight and most importantly of all, his will to fight. A good example of this strategy is Operation 'Desert Storm' in 1991 and Operation 'Iraqi Freedom' in 2003, while a bad example of this strategy is Operation 'Allied Force' in Kosovo in 1999 where air-power alone simply did not work.

The weaponry available today for bombing campaigns is truly awesome, with literally a bomb, a missile or a munition available for every possible type of conceivable scenario-or so it would seem. For instance, we have:

The **E-BOMB**, so called because its microwave warhead generates millions of watts of electricity in a microsecond frying any electronic circuitry in its wake, such as those found in military computers, radar systems and weapons launchers.

The **BLACKOUT BOMB**, which rains carbon filaments onto electrical grid

A stealth bomber returning from a bombing mission in Iraq in which it had to fly half way around the earth to accomplish it.

Four direct hits on concrete aircraft hangars in Ali As-Salim Airfield, Kuwait - 1 March 1991.

systems-causing them to fry and cut out.

The **ETHNIC BOMB**, that only attacks a person or persons of a particular tribe or sect.

The **CONCRETE BOMB** or **BLUE CIRCLE CEMENT BOMB**, as it is often called in the UK- on account of it being filled with concrete rather than high explosives- is designed to knock out tanks or fortifications in urban areas where collateral damage is an issue, as it does not explode on impact.

The **DAISY CUTTER**, is a 7.5 ton bomb that is so heavy that it has to be rolled out of a C-130 transport aircraft, rather than a bomber. Its original purpose was to clear jungles for helicopter landing zones during the Vietnam War, however it is equally effective against troops in open or confined areas, and was used operationally in Afghanistan against Al-Qaeda fighters who were holed up in mountain caves.

The **MOTHER OF ALL BOMBS** or **MOAB** (MASSIVE ORDNANCE AIR BLAST BOMB) as it is officially known is the satellite-guided successor to the **DAISY CUTTER** but weighs in at a staggering 21,000-lbs-making it virtually a mini-nuke.

The **T-BOMB**, is a thermobaric bomb that unleases an expanding wall of fire that quite literally sucks the oxygen out of a building or an underground bunker making it a fearsome weapon as it incinerates everything in its path.

The **BUNKER BUSTER**, is a precision guided 30,000-lb bomb capable of piercing some sixty-five feet of concrete before exploding making it the ultimate leadership decapitation weapon.

In addition to the so-called exotic weaponry, we also have:

The **GENERAL PURPOSE BOMB**, which usually weighs between 500 and 2,000lbs and produces a combination of blast and fragmentation effects.

The **PENETRATION BOMB**, which is designed to penetrate hardened targets such as bunkers before the explosives detonate.

The **CLUSTER BOMB**, which is a fragmentation weapon designed for use against light armour,vehicles,parked aircraft and fielded forces.

SMART WEAPONS - Precision Guided Munitions

A PRECISION GUIDED MUNITION (PGM) is a bomb, missile or artillery shell that has a terminal guidance system that is designed to sense emitted or reflected EMR (electromagnetic radiation) within its field of view. For a PGM to be effective, it must be employed with a target acquisition (TA) system, such as the Mk 1 eyeball, which is the most commonly employed TA system. Others include, TV and forward-looking IR sensor display systems, radar, and laser guidance systems.

The target acquisition cycle is composed of the following five steps:
1 Detection of target area.
2 Detection of the target itself.
3 Orientation of the target.
4 Target recognition.
5 Weapon release.

In 1944, it required 108 B-17s dropping 648 bombs to destroy a point target, while in Vietnam it took 176 bombs, whereas now it only takes a few PGMs to do the same job - that's progress. In the case of the United States, since 'Desert Storm' in 1991, the USAF has:

Tripled its number of precision-capable platforms.Boosted its PGM inventories by some twenty-five per cent and developed a totally new generation of PGMs that have enhanced accuracy, adverse weather capability and are standoff capable.

These include :

The **JOINT STAND-OFF WEAPON** (JSOW), an adverse-weather, short-range, stand-off anti- armour/SEAD dispenser weapon.

The **JOINT DIRECT ATTACK MUNITION** (JDAM) an Inertial Navigation System (INS)/GPS guidance tail kit that converts dumb bombs into accurate adverse-weather capable weapons.

The **WIND CORRECTED MUNITIONS DISPENSER** (WCMD) is basically the same as JDAM in its operation, but is engineered only for cluster munition dispensers.

The **JOINT AIR-TO-SURFACE STAND-OFF MISSILE** (JASSM) a long-range, precision strike weapon that has only limited hard target penetration capability.

Other key air-weapons include the B-52 launched US AGM-86 Cruise missile and the Britsh Storm Shadow, a high precision Conventionally-Armed Stand-Off Cruise Missile (CASOM) that can be utilised day and night and in all weathers. Its primary role is to attack high-value, heavily-protected targets that are deep inside enemy territory where aircrew could be vulnerable to attack from integrated air defence systems. With a range greater than 135 miles, this situation can easily be avoided, as the missile can be fired from a safe distance way outside the range of most SAMs. Storm Shadow navigates by means of either its GPS or its TERPROM (Terrain Profile Matching) system and is virtually immune to jamming.

Storm Shadow is armed with BROACH (Bomb Royal Ordnance Augmented Charge), a high explosive warhead whose shaped Augmentation charge is mounted separately in front of the penetration charge. In operation, the Augmentation charge focuses a jet of molten plasma onto the target to make a circular hole from where the bombs penetrating charge then enters the target through the aperature and detonates- having wasted none of its explosive energy in the penetration process. In trials, BROACH has been demonstrated to penetrate between 6.5ft (2m) and 13ft (4m) of concrete- depending on its impact angle and velocity-making it a highly lethal weapon. Storm Shadow was used for the first time in anger during Operation 'Telic' (Iraq) in 2003, where it proved highly successful- both in accuracy and lethality.

Air-bombing campaigns have played a major role in military strategy for decades now and will continue to do so in future conflicts-albut on a different level.

Just to reinforce this point even further, here is a list of countries that America has bombed in the last half century alone.

US AIR BOMBING CAMPAIGNS SINCE WORLD WAR II

China	1945-46, 1950-53	El Salvador	1980s
Korea	1950-53	Nicaragua	1980s
Guatemala	1954, 1960, 1967-69	Panama	1989
Indonesia	1958	Bosnia	1995
Cuba	1959-61	Sudan	1998
Congo	1964	Former Yugoslavia	1999
Peru	1965	Afghanistan	1998, 2001-?
Laos	1964-73	Iraq	1991-2003
Vietnam	1961-73		
Cambodia	1969-70		
Lebanon	1983-84		
Grenada	1983		
Libya	1986		

COMBAT POWER
AH-64 APACHE LONGBOW

The Apache attack helicopter is the US Armys primary air support weapon system, and first saw action in Panama in 1989. During the first Gulf War in 1991, it played a key role in supporting the ground forces-effectively serving as a flying tank, being faster and better armed than anything else then available to the US Army and its coalition allies.

Above: An Apache shows off its deadly arsenal of weaponry.

Left: The AH-64 Apache Longbow

The US Army has more than 800 Apaches in service, of which a significant number are designated Apache Longbow on account of their enhanced capability and specification compared to that of the original version.

The US Army version of the AH-64 is powered by two General Electric T700-GE-701C gas- turbine engines, rated at 1,890shp each, enabling the aircraft to cruise at a speed of 145 mph (233Km/h) with a flight endurance in excess of three hours. Combat radius is some ninety-three statute miles (150 km), but the addition of a single external 230 gal fuel tank enables this to be extended to some 186 miles (300km), although this is dependent upon a number of factors, including temperature, weather, and payload. Ferry range on internal fuel is 430 miles (690km), but this can be considerably extended by the addition of up to four 230 gal external tanks. The AH-64 is air transportable in the C-5, C-141 and C-17.

The AH-64D Longbow Apache is equipped with the Northrop Grumman millimetre-wave Longbow radar, which incorporates an integrated radar frequency interferometer for passive location and identification of radar emitting threats. This operates in the millimetre bandwhich and is unaffected by poor visibility or ground clutter-therefore making it resistant to countermeasures.

The primary weapon system is the Lockheed Martin/Boeing AGM-114D Hellfire air-to-surface missile which has a millimetre -wave seeker to allow the missile to perform in full fire-and-forget mode. Missile range is 5 to 7.5 miles. The Apache can also be armed with air-to-air missiles (Stinger, Sidewinder, Mistral and Sidearm) and 2.75in rockets. The Longbow Apache carries a combination of armaments- which vary according to the mission profile being flown at the time. In the close support role, a typical combat load would consist of sixteen Hellfire missiles, four air-to-air missiles and 1,250 rounds of ammunition for the 30mm automatic Boeing M230 Chain Gun located under the fuselage.

The Apache is crewed by a pilot and copilot/gunner, who sit in a tandem arrangement- as it offers better visability and presents a smaller target.

The Longbow Apache can effect an attack in less than thirty seconds, by virtue of its radar dome which is unmasked for a single radar scan and then remasked-while the processors determine the location, speed and direction of travel of the target. The Longbow Apache is a highly lethal weapon system, and can detect, target and engage up to 256 targets - either individually or in conjunction with other assets-making it the most feared weapon on the battlefield.

THE TANK		
M1A2 ABRAMS MBT		**CHALLENGER 2 MBT**
Armament	1x 120mm smoothbore cannon 1x 12.7mm machine gun 2x 7.62mm machine gun	1x 120mm rifled gun 1x 7.62mm chain gun 1x 7.62mm machine gun
Crew	4	4
Armour	Passive and Reactive	Passive and Reactive (Chobham)
Weight	125,890lbs	137,500lbs
Top Speed	41mph	35mph
Range	300 miles	280

Left to right: An Abrams and a Challenger train for combat prior to Operation Iraqi Freedom.

LAV-25

One of the most successful armoured fighting vehicles on the battlefield today is the Light Armoured Vehicle-25 or LAV 25 as it is more commonly known.

Designed to meet a US Marine Corps requirement for a light armoured vehicle, the LAV-25 was chosen out of many competing designs as the best possible vehicle then available to meet this demanding requirement with General Motors of Canada selected to build an initial batch of 758 vehicles over a five year period.

The LAV-25 design was based on the Swiss MOWAG Piranha series of vehicles and is available in a number of versions.

Logistics

Mortar

Maintenance and Recovery

Anti-tank

Command and control

Mobile electronic warfare

Anti-Aircraft

and, of course, reconnaissance

All Piranhas feature a similar layout with the driver seated front left, Detroit diesel engine right and the rear of the vehicle occupied by either a six man troop compartment or a utility unit. The idea for this family of armoured fighting vehicles was first conceived in the early 1970s, when MOWAG started development of a range of 4x4, 6x6 and 8x8 configured vehicles.

The concept featured common components and a wide range of roles and was subsequently called Piranha with the first prototype completed in 1972. It was a design concept years ahead of its time.

The LAV-25 is an all weather, all terrain vehicle that is equipped to fight both night and day. It provides strategic mobility for expeditionary forces and is capable of defeating heavy armour. The LAV-25 is air transportable via C-5, C-130 and C-141 aircraft and is fully amphibious. In fact it is capable of fording streams, rivers and shallow beacheads with only minimal preparation.

The LAV-25 is armed with a 25 mm chain gun and a 7.62 mm machine gun. If required an additional M240 machine gun can be mounted on the commanders station in the turret. When combat loaded the LAV-25 carries 210 rounds of 25 mm ammunition ready to fire with an additional 420 rounds in reserve.

During urban combat operations the LAV-25 carries 400 rounds of 7.62 mm ammunition ready to fire with 1,200 rounds held in reserve. The vehicle also carries 16 smoke grenades for self-protection.

The crew of the LAV-25 consists of a driver, gunner and commander. The driver and gunner both have laser protected periscopes to enable operations while under fire, while the commander has the use of seven laser protected periscopes, a DIM 36 target acquisition sight plus a low light 2nd generation image intensification system.

Later versions also include thermal viewers for all members of the crew.

The LAV-25 is a truly impressive armoured fighting vehicle.

MULTIPLE LAUNCH ROCKET SYSTEM (MLRS)

The MLRS in action.

One of the most lethal artillery systems in the world today, is the American MLRS or Multiple Launch Rocket System as it is officially known. MLRS provides the US Army and some its allies with an all-weather, indirect, area fire system that is designed to engage enemy artillery, air defence systems and armoured formations at all depths of the tactical battlefield.

The primary mission of MLRS is to suppress and neutralize possible enemy threats - period. The system is highly versatile and is designed to supplement traditional cannon artillery rather than replace it. It does this by rapidly delivering large volumes of firepower against designated areas that have high value time-sensitive targets, such as air defence tracking radars.

During attacks on fast moving armoured formations, MLRS units can use their 'shoot and scoot' mode which allows them to fire on enemy targets and then move away before enemy counter-fire zero's in on them.

During Operation 'Desert Storm', British and American MLRS units deployed to the region in support of the ground invasion force prior to its advance into Iraq. Once H- Hour arrived they fired huge salvoes of rockets into concentrated areas of the Iraqi lines. The bombardment tore massive gaps in their defences and caused death and destruction on a massive scale.

After the attack ended both British and American forces nick named the MLRS, 'The Grid Remover.' MLRS had its origins in a 1976 feasibility study which was known as the General Support Rocket System. It is a self-propelled platform built on the chassis of the M2 Infantry Fighting Vehicle and features two pods loaded with six rounds each. These rounds might consist of anti-tank mines, fragmentation bomblets, mine-dispensing munitions or chemical warheads. The reload time for MLRS is nine minutes.

MLRS has proved a tremendous success in service and a number of significant upgrades are planned in the future to enhance its combat effectiveness. Options include, a wheeled variant which is currently part of the Future Combat System programme, and a maritime variant for shore bombardment.

BRADLEY MICV

One of the most controversial armoured fighting vehicles in US Army service today, is the M2 Bradley Mechanized Infantry fighting vehicle. The M2 Bradley was born out of the culmination of an early 1960s programme to equip the US

A Bradley Fighting Vehicle of 3-7 Cavalry Squadron, 3rd Infantry Division goes through a test drive after visiting the Unit Maintenance Collection Point.

Army with a well armed tracked vehicle that could operate both with tanks and existing M113 armoured personnel carriers.

Prototypes were completed by FMC Corporation in 1978, with the first production models appearing in 1981 at an initial rate of 600 units per year.

The hull of the Bradley is made of welded aluminium with a layer of spaced laminate armour for added protection. Its main armament consists of one Hughes 25 mm chain gun which is stabilised to allow firing on the move, while for secondary armament it has a twin launcher for Hughes TOW anti-tank missiles and a 7.62 mm coaxial machine gun.

The driver of the M2 Bradley sits front left with a cummins eight cylinder diesel engine to his right. Behind him is a troop compartment, that sits six fully equipped soldiers who enter the vehicle via a large ramp at the rear of the hull or through a roof-top hatch. Also within the troop compartment, there is an individual periscope equipped firing port for each soldier, which allows them to fire their weapons from within the safety of the vehicle, and while on the move.

Night vision, thermal imagers and chemical warfare systems are fitted as standard on the Bradley, and proved very effective in the urban battles for Baghdad during Operation Iraqi Freedom.

When Bradley first entered service with the US Army, it was heavily criticized for being too expensive, too big and too difficult to maintain under field conditions, but in recent years thanks to improved technology many of the reliability issues have been resolved.

There was also great concern over the M2 Bradley's armour, as it was considered insufficient for modern warfare. However, new versions such as the Bradley A3, feature increased armour protection such as explosive reactive panels which are usually fitted around the turret and hull-greatly increasing the vehicles survivability. Although the latest versions of Bradley are proving effective, its long term future is in serious doubt as armoured fighting vehicles such as the LAV-25 offer more or less the same performance for a fraction of the cost. Bradley will eventually be replaced by a version of the FCS (Future Combat System).

AIR CAVALRY
16 Air Assault Brigade (UK)

The UKs 16 Air Assault Brigade was formed in 2000, and is a lethal combination of air assault infantry and attack helicopters. Its awesome capabilities bring a new meaning to the word manoeuvre warfare as it has both the means and method of rapidly inserting a large well equipped force deep behind enemy lines, at very short notice by day or night and in all weathers. Although originally conceived as a hard hitting mobile tank-killing force (when it was 24 Airmobile), its capabilities have grown to encompass many other missions such as; hostage rescue, seizure of strategic assets, infiltration and extraction of Allied forces, counter penetration, flank protection, raids on key targets, humanitarian aid and civil aid.

The Unique capabilities of 16 Air Assault Brigade allow it to ; attack from any direction, concentrate, disperse or redeploy rapidly, delay a larger force without becoming decisively engaged, provide responsive reserve and reaction forces, react rapidly to tactical opportunities, place forces at natural choke points, provide surveillance and target acquisition, react to rear threats, bypass enemy positions, facilitate surprise and deception and to rapidly reinforce committed areas.

The Brigade has an operational strength of some 10,000 personnel and comprises of an;

HQ AND SIGNALS SQUADRON - HQ is responsible for all direction and co-ordination of air assault operations, while the parachute-deployable 216 Signal Squadron is responsible for establishing and maintaining communications between all elements of 16 AAB.

PATHFINDER PLATOON - responsible for reconnaissance, marking of helicopter landing zones and parachute DZs.

3RD, 4TH AND 9TH ARMY AIR CORPS REGIMENTS - responsible for reconnaissance (using Gazelles), anti-tank operations (Lynx and Apache) and light utility support (using Lynx). At present sixteen AAB is scaled for forty-eight Apache Longbow attack helicopters (with each regiment operating two squadrons of eight helicopters).

AIR ASSAULT INFANTRY BATTALIONS - Three battalions are assigned to

16 AAB, of which two are always from the Parachute Regiment. Within each battalion there are five companies, three rifle, one support and an HQ company. Fire-power levels are extremely impressive as each battalion has eighty GPMGs, fourteen .50 Browning heavy machine guns, nine 81mm mortars and sixteen MILAN anti-tank missile systems.

7TH PARACHUTE SQUADRON - RHA; directly supports 16 AAB with three batteries (each with six guns) of 105 mm light guns.

21ST DEFENCE BATTERY, RA - provides air defence for the Brigade (with Javelin and Starstreak MANPADS).

9TH PARACHUTE SQUADRON, RE - provides engineering support.

HOUSEHOLD CAVALRY REGIMENT (HCR) - provides medium reconnaissance as and when required with three troops of four Scimitar armoured reconnaissance vehicles.

47 AIR DESPATCH REGIMENT - responsible for managing and packing equipment into aircraft.

THE PARACHUTE REGIMENT - provides two of the three infantry battalions assigned to 16 AAB.

RAF SUPPORT HELICOPTER FORCE - provides eighteen Chinooks and eighteen Pumas for mobility (The RAF also provides 16 AAB with C-130 Hercules transport aircraft as and when required).

CHAPTER FOUR

THE PLAYERS

AUSTRALIA
SPECIAL AIR SERVICE REGIMENT

Based at Campbell Barracks, Swanbourne, the Australian Special Air Service Regiment has an operational strength of around 600 men and is made up of six squadrons, three Sabre, one Signals, one Support, one Base and a Regimental Headquarters (RHQ). To ensure maximum operational efficiency at any given time the three Sabre Squadrons work on a three-year cycle which provides both training and operational experience.

A typical squadron cycle would, in its first year, process new recruits and work them up, while at the same time the more experienced troopers within the squadron develop new skills and attend refresher courses. The second year would see the squadron train for its overt military responsibilities, which include special operations in conventional warfare. This provides a good contrast for the third year which involves training for covert operations.

The Base Squadron provides logistical and administrative support, while the Operational Support Squadron evaluates new equipment and provides specialist training for new tactics, techniques and procedures. In addition to this support the SASR also has 152 Signals Squadron (SASR) which provides a highly capable communications network.

The SASR has a long and proud history which dates back to the Second World War when the first Australian SAS Squadrons were formed to fight the Japanese, behind their own lines, a task they performed with great success. After the war ended they were disbanded in the same way as the British SAS and had to wait until 1949 before being reformed. For three years the unit was known as the 1st SAS Company and operated out of Swanbourne. In 1951 they were incorporated into the Royal Australian Regiment (RAR) as an airborne platoon, but this was far from ideal and in 1957 they broke away and became the 1st Special Air Service Company.

This unit quickly grew in size and capabillity and in 1964 became the 1st Special Air Service Regiment (SASR) a title that is current to this day. The SASR mirrors the British SAS in many ways, having worked together over many years both in combat and training. The strength of this special relationship was ably demonstrated in the jungles of Borneo from February 1965 to August 1966 where both British and Australian SAS troopers fought side by side against Indonesian forces in very difficult and demanding conditions. This experience was of immense value to the SASR as it soon found itself involved in another difficult operation in Vietnam, fighting in support of the US Armed Forces. The SASR had originally deployed to Vietnam in 1962 as part of the Australian Army Training Team, however as the war dragged on it became necessary to raise another squadron in July 1966, which brought the SASR up to an operational strength of three Sabre Squadrons. Up until 1971 each squadron rotated after completing two tours of Vietnam in what was a highly controversial and unpopular war, both in Australia and the USA. The SASR developed a fearsome reputation during its time in Vietnam, where its troopers gained a reputation for being tough and tenacious fighters that never quit. As a result the VC tended to avoid them.

After Vietnam the SASR was forced to disband one of its Sabre Squadrons, but this was reformed in 1982 following a terrorist bomb attack on the Sydney Hilton Hotel on 13 February 1978. Within days of the terrorist attack the SASR was formally designated the national counter-terrorist unit and immediately set up the TAG/OAT groups as a reaction force. From 1982 the SASR expanded rapidly and soon found itself needing a dedicated Signals Squadron. In response, 152 Signals Squadron was formed and set about providing each Sabre Squadron with a Signals Troop to enable better communications while on operations. The Gulf War in 1991 led to the deployment of one SASR Squadron in support of the Allied Coalition force. This force of 110 men joined up with the New Zealand SAS to form the ANZAC SAS Squadron which worked alongside both British and US special forces against Iraq. In recent years the SASR has been involved in operations in East Timor and Afghanistan and has performed superbly in both.

Australian SAS in their patrol vehicles, look for trouble in Afghanistan.

TAG/OAT

The **TACTICAL ASSAULT GROUP** (TAG) was formed in 1978 in response to the Sydney Hilton Hotel terrorist action. The TAG is known as B Squadron within the SASR and all of its members have to undergo the same selection and training as troopers in the regular SASR. The selection phase lasts for three weeks and is then followed by almost a year of intensive training before the successful troopers are allowed to wear the coveted sand coloured beret. The TAG's training facilities include sniping ranges, aircraft mock-ups, CQB ranges and an urban CT complex.

The **OFFSHORE ASSAULT TEAM** (OAT) is basically an off-shoot of the TAG group and specializes in maritime operations. The unit regularly practices its skills on ferries, small boats and oil rigs and is viewed as a separate but equal element of TAG.

Both the TAG and OAT have a considerable arsenal of weaponry at their disposal. Favourite weapons include, M-16A2s, F-88 5.56 Austeyr assault rifles plus the entire family of MP-5s. Other weapons include the 7.62 Galil, H&K PSG 1, Parker Hale 82, Finnish Tikka .223 plus a variety of Beretta and Remington shotguns. Pistols include the Browning HP 9mm and SIG-Sauer P228.

All TAG/OAT operators are HALO/HAHO qualified as well as being highly proficient in heliborne operations. They frequently cross-train with other countries and have a very close relationship with the US Delta Force and Navy SEALS. During the Sydney 2000 Olympic Games, both the TAG and OAT played a key role in protecting international athletes against possible terrorist attacks.

UNIFORMS AND EQUIPMENT OF THE SASR

The SASR wear standard Australian army combat uniforms with only their sand coloured beret, cap badge and wings differentiating them from any other conventional Australian Army unit. Standard weapons include, the F-88 Austeyr assault rifle, M16 A2, M-249 Minimi SAW and various 40 mm grenade launchers. As with the British SAS, the SASR makes good use of its Land Rover long-range patrol vehicles and operates a large fleet of specially developed vehicles which are 6x6 rather than 4x4 in configuration. Known as the Land Rover Perentie, within the SASR, this excellent vehicle is ideal for operating in Australia's vast and varied landscape and has proved very successful in supporting the SASR in its operations in Afghanistan.

POLAND

Poland's GROM (Grupa Reagowania Operacyjino Mobilnego) counter-terrorist unit was only formed in 1991 and has already gained an excellent reputation within the world's special forces communities. GROM operators are recruited from other Polish special forces units such as the Army's 1st Commando Regiment and the Navy's 7th Lujcka Naval Assault Brigade. Much of Grom's success is down to its commander, Colonel Slawomir Tetelicki, a man who is greatly admired and respected for his dedication and high standards.

GROM is very security conscious about its size and order of battle, however its combat force is believed to number some 250 operatives plus support personnel. As well as standard military training, operatives within GROM must speak at least two langauges and have good medical skills. In fact almost seventy-five per cent of GROM's personnel are either paramedic or nurse qualified and as such, provide excellent support for the unit's doctors. GROM also has female operatives who carry out intelligence gathering and surveillance, both in Poland and overseas.

Generally GROM operates in four-man assault teams in the same manner as the British SAS with specialized support teams available for tasks such as EOD. These teams are often run by Former operators who have been either injured or are too old for operational service but want to continue serving with the unit. All members of GROM must have high standards in weapons handling as all training is carried out using live ammunition. Training is made as realistic as possible to ensure sharp reactions and realism and often involves mock assaults on ships, aircraft and buildings.

In 1994, GROM was selected to participate in Operation 'Restore Democracy', the American led invasion of Haiti. Prior to this operation, fifty-five members of the unit were sent to Puerto Rico to train with members of the US 3rd Special Forces Group. Whilst there, they were briefed in Haitian politics and social systems to help them understand the need for this important operation. On arrival in Haiti, GROM operators were tasked with providing security for several important VIPs, including UN General Secretary Buthros Buthros Ghali and US Secretary of Defense William Perry. While in Haiti they took part in a hostage rescue operation, which involved storming a building, putting out a blaze and rescuing a young boy who had been taken hostage by a group of heavily armed gunmen. The boy was freed without any bloodshed and as a result GROM received enormous praise for its actions which earned its creator and Commander Colonel Petelicki the US Army Commendation Medal; The first time in American history that a foreign unit has been commended in this way.

Further operations in which GROM participated include protecting Pope John Paul II during his visit to Poland in 1995, as well as a tour in Bosnia during 1998 in which they apprehended a suspected Bosnian war criminal.

Weapons used by GROM include the HK-MP-5,Tantal 5.45mm assault rifle,

HK PSG-1 and Mauser 86 7.62 sniper rifles. Personal sidearm selection is at the individual operators discretion.

UNITED KINGDOM

NO.47 SQUADRON (SPECIAL FORCES FLIGHT) RAF

Based at RAF Lyneham, 47 Squadron RAF (Royal Air Force) is tasked with providing the UK's special forces with a dedicated long range transport capability. The Squadron operates a small fleet of specially modified C-130 Hercules transport aircraft that are equipped with TFR (terrain following radar) systems that enable their aircraft to fly at very low level and in all weathers.

Aircrews assigned to 47 Squadron are screened for their ability to fly at low level for prolonged periods of time, as it can cause severe disorientation for some pilots who do not have an aptitude for this type of flying. For those that make the grade, working with the SAS and SBS can be very rewarding as there are numerous opportunites to travel and develop new skills. Techniques regularly practised by 47 Squadron include; TALO, Ghost insertion (technique whereby aircraft fly so close together that they appear on radar as one image) and JATO (this technique is practised in the USA).

NO.7 SQUADRON SPECIAL FORCES FLIGHT. RAF

Known as the 22 SAS taxi service, No. 7 Squadron's Special Forces Flight is responsible for the covert insertion and extraction of the UK's special forces. No. 7 SSF operates a small fleet of heavily modified Chinook H.C.Mk 2s that feature air-to-air refueling probes, state-of-the-art navigation systems, missile jamming devices, long range fuel tanks, mini-guns and M60 machine guns. Although many of their operations are secret they are known to have operated in the Gulf, Bosnia, Kosovo, Sierra Leone and Afghanistan. Selection and training standards for No. 7 SFF are extremely demanding as much of the Squadron's flying is carried out at low level and at night using 3rd generation NVGs.

SAS (SPECIAL AIR SERVICE)

The SAS is the most feared and respected special forces unit in the world with numerous imitators but few equals. Based at Credenhill, Hereford, 22 Special Air Service Regiment (SAS) is one of the most highly trained special forces units in the world with a reputation that is legendary, and certainly lives up to its motto *Who dares wins*.

Prior to 5 May 1980, very few people around the world knew anything about the SAS or even of its existence. However on that eventful day when men wearing black overalls, respirators and body armour, armed with HK-MP5s, Browning HP pistols and stun grenades stormed the Iranian Embassy in London and killed five terrorists, who had been holding a number of people hostage,

The SAS taxi service. Two heavily modified Chinook H.C.Mk 2s, used by No. 7 Squadron's Special Forces Flight.

everything changed, as the entire operation had been witnessed by millions of people on live TV.

Unfortunately, the old saying any publicity is good publicity does not apply to special forces, as they like to work in the shadows and this exposure gave the SAS an image of being invincible, and created a perception of a unit that was large in size and manned by supermen. The reality was somewhat different as the SAS comprises only one regular (22 SAS) and two part-time TA (21 SAS Artist's Rifles and 23 SAS) regiments, that are supported by 264 Signal squadron (regular unit attached to 22 SAS) and 63 Signal Squadron (TA unit that supports both 21 and 23 SAS).

The SAS has some 700 highly trained operators within its ranks who are divided between four Sabre (Fighting) Squadrons. Each squadron consists of four sixteen-man troops who normally deploy on operations as four-man teams or eight man patrols depending on tactical requirements. In addition to the Sabre Squadrons, the SAS also has the support of an HQ squadron, Operations Research Wing Planning and Intelligence Unit, Training Wing, and various attached personnel such as Medics, drivers, cooks, EOD specialists and engineers. Control of the three SAS regiments and their support units is undertaken by the Director of Special Forces.

Colonel David Stirling, founder of the Special Air Service Retiment.

The SAS can trace its history back to 1941, when under the command of its creator, Colonel David Stirling, a unit was formed called L Detachment, Special Air Service Brigade. However despite its grand title the unit was little more than a handful of unconventional soldiers, who were thrown together to form a new unit as part of a massive deception plan to fool the Germans. As a means of sowing further confusion, the name Special Air Service Brigade was created for a bogus formation of parachute and glider units that were supposedly deployed in the Middle East as part of an invasion force.

In Stirling's words the SAS was formed to;

> 'Firstly, raid in depth behind enemy lines, attacking HQ nerve centres, landing grounds, supply lines and so on and secondly, the mounting of sustained strategic activity from secret bases within hostile territory and, if the opportunity existed, recruiting, training, arming and coordinating local guerilla elements'

Within the British Army there was intense suspicion of the SAS and its unique capabilities and the doubts about them never really went away. Even when the SAS was successful it was never enough for its critics, who despised the idea of small, unconventional units that seemed to be totally autonomous.

An early SAS patrol in North Africa during the Second World War.

The SAS, however, did have friends in high places who were so pleased with their performance in North Africa and the Mediterranean that they agreed to form a new force for operations in north-west Europe.

By 1944, the SAS had become a Brigade and consisted of two British regiments, (1& 2 SAS), two French regiments (3&4 SAS), one Belgian squadron (5 SAS) and a number of signal

SAS soldiers laden with equipment, pose for camera during a skydive.

squadrons.

After the war ended the SAS was disbanded along with a number of other elite units that had served their country well throughout the war. The SAS, however, did not go quietly and fought a campaign within the British MOD (Ministry of Defence) to be reformed. In part they were successful as they were allowed to reform in 1950 as the TA Artist's Rifles, a part-time unit that was to eventually become the 21st Special Air Service Regiment (Artist's Rifles) Volunteers.

Not content with just being a TA unit, the SAS saw an opportunity during the Malayan Emergency in 1952 to form a regular SAS unit, as the highly successful Malayan Scouts who were created in Malaya were looking for a new name that would be more representative of their role. Once agreed, the unit became the Malayan Scouts (SAS), later to be redesignated the 22nd Special Air Service Regiment. The SAS were now back in business.

Since reforming in Malaya, the SAS has participated in more wars and conflicts than any other special forces unit in the world and is the most combat experienced.

SAS EQUIPMENT

Weapons used by the SAS include the HK-MP5 assault rifle (entire range), HK-53 SMG, Ingram Model-10 SMG, UZI SMG, M16 A2 assault rifle with 40 mm M203 grenade launcher, Colt M4 carbine, Colt Commando assault rifle, HK-G3 assault rifle, HK-G8 assault rifle, HK-G41 assault rifle, FN 7.62 SLR (although no longer in use with the British Army, the SAS still use it on certain types of operations), Steyr AUG assault rifle, SA-80A2 assault rifle (used by TA SAS only), SA-80A2 LSW (Light Support Weapon) (used by TA SAS only), M249 Minimi light machine gun, Ameli light machine gun, HK-13E light machine gun, Ultimax 100 light machine gun, 7.62 mm GPMG machine gun, Browning M2 .50 heavy machine gun, Accuracy International PM sniper rifle, Tikka M55 sniper rifle, SSG 3000 sniper rifle, Barret .50 long range sniper rifle, Franchi SPAS 12 combat shotgun, Franchi SPAS 15 combat shotgun, Remington 870 combat shotgun, Browning HP pistol, Glock 18 pistol and SIG 226 and 228 pistols.

Heavy weapons include the LAW 80 anti-tank rocket launcher, M72 anti-tank rocket launcher, Milan anti-tank missile, 81mm Mortar, Javelin MANPADS (man portable air defence system), FIM-92 A Singer MANPADS, MK 19 40mm automatic grenade launcher, SB 40 LAG automatic grenade launcher and 20 mm AMW (Anti-Material Weapon).

Vehicles used include the Land Rover 90 'Dinkies', Land Rover 110, Land Rover SOV (special operations vehicle). Light Strike Vehicle (LSV) , (The SAS are well known for their armed vehicles and often use some of

---

the following vehicle mounted weapons; Browning M2, GPMG, M249 Minimi, 25 mm cannon, Milan, TOW, MK-19 40 mm grenade launcher, 0.5 in GAU-19 three barrel machine gun, 51mm and 81mm Mortars), Argocat mini-ATV (all terrain vehicle), Harley Davidson track bike, Quad ATV, Unimog utility truck, DAF utility truck, Pinzgauer light weight utility truck and Range Rover as well as numerous unmarked vehices.

In addition to their large fleet of ground vehicles the SAS also operates a fleet of small boats such as the Rigid Raider, Klepper canoe, Gemini, Zodiac and Submersible Recovery Craft SRC).

The SAS also have their own fleet of Agusta A-109A light utility helicopters (two of which were captured from the Argentinian forces during the Falklands War in 1982) which are flown by pilots of 8 Flight AAC (Army Air Corps). These helicopters are painted in civilian colours and are used for discreetly transporting counter terrorist operators within the UK.

SAS Troopers generally wear standard British Army DPM combats while training along with their famous sand coloured beret and winged dagger badge. However while on operations, they are allowed to wear virtually anything they like, and are given complete freedom in their choice of weaponry. The Troopers generally try to wear clothing that is as comfortable and practical as possible for the environmental conditions that they are operating within. If feasible, they will even dress in the same manner as the local population and blend in with them as best as they can without attracting too much attention to themselves. This particular tactic worked extremely well in Afghanistan where they used SAS Gurkhas for reconnaissance missions as their clothing and facial features were very similar to those of the local Afghanis. However, for counter terrorist operations the Troopers wear black nomex clothing as it allows them to be seen easier by their colleagues while operating in smoke or dust filled rooms (its visual effect is also very psychologically intimidating). In addition they also wear Avon S10 respirators and bullet proof assault vests that have pockets for stun grenades, spare magazines and a knife. SAS CT operators also attach spare magazines to their wrists for quick reloads (these are known as wrist rockets).

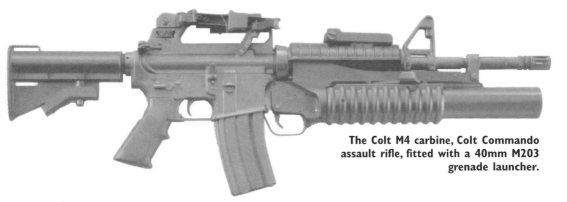

The Colt M4 carbine, Colt Commando assault rifle, fitted with a 40mm M203 grenade launcher.

SBS (SPECIAL BOAT SERVICE)

Based in Poole, Dorset, the SBS (Special Boat Service) is the naval equivalent of the SAS, and warrants a mention in the sea section (See full SBS history in Sea section) since most of its recent operations have taken place on land rather than at sea. This shift in operation is down to the fact that the SBS nows comes under a general UK Special Forces umbrella and plays an important part in supporting the SAS during times of conflict.

This shift in accountability and operational responsibility has not gone down well with the SBS as they see their units identity being eroded to the point that if the SAS gets its way, the SBS will become a maritime roled squadron within the SAS Orbat (order of battle). This process has already slowly started as the SAS made the SBS change its name in the late 1990's from Special Boat Squadron to Special Boat Service, a title it previously held during The Second World War. A further issue relates to maritime operations as the SAS already has its own boat troop. At one time the general rule between the two forces, was that the SAS handled all maritime operations above the surface, while the SBS took care of everything underwater such as, sabotage, equipment recovery and underwater demolitions. This area of responsibilty has now blurred with both units carrying out maritime operations as and when required.

Part of the reason behind these changes relates to the fact that the SAS is understrength at present and cannot meet all of its operational requirements. This is fully understandable as the SAS and SBS have been involved in numerous conflicts in recent years, including operations in the Falklands, Gulf, Bosnia, East Timor, Albania, Kosovo, Sierra Leone, Afghanistan, Somalia as well as ongoing internal security operations in Northern Ireland.

The SBS tends to operate in the shadows far more than the SAS and is very secretive about its exact roles. The unit's operational strength is some 120 regular operators plus a small part- time reserve unit that is highly professional and extremely well trained, and although the SBS is considerably smaller than the SAS, many operations and missions that have been credited to the SAS, have in fact been carried out by the SBS.

During the Gulf War in 1991, SBS units were inserted behind enemy lines to destroy some of Iraq's underground communications systems which were essential for supplying targeting data to the mobile Scud launchers that plagued the Coalition Forces. In 1999, both the SBS and SAS fought side by side in Sierra Leone against a ruthless bunch of armed rebels, known locally as the West Side Boys after they had taken a small group of British soldiers hostage. During the subsequent rescue mission over eighty rebels were killed for the loss of one SAS Trooper, with all of the hostages released unharmed.

However the biggest deployment for the SBS has been in Afghanistan as part of Operation Enduring Freedom following the events of 11 September 2001. First deployed to Bagram Airbase in northern Afghanistan, the SBS were acting in support of US forces who were hunting AQT (Al-Qaeda /Taliban) forces known to be operating in the area. Following a number of military actions by both the British and American forces, who were acting in support of the Northern Alliance, the AQT forces surrendered and were taken to a fortress which was just outside Mazar-e-Sharif. A few days later the AQT prisoners overpowered their guards and a fierce battle took place before order could be restored by British and American special forces. During the insurrection hundreds of lives were lost including those of a number of US personnel who were within the fortress. It was later revealed by the US Department of Defense that at the height of the revolt, six SBS troopers had stormed the fortress and charged a force of some 200 AQT soldiers who were trying to kill American forces, who were trapped within the compound. Despite being totally out numbered they drove the AQT away and rescued the Americans from their predicament. Upon hearing this news, President George W. Bush awarded the SBS troopers the Congressional Medal of Honor.

As SBS operations continued in Afghanistan, Britain's MI6 intelligence service identified a valley where it was believed Osama bin Laden, the Al-Qaeda terrorists' leader was in hiding. In response two SBS Squadrons containing sixty Troopers were deployed in the valley to either capture or kill him. As they awaited further instructions, orders came through from the British government that they were to withdraw from the valley and let American Forces carry out the operation instead. As the SBS withdrew, there was a delay in the Americans deployment, which was to have devastating consequences. Between the British withdrawal and the American Forces arrival, Osama bin Laden slipped out of the valley unnoticed and made his way to Pakistan where border security was slack. Unaware that bin Laden had gone, America launched Operation 'Anaconda' but it ran straight into trouble almost from the beginning. By mistake US Forces landed in the middle of the valley, instead of the outside and all hell broke loose. As the US Forces tried to fight their way out of the valley, they sustained heavy casualties; eleven killed, eighty-eight wounded along with two Chinooks shot down, plus a number of other helicopters so badly damaged that they were sent back to the USA for repair. Although the Americans inflicted hundreds of casualties on the AQT forces, their forces were not trained or prepared for such warfare. Following an urgent request for assistance from the

The M249 Minimi light support weapon.

US government, Britain deployed over 1,800 Royal Marines to the area along with a force of SBS personnel. For several weeks the force carried out intensive search operations in the valley, but there was no reported contact with any AQT forces.

The SBS has an enviable reputation amongst other special forces around the world and will no doubt fight very hard to maintain its independence and identity in the future.

SBS EQUIPMENT

Weapons used by the SBS include the M16 A2 with M203 grenade launcher, Colt M4, Colt Commando, M249 Minimi, SA 80 A2, HK-MP5 (all versions), HK-G3, Steyr AUG, Remington M870, Barret 50. and Browning HP.

USA

75TH RANGER REGIMENT

The 75th Ranger Regiment is one of the finest light infantry units in the world and is a key component of the US Army's Special Operations Command (USASOC) which, in turn, is part of the United States Special Operations Command (USSOCOM).

Based in Fort Benning, Georgia, the Ranger Regiment comprises 2,300 highly trained and well motivated soldiers who are divided between three battalions. Within each battalion there are three combat companies each containing three platoons all of which are supported by a weapons platoon.

RANGER MISSION STATEMENT

The mission of the Ranger Regiment is to plan and conduct special operations and light infantry operations in any operational environment. The primary special operations mission of the Regiment is Direct Action or DA. DA operations conducted by the Rangers may support, or be supported by, other special operations forces. They can conduct these missions alone or inconjunction with conventional military operations. Rangers can also operate as special light infantry when conventional light infantry or airborne forces are unsuited for, or unable, to perform a specific mission. In fact, modern day Rangers conduct basically the same types of missions their forebears conducted 300 years earlier.

The Ranger Regiment is well supported by the US Army and has top priority over other units when it deploys. Its budget alone is that of an entire Infantry Division. The Rangers work very closely with other US special forces units such as Delta Force and the 160th Special Operations Aviation Regiment (SOAR) also known as the 'Night Stalkers'.

The Rangers can deploy anywhere in the world within a few hours as they always have a company at a high level of operational readiness. They are trained to infiltrate enemy territory by land, sea or air and can operate independently without outside support for up to five days. To ensure that maximum firepower and tactical flexibility is maintained at all times, every weapon used by the Rangers must be man-portable.

Although the Rangers can undertake many different types of missions, the areas that they tend to specialize in are rescue and evacuation, snatch and grab, light strike and tactical reconnaissance. They are also experts in urban combat, and primarily operate at night as they are well equipped for such operations as they ably demonstrated in Mogadishu, Somalia.

Training requirements within the Ranger Regiment are extremely demanding as soldiers train for eleven months of the year with only two blocks of leave to break the rigorous programme. The Regiment conducts training all over the world in various environments such as jungle, desert, Arctic and mountain terrain so that its soldiers are physically conditioned for different types of climate.

At present the main training focus within the Rangers is on the Big Four fundamental skills that each Ranger should possess. They are marksmanship, battle drills, medical training and physical training. With a fearsome reputation to protect, the Rangers are very selective in their choice of soldiers as they have very high standards to maintain. Technically within the US Army every soldier is guaranteed a Ranger enlistment option, however the reality is somewhat different as they have to pass the three week long Ranger Indoctrination Phase first. RIP, as it is more commonly known assesses and prepares soldiers for their eight month stint with a Ranger battalion, prior to attending Ranger School.

Before attending RIP, soldiers must first pass through basic training and infantry school. Once this training is completed the soldiers attend a three week parachuting course at the Airborne School in Fort Benning, Georgia. After that it's RIP for them at one of the active duty Ranger battalions.

Soldiers that pass RIP remain with the battalion and work up their skills and physical strength in preparation for Ranger school, which will either make or break them. Ranger School has three phases, all of which are held at different locations within the south eastern United States and all of them hard. The first phase of the course commences at the 4th Ranger Training Brigade at Fort Benning, where the soldiers face a series of long marches in realistic combat conditions. Throughout this phase they receive little food or sleep and are driven to the edge of exhaustion as they have to carry full kit at all times. Once finished here they move on to the 5th RTB in Dahlonega, Georgia where they undergo mountain training, with the final phase jungle/swamp training taking place at the 6th RTB which is located in Eglin Air Force Base.

Throughout this course no rank slides are worn, as all Ranger soldiers are expected to show leadership skills. Those that pass Ranger School can look forward to an exciting career that is both diverse and demanding yet highly rewarding, as few get to be Rangers.

Once qualified, Rangers can undertake further courses in; covert reconnaissance, demolitions, communications, combat medicine, sniping, vehicle operations, watermanship, SCUBA diving and HALO/HAHO parachute infiltration. Service with the Rangers is also seen as a career stepping stone between conventional infantry and special forces, as many Rangers go on to serve with Delta Force.

CHRONOLOGICAL HISTORY OF RANGER OPERATIONS

The Ranger Regiment has a long and proud history that dates back some 300 years and is the oldest regiment in the US Army. The name Ranger dates back to the seventeenth century when American colonists used the word to describe how far they had travelled in a day over rough terrain, i.e. We ranged eight miles this day.

This is the Rangers history.

1754-63: First formed by Major Robert Rodgers of Connecticut, who fought for the British against the French and Red Indians. His most famous operation was against the Abenaki Indians who were based in St Francis, forty miles south of Montreal. Travelling by canoe and by foot, Rodgers and his force of 200 Rangers, covered 400 miles in sixty days without the enemy being alerted to their presence. On 29 September 1759, the Rangers attacked the Abenakis camp and killed hundreds of them before withdrawing to their base. It was a spectacular victory and led to Rodgers being commissioned into the 60th Foot (The Royal Americans) where he wrote his famous nineteen standing orders for the Rangers, many of which are still valid today.

1774-76: Rangers fight on the side of the British during the American War of Independence.

1861-65: Rangers fight on both the Union and Confederate side during the American Civil War, and later for America in the Mexican War.

1942: The Ranger title is revived again for the Second World War, with six battalions deployed in Europe and the Far East. The first unit was, in fact, formed at Carrickfergus, Northern Ireland in 1942 under the command of Major William Derby and fought at Dieppe alongside British Commandos. Other actions fought include North Africa, Sicily and Salerno, Italy, where the 1st and 3rd Ranger Battalions were virtually wiped out in the battle for Cisterna. Their finest hour, however, was during the D-Day landings when Ranger Force A from the 2nd Battalion assaulted the well defended concrete fortifications on the cliffs of the Point du Hoc. For two days they held the position and fought off the German 914th Infantry Regiment in an action that cost them 135 killed and wounded out of a force of 225.

At Dog White beach on Omaha, soldiers of Ranger Force C, 2nd Ranger

Battalion were pinned down by heavy enemy gunfire and were unable to move. Near to the Ranger Force was Brigadier General Norman Cota, assistant divisional commander of the 29th Infantry Division who shouted the famous words; 'Rangers lead the way', which motivated them into breaking out of the deadly killing zone. Since then, 'Rangers lead the way' has become the force motto. Although most of the Rangers better known actions were fought in Europe, they also fought in the Pacific, where they carried out a daring raid on a POW camp at Cabanatuan on Luzon, where they liberated 500 American prisoners.

After the Second World War ended the Ranger units were disbanded. However, Ranger training still continued and eventually became a qualification that was highly valued in the same way as a parachuting or diving qualification.

1950: During the Korean War, Ranger Companies were attached to every Army Division that fought there, and carried out missions such as reconnaissance, hit and run and sabotage.

1969: After the Korean War ended, all Ranger units were disbanded and their soldiers sent to other Army units that had Long Range Reconnaissance Patrols (LRRPs) or Lurps as they were called. The Lurps carried out more or less the same function as Rangers and performed superbly during the Vietnam War, where their skills were highly valued.

At the height of the Vietnam War, the US Army redesignated the LRRPs as specific companies of the 75th Infantry Regiment (which later became the 75th Ranger Regiment) O Company Rangers were attached to the 82nd Airborne, while L Company Rangers went to the 101st Airborne.

In Vietnam, the Rangers were used primarily for reconnaissance and intelligence gathering missions, however on several occasions they made attempts to rescue American POWs.

1980: A small team of Rangers were sent to Iran, as part of the ill-fated Delta Force (Eagle Claw) rescue operation which was mounted after Iranian terrorists took over the American Embassy in Tehran and seized fifty-three hostages. During the operation, Rangers secured the Desert One RV site from where the rescue mission was to be mounted, and whilst there, captured a bus containing civilians that happened to drive through the site before the operation was aborted.

1983: Rangers from both the 1-75th and 2-75th were deployed to Grenada for Operation 'Urgent Fury' and are involved in numerous actions.

1989: During Operation 'Just Cause' two battalions of Rangers were parachuted into Rio Hato airfield, fifty-three miles west of Panama City and ordered to seize and hold the airfield.

1991: During Operation 'Desert Storm', Rangers patrolled behind Iraqi lines in heavily armed vehicles in a manner similar to that of the British SAS and destroyed a communications centre which was located near the Jordanian border.

1993: While performing snatch and grab operations in Mogadishu, against Somali warlords, Rangers suddenly found themselves under attack from hundreds of Somali gunmen and a fierce firefight soon ensued that was to become the most intense action fought by American soldiers since Vietnam. Although the action lasted for less than ten hours, it cost the lives of eighteen American servicemen and left seventy others wounded, while the Somalis lost over 500 killed and over 1,000 wounded. This action was the epitome of everything the Rangers ever trained for as it involved urban combat, night fighting, combat rescue, snatch and grab, sniping, firefights and evacuation of wounded while under fire.

1995: Elements of the Ranger Regiment deployed to the Balkans for operations against the Serbs.

1999: Rangers deployed to Kosovo in support of US forces engaged in operations against Serbian fielded forces.

2001: Rangers deployed to Afghanistan and neighbouring countries as part of Operation 'Enduring Freedom' and help in the search for Al-Qaeda terrorists, in particular their leader Osama bin Laden.

2003: Rangers deployed to Iraq for Operation 'Iraqi Freedom', and were involved in numerous actions throughout the war, including the spectacular rescue of Private Jessica Lynch.

RANGER EQUIPMENT

Weapons and equipment used by the Rangers include the Colt M4 assault rifle, M16A2 assault rifle, Mini 14 assault rifle, Steyr AUG assault rifle, HK-G3 assault rifle, SOPMOD (Special Operations Peculiar Modification) M4A1 assault rifle, CAR 15 assault rifle, Stoner SR- 25 self loading rifle, Colt Model 733 assault rifle. Walther MP-K SMG, HK-MP5SD SMG, MAC 10 SMG, UZI SMG, M249 SAW light machine gun, HK-13E light machine gun, M60 medium machine gun, M240B medium machine gun and Browning M2 .50 heavy machine gun. Remington 870 combat shotgun and Mossberg Cruiser 500 combat shotgun, HK-PSG-sniper rifle, M40A1 sniper rifle, M24 sniper rifle and Barret M82A1 .50 heavy sniper rifle.

Support weapons include the M203 40mm grenade launcher, M79 'Blooper' 40mm grenade launcher, 81mm mortar, Carl Gustav 84mm recoilless rifle, 66mm LAW and Mk 19 40mm automatic grenade launcher, Stinger MANPAD and the M136 AT-4 anti-tank rocket. Beretta 92F handgun and SIG-Sauer P-228 handgun.

Specialist Weapon Sights include Aimpoint Comp M close quarter battle sight, M68 Aimpoint, M28 Aimpoint sight, AN /PEQ2 Infrared Target Pointer/Illuminator/Aiming laser (IPITAL) dual beam aiming device.

Uniforms worn by the Rangers include: standard US army combat fatigues, Lizard suits and Ghillie sniper suits. The Rangers also make extensive use of body armour and night vision devices such as the AN /PVS-7 night vision goggles, and for additional protection they wear Bolle T800 ballistic goggles while operating in open areas. The Rangers also operate an extensive fleet of vehicles that include the Land Rover Defender 110 SOV (Special Operations Vehicle), Humvee, Quad ATV (All Terrain Vehicle) and Harley Davidson Track bike. Vehicle mounted weapons include the Mk 19 40 mm automatic grenade launchers, M60 medium machine guns, M240B medium machine gun and Browning M2 .50 heavy machine gun. Other specialist Ranger equipment includes Zodiac boats and rigid raiders. Rangers also use heavily modified parachutes for HALO and HAHO parachute operations.

In addition to their vehicles, the Rangers also make extensive use of helicopters such as the MH-47 D/E Chinook, MH-60 K/L Blackhawk and MH-6 Little Bird which are operated by the US army's 160th Special Operations Aviation Regiment.

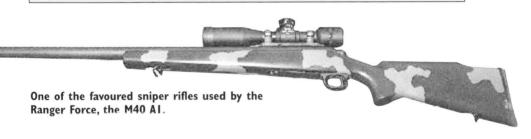

One of the favoured sniper rifles used by the Ranger Force, the M40 AI.

The Rangers are currently among the best equipped light infantry in the world, but from 2005 onwards, they will be the best equipped in the world as they will be the first recipient of the new Land Warrior integrated combat system.

COMBATING TERRORISM US STYLE
DELTA FORCE

Delta Force is the best trained and equipped counter-terrorist unit the world. Although only formed in 1977, it has grown rapidly since its inception and currently comprises some 800 trained operators. Delta Force is based at Fort Bragg, North Carolina, and has the Airborne and Green Berets as close neighbours. The compound they occupy is protected by large razor wire fences and a series of armed checkpoints which are covered with motion detectors and infrared cameras, which make it virtually impregnable. Delta Force was officially formed on 19 November 1977 by Colonel Charles A. Beckwith (known as Charging Charlie) who was both founder and CO of Delta from its inception. The inspiration to create a highly trained special forces unit came about after Beckwith returned to the United States having served in the British SAS (Special Air Service Regiment) on an exchange posting in the early 1960s. Colonel Beckwith was fascinated by the SAS and its methods of fighting in an unconventional manner, as he had deployed with them to Malaya, during the Malayan Emergency of 1950-60, and seen at first hand what they were capable of accomplishing. He greatly admired the multiple skills that each SAS trooper possessed, which enabled small four-man teams to operate with a greater effectiveness compared with that of a larger conventional force.

Beckwith was so impressed with the SAS that he decided to form his own American version that would be virtually identical in terms of training and methods of operation, but would have some local differences; such as choice of weaponry, uniforms and operational accountability. Getting Delta Force off the ground was no easy task for Beckwith, as he had to constantly justify the need for another special forces unit, when at the time there was much resentment of the existing ones due to their poor performance in Vietnam. Eventually however, after much pleading and lobbying, the Pentagon and Congress agreed to his request and the 1st Special Forces Operational Detachment Delta (SFOD-Delta) was born.

Delta Force was set up in great secrecy, initially as an overseas counter-terrorist unit that specialized in hostage rescue. However it soon became clear that Delta could perform other missions such as long range covert reconnaissance and snatch and grab missions. Delta's selection and training programmes were initially based on the tried and tested methods used by the SAS. However as Delta developed they refined the training programmes to better reflect current American thinking on CQB operations, which placed a much greater emphasis on the use of firepower.

Delta's first operational deployment took place in April 1980, after the American Embassy in Tehran was attacked on 4 November 1979 by supporters of the Ayatollah Khomeini, who took sixty-six Americans hostage in a bid to force the USA to hand over the pro-western deposed Shah of Iran.

Once all political avenues had been totally exhausted, US President Jimmy Carter gave Delta Force the go ahead to enter Iran covertly and mount a rescue operation that was code named 'Eagle Claw'. It was an extremely ambitious plan that required Delta to fly into a remote desert area by C-130 where they were to RV with eight Sea Stallion helicopters that were to be used in the actual rescue attempt. However, before the operation had even commenced, there were problems, as two helicopters were lost on their way to the RV point, while another one developed mechanical problems on the ground. In addition, some of the operators had been forced to stop a bus containing civilians as it attempted to drive past the parked aircraft on the ground, and if that weren't enough for Beckwith, another group of his men had been forced to open fire on a fuel truck that failed to stop at one of Delta's roadblocks. As it was hit it exploded in a spectacular manner that lit the night sky for many miles around. It was a nightmare scenario for Beckwith as Delta's rescue plan hinged on the use of at least six working helicopters and he now only had five. Added to his other problems, he had no choice but to abort operation 'Eagle Claw'.

As Beckwith gave the order to withdraw, there was a catastrophic explosion as one of the hovering helicopters hit a C-130 that was about to take off. Despite valiant efforts by the surviving aircrew and Delta to save all those remaining trapped in the burning wreckage, eight American servicemen died and five were seriously injured.

Even though 'Eagle Claw' ended in failure there was no blame apportioned to Delta as many of the contributing factors that caused the operation to fail were down to sheer bad luck and mechanical failure and nothing else. During the official Congress enquiry that took place to examine all of the issues surrounding 'Eagle Claw', no mention or reference was made about Delta as its existence was still highly classified and even to this day it does not officially exist.

After 'Eagle Claw', Delta intensified its training and was deployed to Panama in 1989 as part of Operation 'Just Cause'. During this operation Delta performed to plan and was highly successful in a number of key operations, such as the capture of General Manuel Noriega and the rescue of American citizen Kurt Muse, who was held captive by the Panamanian Defence Force (PDF) in Carcel Modelo prison in Panama City. Prior to the invasion, Delta had conducted a number of mini-missions in Panama as part of an intelligence gathering operation against General Noriega and the PDF. On one occasion Delta received a tip off about Noriega and a number of his known associates, who were believed to be using the island of Bocas del Toro as an operations base. They dispatched a covert reconnaissance team to the island but found nothing of interest apart from an old shack and a couple of squealing pigs.

Although many of Delta's operations remain secret they are known to have participated in a considerable number of missions in South America against Columbian drug cartels who are known to fund organized crime in America.

During the Gulf War in 1991, Delta played a key part in hunting down Iraq's mobile Scud missiles launchers which were causing considerable problems for the Allied coalition force. Delta worked alongside the British SAS in resolving this problem by mounting constant fighting patrols in the areas where Scud launchers were most frequently known to operate, and within weeks of both Delta and the SAS conducting these anti-Scud operations, they had forced the Iraqi's to move out of this area as it was proving very difficult for them to operate without being attacked.

In 1999, Delta deployed a small number of detachments to Bosnia and Kosovo for operations against Serbian war criminals as they were proving difficult to capture. However, their biggest manhunt so far has been in

Afghanistan, where they have been hunting down the world's number one terrorist, Osama bin Laden and his Al-Qaeda terrorists following the events of 11 September 2001.

In 2003, Delta found itself back in Iraq again, only this time the war was far more complicated than before, as they had to contend with conventional Iraqi forces fighting as terrorists which made for some interesting times. Other operations carried out during this conflict, included searching underground bunkers for Saddam Hussein and his henchmen, and mounting search operations in and around the northern Iraqi border near Syria.

Delta is organized along the same lines as the British SAS and consists of three operating squadrons, (A, B and C) which are subdivided into smaller units known as troops. Each troop specializes in a particular skill such as mountaineering, HALO, SCUBA or land mobility For greater operational efficiency each troop can be divided into smaller four-man units that can either operate alone or join up to form a section.

Delta also has its own support squadron which handles selection and training, logistics, finance, technical and medical issues. The technical unit is of particular interest as it provides Delta with highly sensitive equipment such as human tracking devices and eavesdropping sensors, which are used during hostage rescue operations.

Delta operators also enjoy some of the best training facilities in the world, and have access to an Olympic-sized swimming pool, dive tank, three-storey climbing wall, as well as numerous shooting ranges (include a CQB and sniping facility). The vast majority of Delta's recruits come from the elite Ranger and Airborne battalions. However, a significant number of potential candidates also come from conventional army units, including the Army Reserve and National Guard. Selection and training for Delta is extremely demanding with only the best candidates chosen.

TASK FORCE 11

Task Force 11 is a super elite unit, comprising several hundred Navy SEALS, Army Delta Force soldiers plus their respective support units from the Joint Special Operations Command in North Carolina. The unit was formed in late 2001, following the events of 11 September, when terrorists belonging to the Al-Qaeda (The Base) network attacked America without warning.

In response, America's President, George W. Bush, vowed to hunt down all terrorists that threatened the USA and its way of life, and launched Operation 'Enduring Freedom', a rolling campaign of military action that will fight terrorism around the world for decades to come.

Task Force 11 has the prime mission of hunting down senior members of the Al-Qaeda network, and will continue to do so until they are utterly annihilated. Although most of the units, operations are highly classified, they are known to have participated in Operation 'Anaconda', which was mounted during March

2002. This sixteen day counter-terrorist mission involved more than 1,200 US personnel, including 200 special forces who were deployed by the 101st Airborne Division(Air Assault) into the high mountain ranges of eastern Afghanistan in what was to be a dangerous and very difficult operation. Although the operation was successful in that it inflicted hundreds of casualties on the Al-Qaeda/Taliban (AQT) forces and drove them en masse from Afganistan into Pakistan, it was also costly as eight Americans were killed and seventy-three wounded.

After Anaconda ended, numerous follow-up operations were mounted by Task Force 11 throughout Afghanistan, mainly around villages and cave complexes, but some involved hot pursuits over the border into Pakistan. Task Force 11 tries to maintain a low profile as much as possible, and generally operates in small four-man teams, but these can be increased in size if tactically viable. As the President said at the beginning of Operation 'Enduring Freedom', This will be a war that's going to go in various phases, some of which will be visable, some will not.

In September 2002, Task Force 11 played a key part in two significant operations, one in Afghanistan, the other in Pakistan. On 5 September 2002, a small team of US special forces, acting as bodyguards for Afghanistan's President Hamid Karzai, foiled an assassination attempt after his motorcade was attacked by a lone gunman wearing the uniform of the new Afghan Army. During the short firefight, the gunman was killed along with one of the presidents Afgan bodyguard and a US special forces operator, wearing civilian clothing, was slightly wounded as he attempted to protect the president.

The second incident involving Task Force 11 took place in Pakistan on 14 September 2002 and involved other agencies such as the American CIA and the Pakistani intelligence service, the ISI (Inter-Services Intelligence agency). Following a careless satellite telephone call made by one of the world's most wanted terrorists, Ramzi binalshibh the mastermind behind the 11 September attacks. US intelligence agencies and Task Force 11 were able to trace the call to an apartment in Karachi, and immediately launched an operation to apprehend him. For political reasons the arrest was made by members of the Pakistani security services. However, US special forces were on hand in the background, fully ready to take him out if called upon to do so.

As these operations were taking place, members of Task Force 11 were training and preparing for operations against Iraq, following Saddam Hussein's refusal to comply with UN demands to hand over information to western weapons inspectors, acting on a mandate concerning both his nuclear and chemical warfare capabilities.

Although Task Force 11 was set up as a vehicle for carrying out specific missions during Operation 'Enduring Freedom', its success during this campaign has warranted an increase in both its operational responsibilites and military capabilities, leading to calls for it to be turned into a permanent Super Force.

TASK FORCE 11 EQUIPMENT

Weapons and equipment used by Task Force 11 include the Colt M4 assault rifle, M16A2 assault rifle, Mini 14 assault rifle, Steyr AUG assault rifle, HK-G3 assault rifle, SOPMOD (Special Operations Peculiar Modification) M4A1 assault rifle, CAR 15 assault rifle, Stoner SR- 25 self loading rifle and Colt Model 733 assault rifle. Walther MP-K SMG, HK-MP5SD SMG, MAC 10 SMG, and UZI SMG, M249 SAW light machine gun, HK-13E light machine gun, M60 medium machine gun, M240B medium machine gun and Browning M2 .50 heavy machine gun. Remington 870 combat shotgun and Mossberg Cruiser 500 combat shotgun, HK-PSG-sniper rifle, M40A1 sniper rifle, M24 sniper rifle and Barret M82A1 .50 heavy sniper rifle.

Support weapons include the M203 40mm Grenade launcher, 81mm Mortar, 66mm LAW and Mk 19 40mm automatic grenade launcher, Stinger MANPAD and the M136 AT-4 anti-tank rocket. Beretta 92F handgun and SIG-Sauer P-228 handgun.

Specialist Weapon Sights include Aimpoint Comp M close quarter battle sight, M68 Aimpoint, M28 Aimpoint sight, AN /PEQ2 Infrared Target Pointer/Illuminator/Aiming laser (IPITAL) dual beam aiming device.

Uniforms worn by Task Force 11 include standard US army combat fatigues, Lizard suits, Urban Combat fatigues,Ghillie sniper suits and black nomex overalls which are worn during hostage rescue type operations.

Task Force 11 operators also make extensive use of body armour and night vision devices such as the AN /PVS-7 night vision goggles, and for additional protection they wear Bolle T800 ballistic goggles while operating in open areas. During counter-terrorist operations, TF-11 operators wear British Avon S10 respirators, body armour, anti-laser goggles and Nomex clothing.

Task Forced 11 also operates an extensive fleet of vehicles that include the Land Rover Defender 110 SOV (Special Operations Vehicle), Humvee, Quad ATV (All Terrain Vehicle), Harley Davidson Track bike and LSV (Light Strike Vehicle). Weapons mounted on vehicles include Mk 19 40mm automatic grenade launchers, M60 medium machine guns, M240B medium machine gun, General Electric 7.62 mini gun, 20mm cannon and Browning M2 .50 heavy machine gun. Other specialist equipment includes; Zodiac boats, submersibles, high speed patrol boats and rigid raiders. TF-11 also uses heavily modified parachutes for its HALO and HAHO parachute operations.

The Colt M4 assault rifle, complete with laser, night sight and 40mm grenade launcher.

Left: The Barret M82A1 .50 heavy sniper rifle.

An American soldier looks down the sight of a Mk 19, 40mm automatic grenade launcher.

Inset: Mk 19 showing belt fed 40mm grenades

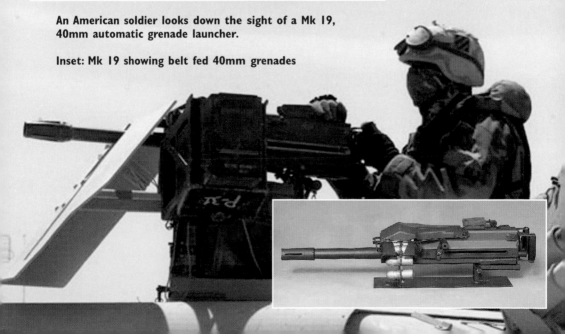

Although the most common means of transport for Task Force 11 is the helicopter, they will use literally anything, including horses as they ably demonstrated in Afghanistan. Helicopter types used include the MH-47 D/E Chinook, MH-60 K/L Blackhawk and MH-6 Little Bird which are operated by the US Army's 160th Special Operations Aviation Regiment. For long range missions, Task Force 11 uses the MH-53J which is operated by the USAF's Special Operations Group (SOG). Task Force 11 is extremely well funded, and can buy any weapon or piece of equipment it wants without going through laborious purchasing procedures. For its size, Task Force 11 is the best armed and equipped unit in the world.

TASK FORCE 11 OPERATIONAL HISTORY

2002: Deployed to the Philippines, Pakistan, Yemen, Saudi Arabia and Afghanistan as part of Operation 'Enduring Freedom'.

2003: Deployed to Iraq as part of Operation 'Iraqi Freedom' and 'Enduring Freedom' following Saddam Hussein's failure to comply with UN resolution 1441. Also during this period, elements of Task Force 11 were deployed to South Korea following a rise in tensions between the United States and North Korea.

101ST AIRBORNE DIVISION (AIR ASSAULT)
THE SCREAMING EAGLES

Based at Fort Campbell, Kentucky is the world's only air assault division, hence the designation 101st Airborne Division (Air Assault). Although not deemed a special forces unit like their neighbours, the 160th Special Operations Aviation Regiment (SOAR), the 101st Airborne Division is nevertheless an elite unit by any military standards and has no equals in terms of its sheer size and operational capability. The 101st Airborne Division (Air Assault) is formed of three brigades plus Division Artillery, Division Support Command, the 101st Aviation Brigade, 159th Aviation Brigade, 101st Corps Support Group and several separate commands. In terms of military personnel, the 101st comprises 26,819 men directly within its ranks and 18,166 support troops, making Fort Campbell the third largest military population in the army and the seventh largest in the Department of Defense.

The 101st can trace its history back to the Second World War when the unit was first formed on 15 August 1942. Within days of its activation, the first commander, Major General William C. Lee, promised his new recruits that the 101st has a rendezvous with destiny, and he was right. During the Second World War the 101st Airborne Division led the night drop prior to the D-Day invasion and when surrounded at Bastogne by the Germans and asked to surrender, Brigadier General Anthony McAuliffe gave the famous answer 'NUTS!'. Despite being outgunned and outnumbered the Screaming Eagles bravely fought on until

A Second World War 'Screaming Eagle', armed with a Thompson machine gun.

the siege ended and were awarded four campaign streamers and two Presidential Units Citations.

After the end of the second World War the 101st faced an uncertain future as there was little need for such a large airborne force during peacetime. However, in 1948 and again in 1950 the unit was temporarily reactivated as a training unit at Camp Breckinridge, Kentucky, until finally in March 1956, the 101st was transferred, less most of its personnel and equipment to Fort Campbell, Kentucky, where it was reorganized as a combat division.

In the mid-1960s, the 1st Brigade and its support troops were deployed to Vietnam, with the rest of the division joining them in 1967 to form the world's first airmobile division. Vietnam, was the birthplace of the air cavalry concept and the 101st were instrumental in its great success, as they proved that the idea of combining helicopters with light infantry in the airborne assault role made for a deadly combination. During their seven years in Vietnam, the 101st participated in fifteen campaigns and earned additional laurels to add to their proud history.

In October 1974, the 101st was redesignated as the 101st Airborne Division (Air Assault), resulting in the 3rd Brigade changing its operational capabilities from that of parachute to air assault. In addition to these changes, and to ensure maximum operational efficiency, the 101st created an Air Assault school that was specifically designed to teach new soldiers about the art of helicopter based warfare. This new generation of Air Assault soldiers was also given permission to wear the new emblem of the 101st, the Air Assault Badge.

In the mid-1970s, the 101st conducted numerous training and

Men of the 101st Airborne Division, clamber out of a Huey in Vietnam.

readiness exercises as part of their work-up phase. They also opened their Air Assault School to other US army units so as to ensure a better understanding of helicopter assault tactics, techniques and procedures used by infantry during combat operations. This training proved highly valuable and put the 101st in good stead for forthcoming operations.

On 12 December 1985, tragedy struck the 101st when 248 members of the division were killed in a plane crash near Gander, Newfoundland, while returning to Fort Campbell from a routine tour of duty in the Sinai.

Although a major set-back for the division on a personal level, the 101st still had a job to do. On 17 August 1990, elements of the 101st arrived in Saudi Arabia as part of the Allied coalition force. Their mission; to support Allied forces in their operations against Iraq. The first units of the 101st deployed in Saudi Arabia comprised 2,700 troops, 117 helicopters and 487 vehicles which were transported on board 110 USAF C-5 and C-141 transport aircraft, while the remainder of the division was transported by sea to the Saudi port of Am Damma, a journey that took forty-six days.

Once in theatre, the 101st established their base camp at King Fuad Airport, which was known to the 101st as Camp Eagle II. After a period of working-up the 101st deployed to a Forward Operating Base (FOB), code named Bastogne. From here they mounted round the clock training operations, that involved practising night assaults, urban assaults and street fighting.

On 17 January 1991, Operation 'Desert Storm', the mission to liberate Kuwait began, with the 101st Aviation Regiment drawing first blood. The initial attacks were carried out by eight AH-64 Apache helicopters against two Iraqi early warning radar sites that were key targets for the coalition forces. Once destroyed, Allied strike aircraft were able to bomb Baghdad with little fear of interception from Iraqi fighters. As these attacks went in, Blackhawk helicopters of 1st Battalion were flying CSAR patrols nearby, just in case any Allied aircraft were shot down. Throughout the air campaign, the 101st flew hundreds of sorties against Iraqi positions until ordered to stand down in preparation for the ground war. On 24 February 1991, the ground war began with the 101st and the French 6th Light Armoured Division advancing on the left flank of the coalition line towards Baghdad and the Euphrates river valley. The first stage of the operation involved 300 helicopters lifting the 101st Airborne to their first

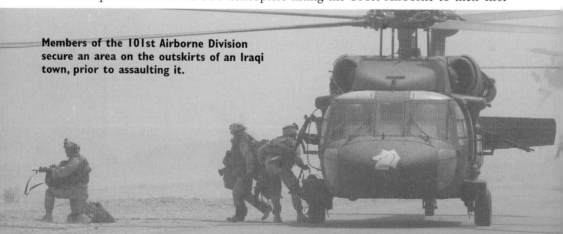

Members of the 101st Airborne Division secure an area on the outskirts of an Iraqi town, prior to assaulting it.

objective, FOB Cobra, located 110 miles inside Iraq. The arrival of the 101st at Cobra took the Iraqis, completely by surprise and following a short firefight, they surrendered. By the end of the day the 101st had consolidated its positions and cut Highway 8 which was Iraq's key supply route. This helicopter assault was the largest in modern warfare history. The following day, 3rd Brigade moved north to occupy positions on the southern bank of the Euphrates River, where they encountered little resistance. While this operation was taking place, the remaining elements of the 101st maintained their positions at Highway 8 and Cobra, effectively acting as a blocking force in the event of an Iraqi counter-attack.

On 26 February, the 101st began accepting the surrender of Iraqi soldiers en masse: the war was over. 'Desert Storm' had been a remarkable success story for the 101st as they had completed the largest helicopter assault in history, without a single loss of life.

After the Gulf War ended, the 101st Airborne Division returned home to Fort Campbell for some well deserved R & R, before embarking on a number of peacekeeping and humanitarian missions in places such as Rwanda, Somalia, Haiti and Bosnia.

Following the events of 11 September 2001, the 101st Airborne were deployed to Afghanistan in January 2002 to relieve the 26th Marine Expeditionary Unit. Their mission: to destroy the Al-Qaeda terrorist network and Taliban regime. As the 101st commenced operations in Afghanistan, they suffered their first casualties, when one soldier was killed and several wounded following a raid on a terrorist cave complex near Gardez.

On 2 March 2002, America launched Operation 'Anaconda'. Its mission; to find, capture or kill Osama bin Laden and his AQT (Al-Qaeda /Taliban) supporters. The mission in the eastern mountain ranges of Afghanistan was to last for sixteen days and involved some 1,000 US troops, including Special Forces and elements of the 101st Airborne and 10th Mountain Division. Anaconda hit problems right from the word go, as the 101st Airborne were given an landing zone right in the middle of the AQT positions instead of a valley that ran parallel to their defensive position.

As a result of this mistake, the American forces were ambushed by a massive AQT force and suffered many casualties, including eight fatalities and seventy-three wounded. The firefight was of such intensity, that every helicopter involved in supporting the ground forces was hit by effective enemy fire, resulting in the loss of two Chinooks and several others so badly damaged that they were unable to be used in Afghanistan again. Despite these setbacks, the 101st fought back with great determination and killed hundreds of Al-Qaeda terrorists before withdrawing. Although the American forces failed to find Osama bin Laden or indeed any of his lieutenants, the operation was deemed successful as it forced the remaining AQT forces out of Afghanistan and into nearby Pakistan.

In 2003, the 101st were deployed to Kuwait, and later Iraq, for Operation 'Iraqi Freedom' where they carried out numerous attacks against Republican Guard units defending Baghdad-culminating in its spectacular fall. This victory was in part achieved through combined operations with the 3rd Infantry Division, who fought their way up through southern Iraq as part of a three-pronged attack. At one stage, a plan was drawn up that involved the 101st mounting a massive air assault on the city of Baghdad but Saddam's regime fell before it could be implemented, much to the disappointment of its 17,000 members.

PRIMARY WEAPON SYSTEMS

Infantry, Attack helicopters, Support helicopters, Field Artillery, Air Defence Artillery.

Helicopter Types used by the 101st Airborne Division (Air Assault) include:

AH-64 APACHE ATTACK HELICOPTER: used for close support, light strike, anti-tank and escort missions.

OH-58D KIOWA WARRIOR: used for armed reconnaissance and scouting missions.

UH-60 BLACKHAWK TRANSPORT HELICOPTER: used for short-range infiltration/exfiltration missions, plus Medevac.

CH-47 CHINOOK: used for medium range support, infiltration/exfiltration type missions plus heavy lift.

MISSION

To deploy within thirty-six hours worldwide to close with the enemy by means of fire and manoeuvre to destroy or capture him, or to repel his assault by fire, close combat or counter-attack.

OVERVIEW OF FORT CAMPBELL, KENTUCKY

SIZE OF POST

At 164 square miles (105,068 acres), the installation is one of the largest in the world. Today, approximately 12,000 acres of the installation have been developed into the cantonment area while the remaining 93,000 plus acres of the reservation are dedicated to training and firing ranges.

Ranges	52
Major Drop Zones	5
Assault Landing Strip	1
A2C2 Air Sectors	10
Bayonet Assault Course	1
Rappel Tower	1
MOUT Facilities	3
Impact Areas	3

Demo Areas	I
Manoeuvre Areas	20
Artillery Firing Points	340

82ND AIRBORNE DIVISION

Based at Fort Bragg, North Carolina is America's illustrious 82nd Airborne Division. The 82nd is made up of a Divisional Headquarters, a Divisional Support Command and three Airborne Brigades. Each Brigade consists of three parachute battalions plus a HQ and support element that is equipped with mortars, anti-tank missiles and heavy machine guns.

Entry into the 82nd is either by direct application or by volunteering from another unit. Before entering the Airborne brotherhood, all candidates must first pass a tough selection procedure, followed by a rigorous training programme and parachute course, after which they get their 'Wings' and maroon beret.

The primary role of the 82nd Airborne is to arrive by air, take control of the ground, and hold it until relieved by a main force unit. At any given time, one parachute battalion is on an eighteen-hour standby, with one of its companies on two-hour standby. One of the Brigades, the Ready Brigade, rotates around the division and is on twenty-four hour notice to move.

Airlift capability for the Division is provided by Boeing C-17 Globemasters, Lockheed C-141 Starlifters and C-130 Hercules of the USAF. During operations each soldier is issued with enough food rations, water and ammunition to last for three days. After that a resupply is necessary.

82ND AIRBORNE EQUIPMENT

Weapons used by the 82nd Airborne Division include the M16A2 assault rifle, Colt M4 assault rifle, M249 SAW light machine gun, M60 medium machine gun, M2.50 cal heavy machine gun, M203 40mm grenade launcher and 81mm mortar.

The 82nd has seen action in places such as Vietnam, Grenada, Panama and Afghanistan.

'BROTHERS IN ARMS' THE ROYAL MARINES AND THE UNITED STATES MARINE CORPS

The Royal Marines

The Royal Marines are an integral part of the Royal Navy, and were formed in 1942 as a commando force. Their current ORBAT (Order of Battle) comprises some 500 officers and 5,500 men, all highly trained and well-equipped for both the rigours of land and sea warfare. By UK standards they are

Royal Marine Commandos in a well armed Land Rover, speed away from a Chinook during a deployment exercise in Kuwait.

only deemed an elite force, but by any other they are Special Forces. The United States in particular, holds them in great esteem as they have a very close working relationship with the US Marine Corps.

The Royal Marines are always ready and willing to deploy at a moment's notice as they are a spearhead unit. The bulk of their manpower is grouped into lightly armed battalion-sized units-known as commandos, of which there are currently three and together they form 3 Commando Brigade. The Brigade is a key component of the UK's Joint Rapid Deployment Force (JRDF), and it played a major role in fighting Al-Qaeda terrorists in Afghanistan.

ROYAL MARINES EQUIPMENT

Weapons used by the Royal Marines include: The SA-80A2 Assault rifle, the SA-80A2 LSW (Light Support Weapon), the 5.56 Minimi SAW (Squad Assault Weapon), the 7.62 GPMG (General Purpose Machine Gun), the Colt M4 Assault rifle, the M16A2 Assault rifle, the M203 Grenade launcher and the HK-MP5 sub-machine gun.

The American M16 assault rifle, also used by the Royal Marines.

THE UNITED STATES MARINE CORPS (USMC)

The USMC comprises some 175,000 active and 40,000 reserve marines, organized into four divisions, making it one of the largest forces in the world today.

Since 1775, US Marines or 'Leathernecks' as they are more commonly known, have been involved in almost all American military activities and have earned an enviable reputation for their fighting prowess. They are a vital part of America's Rapid Deployment Force and have always been considered an elite force.

The USMC divisions (three active and one reserve) are organized, armed and equipped on the same triangular basis as the US Army, namely three infantry regiments, each of three battalions (however USMC units normally have some twenty per cent more manpower than their Army equivalents). The Marines are self-supporting and have assets such as fighters, attack helicopters, transport aircraft, assault ships, tanks, artillery etc.

Within this formidable force are specialists, such as:

- Marine force reconnaissance (in US parlance 'recon') units.
- Marine long-range reconnaissance battalions (LRRP).
- Search and target acquisition platoons (normally one per USMC regiment).
- Fleet radio reconnaissance platoons (one Atlantic and one Pacific).
- Air-naval gunfire liaison companies (ANGLICO).
- Fleet anti-terrorism security teams (to provide swift, short-term, professional protection on a worldwide basis, as and when needed).

US Marines secure a perimeter, prior to launching an assault on an Iraqi position.

Members of such units must undergo similar training to SOF personnel, so that they can undertake their missions by land, sea and air, including, for example, parachuting and SCUBA diving.

Each active marine division maintains a reconnaissance battalion for tactical reconnaissance, and a force reconnaissance company. The latter contains four platoons and three direct-action platoons. The seven platoons each consist of sixteen marines, divided into four-man patrols. As they have to be the eyes and ears of the division they must be expert in aerial infiltration (HAHO and HALO) and SCUBA diving. Considered to be the 'elite' of the USMC, they can volunteer only after three to four years in the Corps and after qualifying on a specialised course (e.g. for selected marksmen) or being a member of a specialized unit such as the Scout Sniper Platoon (SSP). They must also pass the Army airborne test which includes running three miles in eighteen minutes, swimming 500m, retrieving a heavy object from the bottom of a swimming pool and completing a testing obstacle course in under five minutes.

Following an interview they then go on to form part of the Recon Indoctrination Platoon (RIP) to complete their training Later they attend the school of Amphibious Reconnaissance and have to pass a three-week diving course, followed by a month of parachuting.

The standards are exceptionally high, with only two or three out of the original sixty being eventually selected. Following their posting to a unit they will complete their training which will include courses at Survival, Escape, Recon and Evasion (SERE) School, Scout Sniper School (SSS) and Jungle Environment Survival Training (JEST). A chosen few may also be integrated into Delta Force (Army) or Team 6 (Marines).

There are also plans to create a USMC Special Operations Command because so many marines are now trained and experienced in special forces type warfare.

IRAQ
THE REPUBLICAN GUARD

Originally based in Baghdad, and consisting of seven divisions are Iraq's shock troops, the Republican Guard.

Although originally formed to protect the government, its tanks, mechanized infantry and ground troops, the Republican Guard performed so well during the Iran-Iraq war that it also found itself protecting Iraq's President Saddam Hussein as it was now deemed special forces.

The decision to change the Republican Guard status was also in part due to a major reorganization within the Iraqi armed forces that took place during the 1980s. This change affected all aspects of the Iraqi military including its arms suppliers, hieracy, deployments and political character.

Prior to 1991, the Iraqi Army had an estimated strength of 1.7 million personnel, including reserves and paramilitary forces, with the Republican

Guard accounting for a significant percentage of this figure. In 1987 the Iraqi army had seven corps, five armoured divisions (each with one armoured brigade and one mechanized brigade), and three mechanized divisions (each with one armored brigade and two or more mechanized brigades). By the end of the Iran-Iraq war the Iraqi army general headquarters supervised up to ten corps headquarters, which carried out logistical and administrative tasks as well as directing operations. Each corps commanded as many as ten armoured, infantry or mechanized divisions, depending on the operational situation at the time.

Within the Army the Brigade was normally the smallest unit to operate independently. Also subordinate to the general headquarters was the corps size Republican Guard Forces Command which consisted of three armoured divisions, one infantry division and one commando division all of which operated seperately from the regular army.

When Saddam Hussein invaded Kuwait in 1990, the Republican Guard played a major part in the initial invasion and then acted as a theatre reserve force once operations had ceased. The Republican Guard appeared high on the list of targets when western military planners plotted the ousting of Iraqi forces from Kuwait as they posed a significant threat to allied ground forces. From the outset of Operation 'Desert Storm' the Republican Guard was subjected to constant air attack but never broke. This was quite a remarkable feat as it was deployed in open desert where it had little or no cover, yet it stood its ground and put up stiff resistance. During the ground invasion phase of Desert Storm the American 24th Infantry Division encountered heavy resistance from the 47th and 49th Infantry Divisions who were part of the Nebuchadnezzar Division of the Republican Guard. In addition the 26th Commando Brigade also fought with great distinction against both American Infantry and armored units. Eventually the US 1st Armored Division succeeded in defeating elements of the Tawakalna Division, while the 3rd Armoured Division engaged remnants of the Tawalzalaa, Madina and Adnan Divisions of the Republican Guard.

After the end of the Gulf War, the Republican Guard were used to suppress anti-government forces as well as elements of the Iraqi army who mounted a failed coup against Saddam. Since the first Gulf War ended, the Republican Guard has reoganized and re-equipped and is now trained to operate in an unconventional manner for the purpose of mounting guerilla warfare type operations.

The Republican Guard was commanded by Qusai Saddam Hussein, and the Chief of Staff is staff General Ibrahim Abd Al Sattar Mohammad Al-Tikriti.

A typical Republican Guard armoured division consists of the following:

DIVISIONAL HEADQUARTERS
2 Tank Brigades
3 Tank Battalions
1 Motorized Special Forces Company

1 Mechanized Infantry Battalion
1 Engineering Company
1 Medium Rocket Launcher Battery
1 Reconnaissance Platoon
1 Mechanized Infantry Brigade
3 Mechanized Infantry Battalions
1 Tank Battalion
1 Anti-tank Company
1 Motorized Special Forces Company
1 Engineering Company
1 Reconnaissance Platoon
1 Medium Rocket Launcher Battery

Divisional Artillery Brigade
3 Self-propelled Artillery Battalions (155 mm SP)
2 Self-propelled Artillery Battalions (152 mm SP)
2 Self-propelled Artillery Battalions (122 mm SP)

Separate Units
3 Motorized Special Forces Battalions
1 Anti-tank Battalion
1 Reconnaissance Battalion
1 Engineer Battalion

REPUBLICAN GUARD EQUIPMENT

Weapons used by the Republican Guard include the AK-47 assault rifle, AK-74 assault rifle, AKSU-74 SMG, RPK light machine gun, Type 74 medium machine gun and RPG-7 anti-tank rocket launcher.

The Russian made AK-47 assault rifle, used by the Iraqi Republican Guard.

THE IRAQ ARMY

Prior to Operation 'Iraqi Freedom', the Iraqi army had a strength of some 375,000 personnel of which at least a third were reservists, while in 1991 the strength of the army was put at around a million plus.

The Army has been beset with problems ranging from lack of new equipment to lack of officers, as Kurds and Shias cannot become officers, due to the ethnic and religious tensions that exist within Iraq. Adding to these problems, is the fact that the Iraqi army is competing against other organizations with military and quasi-military roles, such as the Republican Guard, Special Republican Guard, Brigade 999 and the Fedayeen Saddam, all of which receive better pay, equipment, status and privileges than those enjoyed by the army proper.

The army operates at a command level of a corps, with each exercising control over a particular geographical area, within which it is responsible for all ground combat operations, along with both logistical and administrative support.

The Iraqi army is composed of seven corps, each of which is allocated a number of divisions, usually numbering three or four, and all have direct control over their, corps assets, such as artillery and helicopters. Corps headquarters are generally located in buldings above ground-level, but in wartime revert to underground bunkers or mobile field command centres.

In 1991, at the start of the first Gulf War, the Iraqi army had some seven armoured and mechanized divisions and twenty infantry divisions. However, following heavy losses in the war, of both men and materiel, as well as numerous reorganizations, the army is now only about seventeen divisions strong-but these are not comparable to a US division.

At the end of 2002, the Iraqi army was organized into three armoured divisions, three mechanized divisions, and eleven infantry divisions. Its estimated equipment levels were put at 2,000 main battle tanks 3,000 armoured personnel carriers and 2,000 artillery pieces.

FEDAYEEN SADDAM (Meaning Men of Sacrifice)

Although not a special forces unit as such, the paramilitary Fedayeen Saddam warrants a mention here as it fought alongside elements of the Iraqi special forces in a way that proved far more successful than any regular unit of the Iraqi army. Formed in 1995, by Saddam Hussein's son, Uday, the Fedayeen has an operational strength of some 40,000 members who are trained to mount operations against dissidents and foreigners alike. Some have even been trained by the Chechens to carry out suicide attacks in the same manner as the Palestinian Fedayeen. Indeed, on several occasions during Operation 'Iraqi Freedom', they were successful in their efforts against US service personnel, who greatly feared them.

At present, some elements of the Fedayeen are still at large, and continue to attack US forces on a regular basis. They now operate in groups of twenty plus, as this is deemed the optimum number when fighting guerilla type operations. More alarmingly, they have formed offshoot groups who are even more extreme in their views and methods than they are. These groups are known as the 'Sons of Saddam' and 'The Return' and operate primarily around central and northern Iraq where they can easily blend in with the locals.

For US forces operating on peacekeeping duties within Iraq, they pose a considerable threat, as they are growing in number all the time and, more alarmingly, are not afraid to take them on. They are without doubt, the most lethal legacy of Saddam Hussein's fallen regime.

SPECIAL REPUBLICAN GUARD

The Special Republican Guard is effectively an elite within an elite, and was formed by Saddam Hussein to overcome the increasing problem of insuring the political reliability of his Republican Guard units. Prior to Operation 'Iraqi Freedom', the Special Republican Guard comprised some 15,000 well equipped troops that were trained to fight as a conventional force if tactically feasible, but as a guerilla force if unfeasable. Their role now also encompasses the support of other forces but these are unconventional militia forces, and include the 'Fedayeen Saddam', the 'Sons of Saddam' and the 'Return' as well as some foreign mercenaries.

The Special Republican Guard, is organized into four 'Special Republican Guard Brigades' and has a reserve force of some 10,000 personnel.

CHAPTER FIVE

FORCES INVOLVED

UK FORCES INVOLVED IN OPERATION IRAQI FREEDOM

ROYAL NAVY

Rear Admiral David Snelson

HMS *Ark Royal* (aircraft carrier)
HMS *Ocean* (helicopter carrier)
HMS *Edinburgh* (Type 42 destroyer)
HMS *Liverpool* (Type 42 destroyer)
HMS *York* (Type 42)
HMS *Marlborough* (Type 23 frigate)
HMS *Richmond* (Type 23 frigate)
HMS *Chatham* (Type 22 frigate)
HMS *Grimsby* (minehunter)
HMS *Ledbury* (mine hunter)
HMS *Brocklesby* (minehunter)
HMS *Blyth* (minehunter)

HMS *Splendid* (Swiftsure class submarine)

HMS *Turbulent* (Trafalgar class submarine)

RFA *Argus*
RFA *Sir Tristram*
RFA *Sir Galahad*
RFA *Sir Percivale*
RFA *Fort Victoria*
RFA *Fort Rosalie*
RFA *Fort Austin*
RFA *Orangeleaf*

A Royal Navy warship
on patrol in the Gulf.

A hovercraft serving with the Royal Marines,
returning from a patrol in the Al-Faw peninsula.

British
soldier on
patrol, armed
with the
Minimi 5.56
machine gun.

A Scimitar driving
through Iraq's featureless
desert plain.

The Gazelle Helicopter, used for observation, reconnaissance and target designation. It is also used as an anti-tank attack helicopter.

An RAF Harrier prepares for a night sortie.

The silhouette of a fully armed Tornado F3, patrolling the 'No Fly Zone'.

ROYAL MARINES AMPHIBIOUS FORCE

Commodore Jamie Miller

Comprising some 4,000 personnel from HQ 3 Commando Brigade

Brigadier Jim Dutton
    40 Commando Royal Marines
    42 Commando Royal Marines
    45 Commando Royal Marines
    29 Regiment, Royal Artillery *(equipped with 105mm light guns)*
    539 Assault Squadron, RM
    59 Commando Squadron, RE

Plus elements of the **SBS** *(Special Boat Service)*

Helicopter air groups deployed on board HMS *Ark Royal* and HMS *Ocean* 845, 846, 847 and 849 Squadrons.

ARMY

Major General Robin Brims

1 (UK) Armoured Division:
Headquarters and 1 Armoured Division Signal Regiment
    30 Signal Regiment *(strategic communications)*
    The Queens Dragon Guards *(reconnaissance)*
    1st Battalion The Duke of Wellingtons Regiment
    (additional infantry support)
    28 Engineer Regiment
    1 General Support Regiment, Royal Logistics Corps
    2 Close Support Regiment, Royal Logistics Corps
    2nd Battalion, Royal Electrical and Mechanical Engineers
    1 Close Support Medical Regiment
    5 General Support Medical Regiment
    1 Regiment, Royal Military Police

plus elements from:
    30 Signal Regiment
    33 EOD Regiment
    32 Regiment Royal Artillery *(equipped with Phoenix UAVs)*

7TH ARMOURED BRIGADE

Brigadier Graham Binns

Headquarters and Signal Squadronn:
    Royal Scots Dragoon Guards *(equipped with Challenger 2 tanks)*
    2nd Royal Tank Regiment *(equipped with Challenger 2 tanks)*

1st Battalion The Black Watch *(equipped with Warrior Infantry Fighting Vehicles)*

1st Battalion Royal Regiment of Fusiliers *(equipped with Warrior Infantry Fighting Vehicles)*

3rd Regiment Royal Horse Artillery *(equipped with AS90 self-propelled guns)*

32 Armoured Engineer Regiment

plus various elements from other units including:

Queen's Royal Lancers *(equipped with Challenger 2 tanks)*

1st Battalion Irish Guards *(equipped with Warrior Infantry Fighting Vehicles)*

1st Battalion The Light Infantry *(equipped with Warrior Infantry Fighting Vehicles)*

26 Regiment Royal Artillery

38 Engineer Regiment

16 AIR ASSAULT BRIGADE

Brigadier Jacko Page

Headquarters and Signal Squadron

1st Battalion The Royal Irish Regiment

1st Battalion The Parachute Regiment

3rd Battalion The Parachute Regiment

7 (Para) Regiment Royal Horse Artillery *(equipped with 105mm light guns)*

23 Engineer Regiment

D Sqn, Household Cavalry Regiment

3 Regiment Army Air Corps *(equipped with Lynx and Gazelle helicopters)*

7 Air Assault Battalion, Royal Electrical and Mechanical Engineers

13 Air Assault Support Regiment, Royal Logistic Corps

16 Close Support Medical Regiment

156 Provost Company RMP

102 LOGISTICS BRIGADE

Brigadier Shaun Cowlan

Headquarters 2 Signal Regiment

36 Engineering Regiment

33 and 34 Field Hospitals

202 Field Hospital *(Volunteer)*

4 General Support Medical Regiment

3 Battalion, Royal Electrical and Mechanical Engineers

6 Supply Regiment, Royal Logistic Corps

7 Transport Regiment, Royal Logistic Corps
17 Port and Maritime Regt, Royal Logistic Corps
23 Pioneer Regiment, Royal Logistic Corps
24 Regiment, Royal Logistic Corps
5 Regiment, Royal Military Police

plus additional support and specialist units from:

12 Engineer Brigade *(airfield engineer support unit)*
11 EOD Regiment
Royal Logistic Corps

ROYAL AIR FORCE

Air Vice Marshal Glenn Torpy

12, 14, 617 Squadrons, RAF Lossiemouth
11, 25 Squadrons, RAF Leeming
43, III Squadrons, RAF Leuchars
6, 41. IV Squadrons, RAF Cottesmore
8, 23, 51 Squadrons, RAF Waddington
33 Squadron, RAF Benson
10, 99, 101, 216 Squadrons, RAF Brize Norton
24, 30, 47, 70 Squadrons, RAF Lyneham
120, 201, 206 Squadrons, RAF Kinloss
7, 18, 27 Squadrons, RAF Odiham

plus composite Squadrons, formed from elements of:

9, 13, 31, 39 (1 PRU) Squadrons, RAF Marham, RAF Regiment

AUSTRALIAN FORCES

HMAS *Kanimbla*
HMAS *Anzac*
HMAS *Darwin*

AIR FORCE

One RAAF squadron (equipped with F/A 18 aircraft)
Three RAAF C-130 aircraft
Two P3C Orion aircraft

ARMY

Special Forces Task Group
(includes SAS and 4 Royal Australian Regiment)

POLISH FORCES
GROM (SPECIAL FORCES)

US FORCES

US ARMY
Special Operations Command

> 5th Special Forces Group
> 75th Ranger Regiment
> 160th Special Operations Aviation Regiment
> Delta Force (deployed with Task Force 20)

3RD INFANTRY DIVISION

> 1st Battalion, 39th Dd Artillery Regiment
> 11th Aviation Regiment

1st Brigade:

> 2nd, 3rd Battalions, 7th Infantry Regiment
> 3rd Battalion, 69th Armor Regiment
> 1st Battalion, 41st Fd Artillery Regiment

2nd Brigade

> 3rd Battalion, 15th Infantry Regiment
> 1st, 4th Battalions, 64th Armor Regiment
> E Troop, 9th Cavalry Regiment
> 1st Battalion, 9th Fd Artillery Regiment

3rd Brigade

> 1st Battalion, 30th Infantry Regiment
> 1st Battalion, 15th Infantry Regiment
> 2nd Battalion, 69th Armor Regiment
> D Troop, 10th Cavalry Regiment
> 1st Battalion, 10th Fd Artillery Regiment

Aviation Brigade

> 1st Battalion, 3rd Aviation Regiment
> 2nd Battalion, 3rd Aviation Regiment
> 3rd Squadron, 7th Cavalry Regiment

82ND AIRBORNE DIVISION

> 2nd Brigade Combat Team

1st, 2nd 3rd Battalions, 325th Airborne Infantry
1st Battalion, 82nd Aviation Regiment

101ST AIRBORNE DIVISION

1st Brigade, 101st Airborne Division

1st, 2nd, 3rd Battalions, 327th Infantry Regiment
2nd Brigade, 101st Airborne Division
1st, 2nd, 3rd Battalions, 502nd Infantry Regiment
3rd Brigade, 101st Airborne Division
1st, 2nd, 3rd Battalions, 187th Infantry Regiment

101st Aviation Brigade

2nd Battalion, 17th Cavalry Regiment
1st, 2nd, 3rd, 6th Battalions, 101st Aviation Regiment

159th Aviation Brigade

4th, 5th, 7th, 9th Battalions, 101st Aviation Regiment

Divisional Artillery

1st, 2nd, 3rd Battalions, 320th Fd Artillery Regiment

173rd Airborne Brigade

1st, 2nd Battalions, 508th Infantry
173rd Engineer Detachment
173rd Brigade Recon Company
Battery D, 3rd Battalion, 319th Airborne Field Artillery

US MARINE CORPS

I MARINE EXPEDITIONARY FORCE

1st Marine Division

1st Marine Regiment
3rd Battalion, 1st Marines
1st Battalion, 4th Marines
1st, 3rd Battalions, Light Armored Recon

5th Marine Regt

1st Battalion, 5th Marines
2nd, 3rd Battalions, 5th Marines

7th Marine Regt

1st, 3rd Battalions, 7th Marines
3rd Battalion, 4th Marines

3rd Battalion, 11th Marines
1st Tank Battalion

2ND MARINE EXPEDITIONARY BRIGADE, 2ND MARINE DIVISION

1st, 3rd Battalions, 2nd Marines
2nd Battalion, 8th Marines
1st Battalion, 10th Marines
2nd Amphibious Assault Battalion
2nd Recon Battalion
2nd Light Armored Recon Battalion
2nd, 8th Tank Battalions

15th Marine Expeditionary Unit

24th Marine Expeditionary Unit

26th Marine Expeditionary Unit

US AIR FORCE
Special OPS

16th Special Ops Wing (AC-130)
20th Special Ops Squadron (MH-53M)
193rd Special Ops Wing (EC130E)

Ali Al Salem AB, Kuwait

386th Air Exped Group
118th Fighter Squadron (A-10)
41st Electronic Combat Squadron (EC-130)

Al Jaber AB, Kuwait

332nd Air Exped Group
52nd Fighter Wing
22nd, 23rd Fighter Squadrons (F-16)
172nd Fighter Squadron (A-10)
332nd Exped Air Support Ops Squadron
332nd Exped Intelligence Flight
332nd Exped Rescue Squadron (HH-60G)
552nd Air Control Wing (E3 AWACs)

Masirah AB, Oman

355th Air Exped Group
4th Special Ops Squadron (AC-130U)

An Australian soldier of 4 RAR, moves carefully through Iraqi territory.

American Chinook helicopter crewmen, converse while AH-64 Apache helicopters prepare for take off.

An F-15E Strike Eagle refuels after a combat mission over Iraq.

A US Navy patrol boat provides protection for a warship after receiving a threat warning of a possible suicide attack.

8th Special Ops Squadron (MC-130E)

Thumrait AB, Oman

405th Air Exped Wing
405th Exped Bomb Wing (B1B)
28th, 34th,37th Bomb Wings (B1B)
55th Wing (RC-135)

Al Udeid AB, Qatar

379th Air Exped Wing
49th Fighter Wing (F-117)
4th Ops Group (F-15)
336th Fighter Squadron (F-15)
93rd Air Control Wing (E8 J-STARS)

Al Dhafra AB, UAE

380th Air Exped Wing
9th, 57th Recon Wings (U2)
11th, 12th, 15th Recon Squadron (RQ1A)

Prince Sultan AB, Saudi Arabia

363rd Air Exped Wing
14th, 22nd Fighter Squadrons (F-16)
67th, 390th Fighter Squadrons (F-15)
457th, 524th Fighter Squadrons (F-16)
363 Exped Airborne Air Control Squadron (E3 AWACs)
38th Recon Squadron (RC-135)
99th Recon Squadron (U2)
VAQ-142 (EA-6B)

Diego Garcia

40th Air Exped Wing
509th Bomb Wing
20th,40th Bomb Squadrons (B2)

RAF FAIRFORD, UK

457th Air Exped Group
23rd Bomb Sqn (B52)
509th Bomb Wing
9th Recon Wing

US NAVY

THEODORE ROOSEVELT CARRIER BATTLE GROUP

USS *Theodore Roosevelt* (CVN 71)
Carrier Air Wing 8
USS *Anzi* (CG 68)
USS *Cape* St. George (CG 71)
USS *Arleigh Burke* (DDG 51)
USS *Porter* (DDG 78)
USS *Winston Churchill* (DDG 81)
USS *Stump* (DD 978)
USS *Carr* (FFG 52)
USS *Arctic* (AOE 8)

HARRY S. TRUMAN CARRIER BATTLE GROUP

USS *Harry S. Truman* (CVN 75)
Carrier Air Wing 3
USS *San Jacint* (CG 56)
USS *Oscar Austin* (DDG 79)
USS *Mitscher* (DDG 57)
USS *Donald Cook* (DDG 75)
USS *Briscoe* (DD 977)
USS *Dey* (DD 989)
USS *Hawes* (FFG 53)
USNS *Kanawha* (T-A196)
USNS *Mount Baker* (T-AE 34)
USS *Pittsburgh* (SSN 720)
USS *Montpelier* (SSN 765)

KITTY HAWK CARRIER BATTLE GROUP

USS *Kitty Hawk* (CV 63)
Carrier Air Wing 5
USS *Chancellorsville* (CG 62)
USS *Cowpens* (CG 63)
USS *John S. McCain* (DDG 56)
USS *O'Brien* (DD 975)
USS *Cushing* (DD 985)
USS *Vandergrift* (FFG 48)
USS *Gary* (FFG 51)
USS *Bremerton* (SSN 698)

ABRAHAM LINCOLN CARRIER BATTLE GROUP

USS *Abraham Lincoln* (CVN 72)

Carrier Air Wing 14
USS *Mobile Bay* (CG 53)
USS *Shiloh* (CG 67)
USS *Paul Hamilton* (DDG 60)
USS *Fletcher* (DD 992)
USS *Crommlein* (FFG 37)
USS *Reuben James* (FFG 57)
USS *Camden* (AOE 2)
USS *Honolulu* (SSN 718)
USS *Cheyenne* (SSN 773)

CONSTELLATION CARRIER BATTLE GROUP

USS *Constellation* (CV 64)
Carrier Air Wing 2
USS *Valley Forge* (CG 50)
USS *Bunker Hill* (CG 52)
USS *Higgins* (DDG 76)
USS *Thach* (FFG 43)
USS *Ranier* (AOE 7)
USS *Columbia* (SSN 771)
USS *Milius* (DDG 69)

NIMITZ CARRIER BATTLE GROUP

USS *Nimitz* (CVN 68)
Carrier Air Wing 11
USS *Princeton* (CG 59)
USS *Chosin* (CG 65)
USS *Fitzgerald* (DDG 62)
USS *Benfold* (DDG 65)
USS *Oldendorf* (DD 972)
USS *Rodney M. Davis* (FFG 60)
USS *Pasadena* (SSN 752)
USS *Bridge* (AOE-10)

AMPHIBIOUS TASK FORCE EAST

USS *Saipan* (LHA 2)
USS *Gunston Hall* (LSD 44)
USS *Ponce* (LPD 15)
USS *Bataan* (LHD 5)
USS *Kearsage* (LHD 3)
USS *Ashland* (LSD 48)
USS *Portland* (LSD 37)
Marine Aircraft Group 29

AMPHIBIOUS TASK FORCE WEST

USS *Boxer* (LHD 4)
USS *Bonhomme Richard* (LHD 6)
USS *Cleveland* (LPD 7)
USS *Dubuque* (LPD 8)
USS *Anchorage* (LSD 36)
USS *Comstock* (LSD 45)
USS *Pearl Harbor* (LSD 52)

TARAWA AMPHIBIOUS READY GROUP

USS *Tarawa* (LHA 1)
USS *Duluth* (LPD 6)
USS *Rushmore* (LSD 47)

NASSAU AMPHIBIOUS READY GROUP

USS *Nassau* (LHA 4)
USS *Austin* (LPD 4)
USS *Tortuga* (LSD 46)

IWO JIMA AMPHIBIOUS READY GROUP

USS *Iwo Jima* (LHD 7)
USS *Nashville* (LPD 13)
USS *Carter Hall* (LSD 50)

MINE COUNTERMEASURES DIV 31

USS *Ardent* (MCM 12)
USS *Dextrous* (MCM 13)
USS *Cardinal* (MHC 60)
USS *Raven* (MHC 61)

CHAPTER SIX

THE WAR

Giving pep talks and speeches before a battle or a war is not uncommon, but very few are as poignant and moving as the one given by Lieutenant Colonel Tim Collins, of the 1st Battalion of the Royal Irish at Fort Blair Mayne on the Iraqi border just prior to the conflict, a copy of which now hangs in the White House.

'It is my foremost intention to bring every single one of you out alive but there may be people among us who will not see the end of this campaign. We will put them in their sleeping bags and send them back. There will be no time for sorrow.

'The enemy should be in no doubt that we are his nemises and that we are bringing about his rightful destruction. There are many regional commanders who have stains on their souls and they are stoking the fires of hell for Saddam. He and his forces will be destroyed by this coalition for what they have done. As they die they will know their deeds have brought them to this place. Show them no pity.

'We go to liberate not to conquer. We will not fly our flags in their country. We are entering Iraq to free a people and the only flag which will be flown in that ancient land is their own. Show respect for them.

'There are some who are alive at this moment who will not be alive shortly. Those who do not wish to go on that journey we will not send. As for the others I expect you to rock their world.

'Wipe them out if that is what they choose. But if you are ferocious in battle remember to be magnanimous in victory.

'If someone surrenders, ensure that one day they go home to their family. The ones who wish to fight, well, we aim to please.' 'If you harm the regiment or its history by over enthusiasm in killing or in cowardice, know it is your family who will suffer. You will be shunned unless your conduct is of the highest, for your deeds will follow you down through history. We will bring shame on neither our uniform or our nation.

'It is not a question of if, it,s a question of when. We know he has *already devolved the decision to commanders, and that means he has taken the decision himself. If we survive the first strike we will survive the attack.*

'Iraq is steeped in history. It is the site if the Garden of Eden, of the Great Flood and the birthplace of Abraham. Tread lightly there. You will see things that no man could pay to see and you will have to go a long way to find a more decent, generous and upright people than the Iraqis. You will be embarrassed by their hospitality even though they have nothing.

'Don't treat them as refugees, for they are in their own country. Their children will be poor, in years to come they will know that the light of liberation in their lives was brought by you. If there are casualties of war then remember that when they woke up and got dressed in the morning they did not plan to die this day. Allow them dignity in death. Bury them properly and mark their graves.

'As for ourselves, lets bring everyone home and leave Iraq a better place for us having been there. Our business now is north.'

TUESDAY 18 MARCH

Late in the evening of Tuesday 18 March, some fifty dhows arrived in the Gulf, having left southern Iraq earlier in the day, in somewhat suspicious circumstances. As a precaution, warships of the coalition forces intercepted them and carried out search and seize boarding operations, as their were well founded fears that they were carrying explosives for use in possible suicide attacks. However, after carrying out thorough searches in which nothing of significance was found, the dhows were released to go about their normal business.

WEDNESDAY 19 MARCH

Coalition aircraft attack Iraqi targets in the southern no-fly zone, after friendly aircraft are engaged by anti-aircraft fire during a routine CAP (combat air patrol). Armed with precision guided weapons, the coalition aircraft attacked: communications sites near Az Zubayr, Mudaysis, and Ruwayshid; a mobile early warning radar and an air defense command centre at an Iraqi air base in the west of the country; an air traffic control radar near Basra, and in addition, in what Britain's Defence Secretary Geoff Hoon described as certain preliminary operations, they hit long-range artillery on the Al Faw peninsula, long-range artillery positions near Az Zubayr, and a surface-to-surface missile system near Basra-leading to speculation that the war had already started.

Elsewhere in southern Iraq, a USAF MH-53 Pave Low helicopter, carrying US Special Forces, made a crash landing in the region, after developing complications, thankfully without loss of life.

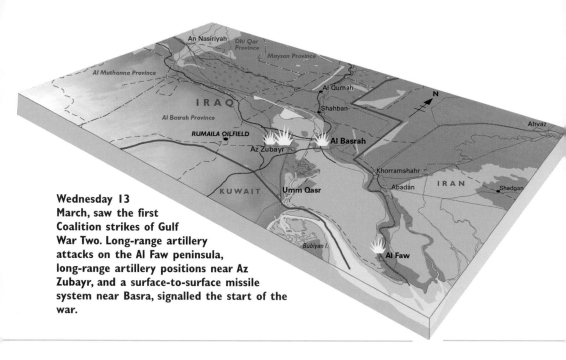

Wednesday 13 March, saw the first Coalition strikes of Gulf War Two. Long-range artillery attacks on the Al Faw peninsula, long-range artillery positions near Az Zubayr, and a surface-to-surface missile system near Basra, signalled the start of the war.

The helicopter, had been part of a major coalition operation to insert SF personnel into southern and western Iraq in advance of the main ground operations phase, and was destroyed so as to prevent it from falling into Iraqi hands.

The weather conditions prior to the assault were not good. Even though they can't see much, soldiers of the 101st Airborne Division try to carry on business as usual during a fierce sandstorm in northern Kuwait.

A formation of Black Hawk helicopters from the 101st Airborne Division (Air Assault) cross the Kuwaiti sky, 18 March.

THE BEGINNING OF THE END

On 19 March, after giving Saddam Hussein just forty-eight hours to leave Iraq or else face the consequences, President George W. Bush gave the go-ahead for a pre-emptive 'decapitation attack', the idea being to terminate the top Iraqi leadership in one precise surgical strike. Although not pre-planned as part of the 'Shock and Awe' campaign, the opportunity to take out Saddam in one single decisive action was just too good to overlook, as it would have saved thousands of lives, both friendly and enemy alike. The decision to circumvent the original OPLAN (Operational Plan) was taken by George W. following a tip-off by the CIA's super secret Special Operations Group (SOG) which had been operating covertly within Baghdad for several months prior to the outbreak of hostilities; its role being to gather intelligence and encourage insurrection.

The Americans call such an operation, a 'stake through the heart' mission, as its effects can be awesome if successfull, but disastrous if poorly planned and executed, a good example being Operation 'Market Garden' during the Second World War.

Essentially the attack comprised Tomahawk cruise missiles launched from both warships and submarines in the Gulf and a pair of F-117A Stealth fighters dropping laser-guided munitions on to a military compound. The attack began on 20 March, at approximately 05.30 hours local time ((02.30 GMT) with the munitions impacting on the city of Baghdad in a spectacular manner. For the watching media it was something of an anti-climax as they had been assured of an initial air attack consisting of some 3,000 cruise missiles.

As dawn broke in Washington DC, news of the attack started to filter through the media wires that Saddam had been either killed or mortally wounded during the initial attack, as spies on the ground had seen ambulances arrive at one of his compounds under heavy escort, but this proved to be a case of wishful thinking.

Meanwhile in the desert of Kuwait, at the time the world's biggest military parking lot- troops, tanks, APCs, artillery and support vehicles were being moved up to the Iraqi border in anticipation of the order to commence the ground phase of Operation Iraqi Freedom.

COMBAT REPORT
LOCATION: KUWAIT /IRAQ BORDER
Account from: A British Army NCO based with the Infantry.

'I had just heard through rumour control, that it had already kicked off and we were on our way. Most of us had thought that the ground phase would not commence until the end of the week, but hey, shit happens.

'The atmosphere amongst the men was mixed. Some were excited, some were scared, but most were just apprehensive, which is understandable. What I found reassuring however, was the ability of the men to still crack jokes, it seemed the more scared that they were, the more they larked about. What concerned me, was the fact that we were being bunched up, and had no cover. Had the Iraqi's known our situation, I'm sure that they would have targeted us, we would have been sitting ducks for their artillery, as we had no where to go. Even the Boss (the CO) looked edgy, which is saying something. He looked like an expectant father to be as he walked around the Warriors, checking on the men and their equipment, I guess that this was his way of dealing with things.

'As night fell the tension mounted. Everyone just wanted to get under way but we were on a no move for six hours.

'It's funny how although you are scared of what lies ahead one side of you just wants to get it over and done with. I guess the best comparison I can give is that of a footballer who trains and trains and just wants to play in a big game, like the FA Cup. This is my FA Cup, and its about everything I've ever trained for.

'Anyway it's for a good cause isn't it and as long as we don't lose anybody it will all have been worth it, at least thats my view anyhow.'

THURSDAY 20 MARCH

At around 05.30 hours, word came through that the first stages of ground operations against Iraq were now underway. In America it was designated Operation 'Iraqi Freedom', while in the UK it was Operation 'Telic', but either way the objectives were exactly the same, find the weapons of mass destruction and remove Saddam Hussein and his evil regime.

Essentially, the plan was as follows:

The British forces, supported by US Marines were to spearhead an operation to capture the ports of Umm Qasr and Basra in the south-east of the country, while US forces were to launch a two-pronged attack on the capital, Baghdad, with 5th Corps, led by the 3rd Infantry Battalion tasked with assaulting the city from the west, while the 1st Marines Expeditionary Force was to move on the city from the east.

As the ground force element of Operation 'Iraqi Freedom' advanced forward, some forty Tomahawk Land Attack Missiles (TLAMs) began impacting on Baghdad. These were launched by four ships and two submarines assigned to the US Navy's 5th Fleet. The four ships were: the cruiser USS *Cowpens* and the destroyer USS *Donald Cook* in the Red Sea and the cruiser USS *Bunker Hill* and destroyer USS *Milius* in the Persian Gulf. The submarines involved were the USS *Cheyenne* and the USS *Montpelier*. General Richard B. Myers, of the US Joint Chiefs of Staff, said:

> 'We took advantage of a leadership target of opportunity in Baghdad. We struck at one of the residences in south-eastern Baghdad where we thought the leadership was congregated. We also struck intelligence service headquarters in Baghdad and a Republican Guard facility.'

In retaliation, Iraq fired surface-to-surface missiles into Kuwait.

At around 20.00 hours the main ground attack began, when British artillery in northern Kuwait opened fire on Iraqi positions in and around the Basra and Al Faw areas- with a ferocious barrage that lasted for some twenty-five minutes.

At around the same time, three US warships and two Royal Navy submarines, HMS *Splended* and *Turbulent*, launched a TLAM attack against eight targets in Baghdad, firing some twenty missiles in the process.

The US warships were the destroyer USS *John S. McCain*, and the submarines *Columbia* and *Providence*. The target included, Saddam's main presidential complex; two of his palaces and the intelligence service headquarters.

In addition to this attack, a further one involving some ten TLAMs was also launched, the target being the Republican Guard units located in and around the Kirkuk area of northern Iraq. In the previous twenty-four hours, coalition Special Forces had seized an airfield in western Iraq and two major gas and oil terminals in the northern Persian Gulf.

That night, the land phase got underway with Royal Marines and US Marines heading eastwards to capture the Al Faw peninsula and Iraq's second city of Basra, while at the same time, US Forces drove 'hell for leather' for the town of Nasiriyah.

The attack on the Al Faw peninsula, comprised men of 3 Commando Brigade, Royal Marines, the 15th Marine Expeditionary Force, who were part of the US 1st Marine Expeditionary Force, and elements of the Special Boat Service. Their key objectives were the oil wells in the Ramaila oil fields, as well as the ports of

The coalition architects of war pose for the worlds media at a press conference.

Umm Qasr and Basra.

Air insertion for the Royal Marines was courtesy of RAF Chinook and Royal Navy Commando helicopters, while the US Marines were flown in by both US Navy and US Marine Sea Knight helicopters.

Sea insertion was provided by landing craft, raiding craft and hovercraft, while warships offshore provided gunfire support as they landed. On the gunline were the warships, HMS *Chatham*, *Marlborough* and *Richmond*.

Also offshore, there was gunfire support from British artillery units that had been landed on Bubiyan Island, while overhead, RAF Tornado aircraft provided top cover and close air support-bombing Iraqi artillery positions as well as other military installations on an 'as and when' needed basis.

As the main assault force went in, its flank was covered by two battlegroups of the UK's 7th Armoured Brigade, including the Black Watch and the 1st Battalion Royal Regiment of Fusiliers. Meanwhile, the US Army's 3rd Infantry Division began moving out across southern Iraq on a wide front, heading towards Nasiriyah.

The Division comprised 20,000 troops, 300 Abrams tanks and 300 Bradley Mechanized Infantry Combat Vehicles (MICV), making it a truly awesome force.

During the initial breakout, the Division was supported by the Royal Engineers as they sped into the desert on their way northwards, under cover of an artillery barrage that featured both guns and multiple launch rocket systems (MLRS).The force was led by the 3rd Squadron, 7th Cavalry Regiment, with the first tank over the border being an M1 Abrams of A Company, 3rd Battalion, 69th Armor Regiment.

As advance elements of the Division moved into Iraq, resistance was encountered from regular Iraqi Army units, but this was quickly eliminated by the heavily armed vehicles within the pack.

Elsewhere in the eastern Mediterranean, twenty F-14 Tomcats and F-18 Hornets, armed with a mixture of bombs and missiles left the aircraft carrier USS *Theodore Roosevelt* for Iraq, their targets being a palace complex and a broadcasting station.

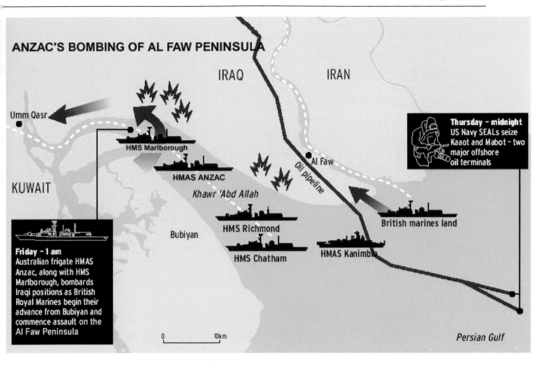

ANZAC'S BOMBING OF AL FAW PENINSULA

IRAQ   IRAN

Umm Qasr

HMS Marlborough

Thursday – midnight
US Navy SEALs seize
Kaaot and Mabot – two
major offshore
oil terminals

HMAS ANZAC

Al Faw

Oil pipeline

KUWAIT

Khawr 'Abd Allah

British marines land

Friday – 1 am
Australian frigate HMAS
Anzac, along with HMS
Marlborough, bombards
Iraqi positions as British
Royal Marines begin their
advance from Bubiyan and
commence assault on the
Al Faw Peninsula

Bubiyan

HMS Richmond

HMS Chatham   HMAS Kanimbla

0   10km

Persian Gulf

On this day, some 700 coalition aircraft flew missions against more than 100 Iraqi targets, including early warning radar sites, command and control facilities and surface-to-surface missile systems.

COMBAT REPORT

Compiled by Lieutenant Helena Bevan and 2nd Lt Ben Watson of 17/16 Battery, 26 Regiment.

The plan was that 17/16 Battery should move north in support of 1 MAR Division (US Marines) and through the breach at H+3 hours. As with all plans it changed and on March 18 we moved east, confidence boosted by recently-issued beige kit, to join D battery.

'Our mission was to provide fire support for 15 MEU, an American all-arms formation, whose aim was to push into Iraq through Umm Qasr. It was an impressive sight to see our vehicle fleet on the move. Having been used to training with six guns, a command post and a few 432 armoured fighting vehicles, we were now at full war-fighting establishment.

'On 20 March, following Scud and SAM missile attacks, we moved toward our H-hour firing position with eight AS90s, twelve 432 AFVs, an armoured ambulance, a REME fitter section with recovery vehicle and 434, and a huge echelon consisting of eleven Drops vehicles, two

JCBs and other supporting vehicles.

'H-hour, 0400 hours on 21 March, found us deployed a few kilometres south of the Iraqi-Kuwaiti border firing HE and smoke in support of the Americans on to observation towers and police posts along the Iraqi border and into Umm Qasr. We remained on the position that day firing sporadically and at nightfall moved through the breach. Evidence of former artillery and tank positions dotted the roadside, along with abandoned ammo and ramshackle shacks from which emerged smiling, waving locals.

'The battery move to its first position in Iraq involved a close encounter with a developing tank battle in which the recce party, led by Captain Charlie Holland, managed to get themselves embroiled. Luckily their Union flag was hoisted high and ensured their protection, and the incident yielded many good photographs. After waiting on the sidelines for the battle to end we deployed through the remnants of the Iraqi vehicles to our next gun position just south of the town of At Tubah Al Hamra. We remained there for three days, firing in support of 7 Armoured Brigade as it engaged regular and irregular forces between Az-Zubayr and Basra. Our next location was the former military airport at Shaibah. Reassuringly it was surrounded by huge stone bunkers, which were used to house the brigade HQ. We also shared the airfield with Challenger tanks, armoured infantry, engineers and a battery of Phoenix from 32 Regiment RA.

'From this position we fired large amounts of HE and bomblet into Basra and the surrounding area. Battle-damage assessments indicated that our use of L20 bomblet round was highly effective, destroying tanks, mortars and enemy positions as well as aiding numerous forays and allied advances.

'Great care was taken to ensure collateral damage was minimised. We also prosecuted a number of night gun raids to positions closer to Basra to take on targets that would otherwise have been out of range. The threat from rocket-propelled grenades in the area was high, which made road moves back to our base, in the early morning, unnerving. This was compounded by evidence of former Iraqi positions, burnt-out tanks, artillery pieces, rubble and junk littering the area.

'The guns rapidly won the confidence of tank and infantry commanders. But we proved too noisy and were ordered to collocate with J Battery in a nearby factory compound to ensure HQ's slumber remained undisturbed. We made ourselves comfortable in the new surroundings and found ourselves hosting news teams from GMTV, Sky and the BBC.

*'Following the discovery of drums of chlorine on our position, 17/16
and J Battery rapidly relocated to an abandoned military detention
centre on marshy ground 5km outside Basra. From there we fired more
illuminating and bomblet missions as troops from 7th Armoured
Brigade secured Basra. Events moved swifter than anticipated and
troops met with little resistance and much celebration from civilians.*

*'To the relief of the battery, orders were received to deploy out of
our swamp to Basra international airport and from there to a position
70km north of Basra to work with 7 PARA RHA in support of 16 Air
Assault Brigade. But the threat melted away and we headed south
again to rejoin 3 RHA and prepare for peacekeeping operations.*

*'Our entrance into Basra was a humbling experience as people
waved and cheered us and bashed at images of their former dictator
with sticks and rocks. By mid-April the whole of 3 RHA was sharing
the area of Basra University, where we conducted deep maintenance on
the guns and awaited further orders'.*

One of the strongest aspects of this war was that of the media coverage it
received, made possible by the fact that over 700 reporters, American and non-
American were assigned or embedded, to use American military parlance, to
both British and American forces operating in southern, central and northern
Iraq. The idea of the so-called 'embed', was to ensure that coalition operations
were portrayed in a positive light, while negative press from the Iraqis was
discredited as soon as possible, preventing any chance of allegations being made
of cover-ups in the event of things going wrong. In essence, the embedded
journalists lived, slept and eat with their hosts, sharing both the good and bad
experiences together in a manner likely to foster positive reporting, rather than
that of negative. The idea stemmed from previous wars, such as Vietnam, where
reporters were blamed for fuelling anti-war protests and negative combat
coverage reporting, on account of them feeling left out of the war. This contrasts
sharply with the last Gulf war, where correspondents got much more help and
support from the military, but access to the action itself , was strictly via videos
in briefing rooms, leading to the war being called the 'Nintendo War'. The jury
however, is still out as to whether embedded coverage is a good thing or a bad
thing, as many felt that the embeds lost their sense of objectivity, on account of
them working with the same group of people for the duration of the war.

In contrast, on the other side of the journalistic fence, there was the unilateral
journalist, a title pinned on those who operated independently of the embedded
forces, and consequently faced both higher rewards and higher risks, with many
paying the ultimate price for their professional desire to get the story behind the
story.

Covering the war from Saddam Hussein's perspective however, we had the
king of spin, Mr Mohammed Saeed al-Sahaf, Iraq's Minister of Information.

M2A2 Bradley Fighting Vehicles line up in the Kuwaiti desert, poised for the ground assault into Iraqi.

This man warrants an entire book alone, as the likes of him have never been seen before, and I doubt will ever be seen again.

Within days of his introduction to the world's media stage, he was nicknamed 'Comical Ali' on account of his outrageous claims and comments, while the British forces called him 'Baghdad Bob.' Usually, most official mouthpieces representing a tyrant or a dictator become the focus of unified hate and loathing, but not our 'Comical Ali', he actually became a cult hero and developed a world wide fan club who hung on to his every word. Amongst his fans were the US military, the Pentagon and the White House, who loved his daily briefings so much that they practically guaranteed his safety. When eventually captured by US Forces, he was treated with the utmost respect and compassion, and was only detained for a few days, while his fellow regime members when caught were treated with utter contempt and are now in long-term detention centres.

Mohammed Saeed al-Sahaf, (Comical Ali), Iraq's Minister of Information

FRIDAY 21 MARCH

Day Two of the conflict and the first operational casualties occur following the crash of a US Marine CH-46E Sea Knight helicopter in a non-combat related crash in northern Kuwait while participating in the Al Faw operation, killing eight British troops and four US aircrew. At the time of the crash there was

A plume of fire and black smoke billow into the sky as Marine aircraft from the 15th Marine Expeditionary Unit (Special Operations Capable) engage targets near Umm Qasr Iraq.

much speculation that it had been brought down by an Iraqi SAM but this theory was quickly dismissed, it was sheer bad luck and nothing more.

Key events of the day were the taking of the Al-Faw peninsula by members of the Royal Marines and the US Marines, their targets being the strategically important deep water port of Umm Qasr and the town of Safwan. As these operations were taking place, special forces secured the vital pumping stations in the Ramaila oilfield, as there were serious concerns following Saddam's threat to destroy them. In fact Saddam had ordered his forces to mount a scorched earth policy as a matter of course, but this failed in the main, on account of the Iraqi Army being reluctant to destroy their own country's precious assets, not to mention the fact that the British and American forces were advancing so fast now, that there was little chance of anyone implementing such a policy.

The fight for the Ramaila oilfield however, was not to be an easy one as the Iraqi's put up stiff resistance- killing a US Marine in the process, the first US serviceman to die in action during this war.

One problem the coalition forces were now encountering was that of mass surrender by the Iraqi troops-as there were just too many to document and

A Patriot interceptor from Battery E, 2nd Battalion, 43rd Air Defense Artillery Regiment, is launched just outside Camp Doha, Kuwait. The Patriot interceptor successfully engaged an Iraqi surface-to-surface missile, aimed at Coalition Forces.

process with the manpower available. Yes, they were prepared for taking prisoners, but not on this scale in one small area. In one case, the entire Iraqi 51st Mechanized Division surrendered en mass, causing considerable logistic problems for their captors.

As the day moved on, US Marines, supported by British armour and troops, reached the outskirts of Basra, while by sunrise, the 3rd Infantry Division's 1 Brigade Combat Team had advanced ten kilometres into Iraq- seizing an airfield south of Jalibah without any resistance. Meanwhile, offshore in the Khor Abdulah waterway in the approaches to Umm Qasr, Australian forces boarded three suspicious Iraqi vessels and found more than 130 sea mines primed and ready for use.

Just after 20.00 hours local time as night fell in Baghdad, a massive air assault commenced that comprised B-52H bombers operating out of RAF Fairford in the UK, B-1 Lancer bombers and ship launched TLAMs. In all the attack lasted for some forty-five minutes, and involved the firing of more than 400 TLAMs from both Royal Navy and US Navy ships deployed in the region. They included the British submarines *Splended* and *Turbulent*; the US cruisers, *Bunker Hill*, *Columbia*, *Cheyenne*, *Cowpens*, *San Jacinto*, *Mobile Bay* and *Shiloh*; the destroyers, *Arleigh Burke*, *Deyo*, *Briscoe*, *Donald Cook*, *Higgins*, *Fletcher*, *John S. McCain*, *Milius*, *O. Kane*, *Oscar Austin*, *Paul Hamilton* and *Porter*; US submarines included, *Key West*, *Augusta*, *Louisville*, *Montpelier*, *Newport News*, *Pittsburg*, *Providence*, *San Juan* and *Toledo*.

By the end of the day, coalition aircraft had flown more than 1,000 sorties in total since the conflict first began, dropping some 100 air-launched cruise missiles and 700 precision guided munitions. The night of 21 March, also saw RAF GR4 Tornado's fire for the first time in anger the UK's new Storm Shadow missile – a highly accurate weapon designed for long-range deep penetration bunker-busting missions.

And 'Comical Ali's' thoughts for the day were:

> **'Britain is not worth an old shoe,**
> **We will welcome them with bullets and shoes'.**

COMBAT REPORT

Night One – 21 March 2003 by RAF Tornado Pilot, Wing Commander 'Moose' Poole MA.

It was a straight forward night sortie as op missions go. Find a tanker, get some fuel, press to the target, drop some bombs, find another tanker to get enough fuel to land back at the base we started from. The KISS principle (Keep It Simple, Stupid) is always a good one to follow, yet there are times when even that isn't going to be enough – times when a huge slice of luck is definitely needed.

'The pre take-off preparations went reasonably smoothly, though I made life uncomfortable for myself by whacking my head on one of the undercarriage doors whilst doing the weapons checks. Fortunately, there was no blood, but the pain was an unnecessary "extra" on such a long mission. As soon as we taxied, it became clear that getting off the ground was going to take a bit more planning. With aircraft everywhere, both four-ships were baulked by US fighters doing their final arming checks. I sat in the lead of the second four, my access to the runway blocked by four F-15Es, the back pair of my formation behind two "blacks", as the F-117s are called. With gridlock similar to a Monday morning in Central London, I enquired over the radio whether the Eagles would like to get a "wiggle on" (a move on), as time was pressing. Finally they got out of the way and we launched on a round trip of 2,000 nautical miles, twelve minutes late.

'On the equivalent of the Hammersmith flyover, we joined the "commuters" flying up the Gulf, all in search of the mission critical tankers. Fortunately, the pre-arranged traffic flow meant that although we couldn't raise anybody on the radios apart from the Navy, this didn't matter – at this stage, anyway. For the ensuing tanker "goat" (a word used for getting fuel from a tanker), radios were to play their part.

'We arrived at the refuelling rendezvous (RV) some four minutes late, short of fuel and with no idea where the tankers were. With zero help from AWACS due to poor radio performance, no air-to-air TACAN (Tactical Aid to Navigation) and several options to choose from on the radar, it seemed highly likely that we would be spending the night on a remote strip in Saudi Arabia, having failed to complete the mission.

'My number two aircraft, with Dozy and Humpo on board, with a note of increasing concern, declared that they were really down on fuel. So are we, fellas – where the fuck are the tankers?

'Dozy spotted them on his night vision goggles (NVG) and called out: "Left 9 o'clock". The blob I was chasing on the radar was clearly not one of ours. We snapped left, giving our wingman some interesting challenges to remain in close formation – every man for himself in a situation like this. What a wonderful sight it is, when you've run out of fuel and ideas, to see those fuel hoses in your 12 o'clock – I'd rather be lucky than good. Still unable to talk to the tanker on the radio, we joined and plugged in, finally speaking to him on a totally different frequency. Only then did we find out that he was well down on the plan and that he couldn't give us as much as we needed. I heard the back pair join on the second tanker – God knows how they had stayed in, with us manoeuvring so much. Bouncing around on the top of the weather made refuelling particularly difficult and having taken

A brace of Tornado F3 interceptors perform a combat air patrol (CAP) over Iraq at the height of the air campaign phase.

several attempts ourselves, I watched young Dozy joust on the left hose. The weather was awful. Extreme turbulence made the trailing hose leap all over the place, as though possessed by demons. After some ten minutes, he got in, by which time we had taken our now limited fuel and were ready to go. Number Four had suffered a computer failure and, though refuelled, was not in a fit state to push. We decided to press on with just

Taking on fuel in mid-air is dangerous and demanding and requires the utmost patience and skill from all concerned in the operation. Here an RAF Tornado F3 tops up after an extended combat air patrol (CAP) over Iraq.

Number Three, being unable to wait for Dozy who had valiantly managed to get his fuel in the most extreme tanking conditions I have ever witnessed.

'So Moose (yes, another one!) and I and Lager and Jock pressed on. Still five minutes late, we had no catch-up on the four ahead. The radio situation didn't improve – we were still unable to raise the AWACS with the limited range of our Havequick radio, and where we were going it was unlikely to get better.

'As we pressed north, with radars on and with warning receivers showing little activity, we watched the bombing of Baghdad. Explosions under the cloud cover looked like the sort of light show Jean Michel Jarre might use, only this outdoor concert wasn't at

Houston. *Imagining the soundtrack, we watched missiles streak into the air in a volley of desperation, blindly hoping to find a coalition aircraft.*

'*After what seemed like eons, we reached the target. Always a tense place to be – the simplest of tasks becomes difficult as you struggle to funnel and restrain the adrenaline and get on with the job in hand. The training in the RAF is second to none – and boy do you depend on what has become your instinct when the enemy are shooting at you! There is no time to think what needs to be done, you need to do it automatically. We proceeded to pepper the target with precision strikes against carefully calculated pressure points – I was not surprised to see the Iraqis respond, albeit in vain. The missiles were never going to reach us, but at the time it takes some self-convincing, as you watch the mesmerising glow of each rocket motor eventually fade. Willing the jet higher and faster, we took what seemed an eternity to egress. We were vulnerable up here – should they be bold enough to launch fighters against us and whilst we had cover around, it would take a few minutes to get to us. Thankfully, that threat did not materialise and we slogged our way home, hoping the aircraft's engines would continue to put up with the strain. That the Tornado does so well at medium level is a blessing as it was designed for high speed, automatic terrain following at very low level; its natural environment. Apart from more firework displays and another light show, the push south to the tanker towlines was reasonably quiet. Still nobody to talk to on the radios, so a good chance of a repeat of the first tanker goat – the Saudi night stop beckoned once more. We could hear the formation ahead, and having noted the frequency earlier, made remarkably easy radio contact with our flying petrol stations. The weather had clearly not improved and despite having them on the radar and the TACAN, we did not see the tankers until we were within a mile of them. Another jousting session was made easier when they were persuaded to climb above the weather. There was no shortage of giveaway fuel this time and we took enough to get home, with a healthy reserve.*

'*The recovery was uneventful, even to the point where I was finally able to talk to someone on the Havequick and pass them our in-flight report: as tasked, successful (apart from 2 and 4). Disappointing for those guys to have had bad luck on the way in but then, shit happens.*

'*On landing, we discovered more than five hours after our departure, that Number Four had diverted with additional fuel problems – it really wasn't their night, so it was just as well they didn't push. As we got together with the front four-ship and debriefed the engineers, the banter and chat was wild and colourful. Only two of us had flown in the first war and we smiled at the fevered exchanges of the other dozen air-crew. It hadn't been as bad as night one of Desert Storm by a long way, but the risks and the dangers are still very real.'*

SATURDAY 22 MARCH

It is announced that Umm Qasr has fallen to coalition forces, but is not under their control as yet, due to sporadic fire fights with local militia wearing civilian clothing, making identification of enemy forces extremely difficult.

As operations continue to secure the port, word comes through that the 7 Armoured Brigade is on the outskirts of Basra and encountering heavy resistance, while 16 Air Assault Brigade is occupying the southern oilfields and consolidating the coalition position there. During these operations the Iraqis put up some resistance, but were subdued very quickly by both UK and US forces. However they did manage to set alight nine well-heads before being either killed or captured.

Other developments relating to the oilfields concerned the fact that practically all of the oil and gas separation platforms, including the oil platforms in the mouth of the waterway up to Basra, had been either mined or booby-trapped and had to be made safe by EOD teams.

The task of clearing the port facilities and oil rigs of demolition charges fell on the shoulders of both the Royal Navy and the Royal Australian Navy Clearance Diving Teams, who worked around the clock to make the area safe, both for the benefit of military and humanitarian operations alike, as the port of Umm Qasr was of key critical importance to the success of Operation Iraqi Freedom.

As the mine clearance operations were taking place in the port, the British mine countermeasures vessels HMS *Brocklesby*, *Blyth* and *Bangor* were hard at work clearing any submerged mines that were in the waterways leading up to Umm Qasr. Also present in this region was Poland's special forces, the GROM, who worked with the British, American and Australian forces in and around the port of Umm Qasr, their operational role being to provide diving teams, security and boarding parties.

Elsewhere on the Al Faw peninsula, 3 Commando Brigade began securing the area in preparation for the arrival of more reinforcements and supplies. Although resistance was encountered, it was light and ineffective, as elements of the British Special Boat Service (SBS) had already neutralized or identified any known Iraqi threat prior to the main assault.

Just as everything seemed to be going so well for the British, news came through that seven people had been killed following a mid-air collision between two Royal Navy AEW-7 Sea King airborne early warning helicopters from 849 Squadron. The accident happened in darkness over international waters south of Iraq, some five miles from the aircraft carrier HMS *Ark Royal*, when one helicopter departing on a mission hit another on its final approach. Although a huge search and rescue operation was immediately mounted for survivors amongst the six British and one American aircrew on board, there were sadly none. The accident was a bitter pill to swallow for the British forces, especially so, as it was non-combat related and could have been avoided.

Around Basra, British and US Marine tanks engaged Iraqi forces in a major battle for the city's airport before turning their attention to a vital bridge that led from the main Kuwait to Basra highway straight into the main urban and commercial centre of the city. Heavy resistance was encountered from both regular and irregular Iraqi forces during this phase, leading to a decision to mount a siege against Basra, rather than an all-out assault. The military, however, hate the word siege as it implies an exhaustion of options. They prefer the term containment but either way it amounts to the same thing.

With the city of Basra now almost totally encircled by the British, the US 15th Marine Expeditionary Unit decided to join up with their army buddies and head northwards towards Baghdad, the key to the lock of power in Iraq. With their American friends now on the move, the British consolidated their positions around the city, as there was a very high risk of an Iraqi counter-attack. Basra, was mainly populated by Shia muslims who detested Saddam and his regime, but after the crushed insurrection of 1991 they were understandably very reluctant to rise up again as they had been very let down in the past by the Americans. This time around they wanted to see action first, and talk second.

The British were very cautious about Basra, as their timing had to be perfect. If they went in too soon and encountered heavy resistance, they would have had to retreat, which would have caused confidence issues with the Shia's and increased the Iraqi forces will to fight. If they waited too long, they risked the Shia's being massacred. However, help was at hand in the shape of British special forces who were already embedded in Basra, both for intelligence and tactical purposes. In essence, the British used their special forces as something of a barometer to gauge public opinion and military activity. They had already recommended that a gap be created in the British forces around the city, so as to serve as an escape route for the Iraqi army, thus making their will to fight less as they could escape if things got too hot. It made perfect sense and suited the forces outside the city as they simply did not have enough manpower to cover the entire area. Some aspects of their redeployment were already made easier by the fact that Basra has a natural barrier on its eastern side in the form of a marsh, making tank movement impossible both to the British and the Iraqi's.

As the British mounted their operations around Basra, aircraft from the USS *Kitty Hawk* flew seventy-four CAS (close air support) missions in support of them, while RAF and USAF aircraft bombed Baghdad throughout the day. The Iraqi's tried in vain to hinder the coalition aircraft by means of giant smokescreens which were created from oil-filled trenches sited in and around the outskirts of the city of Baghdad. Their efforts, however, failed.

Elsewhere in Iraq, US forces were pushing rapidly towards Baghdad from the

Vehicles from the 3rd Infantry Division (Mechanized) roll through sand in southern Iraq, 22 March. US Army photo by Staff Sgt. Kevin P. Bell

south-west, with a force led by the 3rd Infantry Division, who were advancing to the west of the River Euphrates, while to the east of the Euphrates, the 1st Marines Expeditionary Force were making their way towards the south-east of Baghdad, basically in a good old fashioned pincer movement.

Further to the west, the US 5th Corps had captured the Talil airfield near

Nasiriyah as well as securing a key bridge over the River Euphrates. During their advance, the general commanding the Iraqi 51st Infantry surrendered to them at Nasiriyah, providing good intelligence and information on the state of the Iraqi army. Around the same time, the 3rd Infantry Division's 1 Brigade Combat Team began a thirty hour run north, during which more than 250 vehicles were refuelled.

Meanwhile outside the city of Samawah, the 2nd Battalion, 7 Infantry Regiment, engaged in a firefight with Iraqi soldiers, the net

Two CH-47 Chinook helicopters head north towards Iraq, carrying soldiers of the 3rd Battalion, 101st Aviation Regiment, 101st Airborne Division. Their task was to set up a forward fuel supply point that would allow the division to conduct further air assaults deep into Iraq. US Army photo by Pfe. James Matise

Black Hawk helicopters head out for Iraq with members of the 187th Infantry Regiment, 101st Airborne Division, while a line of AH-64 Apache attack helicopters are made ready for their next mission.

Army photo by Pfc. James Matise

result being fifteen Iraqi prisoners of war and no reported casualties.

It was also announced that units of the US Army's elite 101st Airborne Division (Air Assault) had left Kuwait and were heading north across the desert, their destination classified. As the day progressed news came through that the Turkish Government had refused the US permission to move their 4th Infantry Division across Turkey and into northern Iraq-effectively prohibiting a northern front, as they were to have moved south on Baghdad and linked up with other US Forces advancing on the City from the south. As frustrating as this news was at the time, the decision wasn,t a show stopper as the US could insert forces by other means-such as an air-bridge or a further thrust from the south- however this would of course take time to organize.

Behind the scenes, George W. was furious with the Turks, as he felt that he had been personally betrayed by them. However, he was forced to contain his anger, as the coalition forces were still using Turkish air bases, such as Incirlik, for operational purposes, not to mention their air space. The Turks of course had their own agenda to pursue, that being to pre-deploy their own troops on the border with northern Iraq, so as to be able to move rapidly against the Kurds in the event of them attempting to form their own state. With the Americans all bottled up in ships offshore and unable to move through Turkey, there would be no one to stop them.

Frustrated at the Turks, the Americans ordered thirty of their Sealift Command ships loaded with equipment for the 4th Infantry Division to sail through the Suez Canal at full speed and make for the Gulf, where the troops that had been denied permission to use Turkey would meet them, having been flown from their US base directly. Also that day as an act of defiance against the Turks, America began flying troops into northern Iraq, effectively giving them the 'political finger'. That day also saw some seventy TLAMs, hit Kurdish areas in northern Iraq which were under the control of the hardline Islamist group,

Ansar al-Islam, a group said to have direct links with the terrorist group Al-Qaeda.

And 'Comical Ali's' thoughts for the day were:

'The United Nations... is a place for prostitution under the feet of the Americans. - We have destroyed 50 tanks today. That 5-ohhh tanks - They are superpower of villains. They are superpower of Al Capones.'

COMBAT REPORT

Location: Umm Qasr in southern Iraq

Account by a US Marine soldier.

'It's been barely a week, and already I feel this war is going to be a mother cluster-fuck! Nothing seems to be on schedule, and the I-raqs are not fighting as expected, but hell that's war for you. You never seem to get what you came for.

'When we first landed in this ass hole of a place, we thought that we would be done here in a couple of days, but it sure ain't happening. At least not here.

'Only yesterday, we engaged the I-raqs near the port, and they put up a hell of a fight, until we called in air support and arty (Artillery). But the real problem here, and it's a big problem let me tell you, is the way these 'Mothers' fight. Some wear uniform, but most don't, and that's the problem out here. How the heck are we supposed to know who is friendly and who ain't.

'Our mission, once we're done here, is to make Baghdad. But as and when, that's gonna be, I have no idea.

And that's because this war, is just not going to plan. I have no doubt that we will win in the long term, but it's now that concerns me.

'So far, we've been real lucky with casualties, in that we've had no fatacs (fatal casualties) so far, but being realistic, that situation is not going to last forever.

'Seeing how these guys fight, it ain't going to be easy, no sir. Take yesterday, when the I-raqs fought with us they fought as a guerilla force and not as an army. They were pretty darned clever too, in the way they used old tanks and APCs as decoys, that really fooled us. Basically, what they would do is ambush us from behind, as we *engaged what we thought were real vehicles. There were only ever about twenty of them, but they really fought hard, and rarely surrendered. I'm not so sure about what unit they were from, as most didn't wear any sort of uniform. And those that did, quickly discarded it when they ran away towards the urban areas, making it real difficult to pick em up.*

'*It's gonna be a long war, that's for sure, and certainly no cake walk.*'

SUNDAY 23 MARCH

By Sunday 23rd, US ground forces had pushed to within 100 miles of Baghdad, with Apache helicopters and fighters attacking Republican Guard positions just sixty miles from the capital. The advance however was meeting stiff resistance along the way, with irregular Iraqi forces and militia ambushing US convoys at every opportunity that presented itself. When only about 100 miles from Baghdad, the 3rd Infantry Division met with fierce resistance near the city of Najaf. Elsewhere, US forces north of Nasiriyah encountered heavy resistance from irregular Iraqi forces, while in the urban areas of Nasiriyah, a US supply convoy was ambushed with twelve US troops reported missing and five taken prisoner. This was a major blow for the US forces, as they had, prior to this event, captured the city centre and a number of significant bridges over the River Euphrates.

By now it was becoming obvious to all, that this war was not going to be a seven day 'cake walk' as the neo conservatives in America had promised, but a long and protracted guerilla war that would be costly both in terms of money and manpower. Essentially, the Iraqis were adopting what is called a rollover strategy, that being to allow the coalition spearhead forces to over run their positions and move on, while irregular militia hit their rear echelon support troops later. This tactic was proving highly effective, as the US forces simply did not have the manpower to secure the areas that they had just captured or been through, as it was a case of 'Baghdad or Bust.'

Also causing some degree of concern, was the fact that the Iraqi's had also set up a series of defensive rings around the city of Baghdad, with the Republican Guard and its conventional forces defending the outer rings, while the Special Republican Guard and the Fedayeen Saddam (a paramilitary force) defended the inner one. Considering Saddam's plight at the time this was a good strategy as it gave the Iraqis a layered defence in depth and prevented the coalition forces from launching a direct assault in any one area.

The problems encountered by the US forces were by no means unique to them, as the British were also still having difficulty mopping up the pockets of resistance that still existed around the port of Umm Qasr. At one stage during the day, both the Royal Marines and the US Marines battled with snipers that were harrassing the ground support teams as they went about their business.

The operation to secure Umm Qasr, even involved tanks of the 7 Armoured Brigade, their role being to act as bullet magnets.

North of Umm Qasr in Basra, British forces were engaging in probing missions, the idea being to pin-point the strong and weak points of the city, as well as a break-in point for the armoured thrust that would eventually follow.

Other significant events of this day included the loss of an RAF GR4 Tornado aircraft from 9 Squadron, which was brought down by a US Patriot surface-to-air missile battery near the Kuwaiti border as it returned from a mission. At the time, this incident caused great upset amongst the British forces and public alike, as both aircrew were killed, leading to accusations that the Americans were being trigger happy as usual and a repeat of the numerous friendly fire incidents that marred the first Gulf War was looking likely again.

Further up country, the US 3rd Infantry Division's 1 Brigade Combat Team was still on the move, while the 2nd Battalion, 7th Infantry moved up to high ground where the troops found Iraqi soldiers and their equipment scattered over a two kilometre square area.

During the operation, the 2nd Battalion came under highly accurate Iraqi artillery fire, which was eventually located and destroyed by an AH-64 Apache helicopter. During the follow up phase of the operation, US forces came across a military compound, complete with bunkers, watchtowers and barracks that were fully enclosed by barbed-wire and a chain-link fence. As they reached the compound, the 2nd Battalion came across ninety-seven Iraqi soldiers sitting on the ground in a circle, with their uniforms off, as they wished to surrender. By the end of this day, some 249 Iraqi's were apprehended and taken prisoner by the 1 Brigade Combat Team. Since leaving Kuwait, they had located and destroyed numerous pieces of Iraqi equipment, including small arms, artillery, mortar tubes, armoured personnel carriers, vehicles and air defence guns.

In one period of action, the 1 Brigade Combat Team covered a distance of

A British soldier cautiously examines an abandoned Iraqi field gun for possible booby-traps.

A British soldier manning his .50 calibre machine-gun from a tank turret.

200 miles in thirty-six hours and engaged enemy forces regularly throughout the journey. By the end of 23 March, coalition aircraft including those of five US Navy carrier battle groups, had flown more than 6,000 sorties in support of the ground forces, with the main focus of the air campaign being on Republican Guard units situated around Baghdad, Mosul and Tikrit. 23 March, was described by the US Military as the toughest day of resistance in the four days' of war.

As the day's events were being analyzed by the world's media, both embedded and unilateral, a negative atmosphere began to develop over the way the war was being fought and indeed how it was going. This mood emanated from the fact that Operation 'Iraqi Freedom' was seen to have got off to a bad start, some would even say a clumsy one, thus creating an image of incompetence at the highest level. The loss of so many servicemen through accidents and friendly fire incidents so early in the conflict only helped to compound this perception and belief, leading to the conclusion that all was not going well. But the biggest reason for these feelings, lay in the fact that the Iraqi's, were fighting back, and that was not in the script.

And 'Comical Ali's thoughts for the day were:

> **'Americans and Brits are sick dogs.**
> **They are retreating on all fronts. Their military**
> **effort is a subject of laughter all over the world.**
> **They are nowhere.... they are nowhere, really.'**

COMBAT REPORT

ARMOURED INFANTRY OF THE 'DESERT RATS' TELL THEIR STORY OF THE BATTLE FOR THE BRIDGES OF BASRA.

Corporal Jason Thomas, Y Coy, I RRF

'Even though it was my first fire fight it is hard to remember any details because everything seemed to happen so quickly. It was a real buzz and to be honest fear really didn't play a big part because, like a lot of the lads, I was just relieved to actually be doing something.'

Lance Sergeant Mick Welch, 1IG

'When it was all happening I fell back on my training and automatically did what I needed to do.

'The main difference between war, fighting and training is that you have a fear inside you, but that is not a bad thing. Fear makes you sharper in everything you do.'

Guardsman Gavin Meers, 1 IG

'Being on the bridge was different from anything else I have experienced. The training kicks in and you just get on with it. I've enjoyed being out here and it's exactly what I joined the Army for.'

Guardsman Ricky Banner, 1 IG

'It was a hairy time and it made us realise we were at war and that this was where the fighting was going to start. I kept asking to have a Challenger 2 by our side. Being in an APC was a bit nerve-racking and it was a case of seventy-two hours of wanting someone there next to us.'

Fusilier Lee Wines, Y Coy, 1 RRF

'When the mortar rounds came in I have never been so scared in my life. I'm glad we can look back and laugh about it now.'

Lance Corporal Maddar Maddar, 1 IG

'I didn't fear for my own safety because I had complete faith in our equipment and the support that we had, especially from the tankies. All my skills and drills came to the fore and I just got on with the job in hand.'

Fusilier Dan Moran, Z Coy, 1 RRF

'We were expecting trouble when we went up there and were prepared for it. The worst bit was not when we got out of the wagon but as were waiting to get out, not knowing what was going on outside. Once we hit the ground it felt like seconds, but we were probably on the ground for about twenty minutes.'

Lance Corporal Lee Morris, Y Coy, 1 RRF

'I was nervous at the time and have never experienced anything like being mortared. Training takes over and you don't really think about what you are doing, you just do it instinctively. It's not till you sit back *afterwards that you begin to analyse things in more detail.'*

Fusilier Neil Watson, Z Coy, I RRF

'It was my first experience of a fire fight and I was quite scared when we de-bussed on the bridge, but after a short while adrenalin just took over. You can not compare it to training – nobody shoots back at you on an exercise.'

Drummer Andrew Carr, Y Coy, I RRF

'Being in a live situation is totally different from training – it is one hell of an experience and a complete adrenalin rush. Your personal safety is always at the back of your mind but you just crack on with your job.'

Sergeant Stu Wickham, Z Coy, I RRF

'There was certainly a lot of excitement but it was tempered with nerves. There were a lot of young lads in my wagon and I was impressed and proud with the way they handled themselves under pressure.'

MONDAY 24 MARCH

As crippling sandstorms swirl across the desert, US tanks punch to within seventy miles of Baghdad, while units of the 3rd Infantry Division reach Karbala, sixty miles from Baghdad. Paving the way for them are US Army AH-64D Apache helicopters that have been attacking Republican Guard units ringing Baghdad. In one of these missions, an Apache is downed south of Baghdad and its crew captured. The helicopter however is later destroyed by a coalition long range surface-to-surface missile. In another non-combat related incident, an Apache is lost in a brown out (dust or storm), but the crew are recovered. The Iraqis however, claim that they have shot it down.

In the north of Iraq, some ten cruise missiles hit the city of Mosul, prior to an air attack by coalition aircraft who also attacked Kirkuk. Throughout the day, a total of 1,000 sorties are flown-mainly against Republican Guard units, but some are prosecuted in support of both ground forces advancing from the south and special forces operating in the west of Iraq around the H2 and H3 airfields.

In the south of Iraq, there are extensive operations around the Ramaila oilfield that include providing security for firefighters as they attempt to deal with the wells set alight by the Iraqi's. Off shore, the Australian frigate HMAS Anzac fired on Iraqi artillery positions and bunkers on the Al Faw peninsula following an incident the night before. Further inshore, a US Navy F-18 aircraft

Soldiers from the 3rd Infantry Division (Mechanized) in firing positions during an enemy approach on their position at objective RAMS, in Southern Iraq on 24 March.

destroyed an Iraqi patrol boat on a waterway in southern Iraq.

News also comes through of ten American soldiers killed in the battle for Nasiriyah, while the British suffer two killed following an ambush on a Land Rover vehicle near Basra. The Arab television station Al-Jazeera later broadcast images of the dead British soldiers, causing outrage in the UK.

During the day, eight Iraqi surface-to-surface missiles are fired at Kuwait, but six are brought down by Patriot surface-to-air missiles.

Saddam's forces are still fighting back.

And 'Comical Ali's' thoughts for the day were:

'We will push those crooks, those mercenaries back into the swamp...

...the insane little dwarf Bush.

The midget Bush and that Rumsfeld deserve only to be beaten with shoes by people everywhere.'

TUESDAY 25 MARCH

The day commences with violent windstorms that bring the advancing columns to a halt, as visability is virtually zero. Air operations over Baghdad are also reduced on account of the collateral damage risk. Taking advantage of the poor weather, the US Army's 3rd Infantry Division consolidated their position north-west of the town of Najaf, some sixty miles from Baghdad. After a five-day push across Iraq this break was well deserved and much needed. During the day, the Pentagon released details of the Battle of Najaf, in which 300 Iraqi troops were killed. It was the biggest battle of the war so far, the series of engagements lasted some four hours.

Near Nasiriyah, the US 1st Marine Expeditionary Force gained control of a hospital that was in use as a paramilitary headquarters, staging area and storage area. As well as weapons and a tank, the Marines discovered 3,000 chemical protection

A US soldier mans a MK-19 40 mm Grenade Launcher mounted on a HUMVEE in Central Iraq. Photo by Sgt. 1st Class David K. Dismukes/CFLCC Public Affairs

suits and nerve agent antidote injectors. They also took 170 prisoners. There was still fierce fighting around Nasiriyah, despite Cobra helicopters attacking Iraqi forces for several hours prior to the main US ground assault. Fierce fighting also took place in the Euphrates valley, as it was a key junction point for US forces and the Iraqi's knew it. In all, their defence of this area cost them some 200 killed and wounded.

In the west of Iraq, coalition special forces took control of two airfields for use as forward operating bases. These were designated by the Iraqi's as H2 and H3.

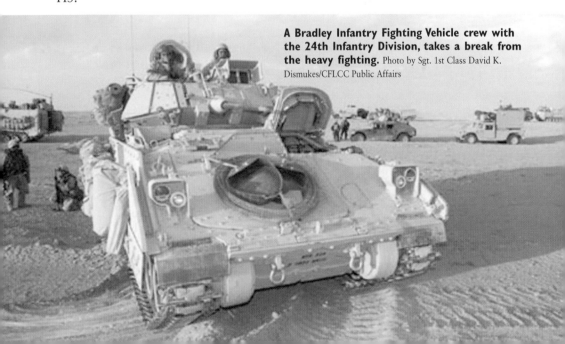

A Bradley Infantry Fighting Vehicle crew with the 24th Infantry Division, takes a break from the heavy fighting. Photo by Sgt. 1st Class David K. Dismukes/CFLCC Public Affairs

In Washington, General Myers said that coalition forces were nearing Baghdad, and that they had moved some 200 miles into Iraq in just five days of the ground campaign, while in Qatar, Royal Marines Brigadier Jim Dutton said that the port of Umm Qasr was now safe and open, with the first ship carrying humanitarian supplies due to arrive within forty-eight hours.

Overnight, Royal Marines moved to positions along the Iraq-Iran border in preparation for 'sweep and clear' operations. In the early hours, Iraqi forces, including tanks and personnel, moved south-east from Basra towards 3 Commando Brigade on the Al Faw peninsula. Using just Milan anti-tank missiles and hand held anti-tank weapons, the Marines managed to stop a number of tanks. When the scale of the attack was realised, coalition aircraft, helicopter gunships and artillery were called in to provide support. 3 Commando confirmed that during the attack, nineteen enemy T-55 tanks were destroyed for no losses to the British.

Meanwhile, to the north of Al Zubayr, tanks of the British 7 Armoured Brigade along with strike aircraft, destroyed the headquarters of the ruling Ba'ath Party in the south of the town. In other attacks, coalition aircraft destroyed two large patrol boats of the Iraqi Navy and severly damaged Saddam's presidential yacht *Al Mansur*. This luxurious vessel weighed in at 7,359 tonnes, and was built by Wartsila, Turku in 1982.

Elsewhere in the Gulf, coalition warships were placed on high alert amid fears of suicide attacks by Iraqis using small boats and jet-skis.

By the end of the day, helicopter operations were now able to resume operations after being grounded for several days due to the severe sandstorms and gusts of wind that were ravaging the country, some were, infact, in excess of eighty-five mph.

As these events were taking place, President Bush asked congress for $75 billion to pay for the war.

WEDNESDAY 26 MARCH

26 March, saw some of the fiercest fighting yet, especially around the cities of Najaf and Nasiriyah. The fighting mainly involved the US Marines and the Saddam Fedayeen paramilitary force, a group of fanatics who were under the command of Saddam's son, Uday. As the Americans fought their way through the cities, word came through that a massive convoy of some 1,000 vehicles had left Baghdad, and were heading south towards US forces, principally the 7th Cavalry, near Najaf. The number of vehicles in the convoy, however, proved to be exaggerated, but the intention of the Iraqi,s to fight wasn't. During the engagement that followed, several hundred Iraqi's were killed and thirty vehicles destroyed.

As this action was taking place, word came through from Basra, that another convoy of around 100 vehicles was heading south towards the Al Faw peninsula. In response, the 7 Armoured Brigade was sent to intercept them, and this they did outside the city of Basra, engaging in what was to be the biggest tank battle fought by the British since the Second World War. The British, with their Challenger 2 tanks, destroyed the Iraqi armoured force in no time and left fourteen tanks burning, along with many of their support vehicles. Nearby, resistance was finally crushed in Al Zubayr, leaving British forces free to reinforce the cordon around Basra.

Elsewhere in the south, it was announced by the British Defence Secretary Geoff Hoon, that the Al-Faw peninsula, the port of Umm Qasr and the southern oilfields were now secure, as the Iraqi forces defending them had been defeated. He also confirmed that 3 Commando was now in control of these areas, and that the US 15th Marine Expeditionary Unit had been released to rejoin the 1st Marine Expeditionary Force, now heading north towards Baghdad.

Meanwhile in the same area, the MCM task force, which comprised Royal Navy, Royal Australian Navy and US Navy elements, was still making steady progress in clearing the Khawr Abd Allah waterway approach to Umm Qasr of any mines that had been deployed by the Iraqi's prior to their defeat. They had already cleared an area some forty miles long, by 200 yards wide, blowing up over 100 suspicious items in this one section alone.

In the north of Iraq, 1,000 assault troops of the US 173rd Airborne, parachuted into the Kurdish-controlled area of the country as part of a spearhead force sent in to seize and secure an airfield that was of great tactical importance as an air-bridge for future operations.

By the evening of 26 March, US forces were spearheading an advance northwards, with lead elements already at Karbala. News also came through that the US Marines had crossed the Euphrates River and were proceeding northwards.

Up until today, some 5,000 sorties had been flown, along with over 600 coalition TLAM launches. However, the day was marred by news of a bomb attack on a market in Baghdad that killed thirty-six civilians. The Pentagon denied that the area was a target for coalition forces, but the Iraqis insisted otherwise.

COMBAT REPORT

One soldier recalled experiencing a type of blindness caused by darkness and the 'fog of war', while the other noted it was hard to see the enemy because of deception.

These were the views of Marines 1st Sergeant Bruce Cole and Marine Unwins, wounded in combat in Iraq. The two were treated at Landstuhl Regional Medical Centre, in Germany. Unwins, aged twenty-six, remembered a gruelling forty-eight hours, trucking supplies to Marines striving to secure a bridge over the Euphrates River near the town of Nasiriyah.

Near nightfall on 26 March, Unwins and his group of drivers and mechanics from the 2nd Battalion, 8th Marine Regiment, had established a temporary rest-

A knocked out Iraqi tank bears testimony to the fierce fighting that took place around the city of Basra.

and-refit stop at an abandoned Iraqi petrol station. Marine bulldozers piling up berms or mounds of earth around the station improved security, he noted.

'It was looking like a pretty good place to spend a couple of days,' the lieutenant recalled. 'We had Marines set up on the perimeter around this berm, so our security was in place.'

Darkness had fallen when Unwins 'was pulling my sleeping bag out. Suddenly, we started having a kind of sporadic fire... I saw the tracer rounds passing over the berm of the camp,' Unwins remarked. At first, he thought 'it was

A fearsome sight for the Iraqi tank crews. The mighty British Challenger 2 tank, seen here on patrol outside the city of Basra.

just someone kind of sniping the camp.' Then, *'we really started to take heavy fire, and that's when the small-arms fire escalated to rocket-propelled grenades and mortars.'*

At that point an RPG round ploughed into a nearby vehicle and shrapnel shot toward the lieutenant. Hot metal struck his lower right leg, then went all the way up to the left leg, then, another piece of metal sliced his left arm. *'The shrapnel in the leg kind of took me out of the fight,'* Unwins said, noting that a medic quickly began treating him.

The night's darkness really created the 'fog of war' during the fight, the lieutenant emphasized. Consequently, there was no clue, he declared, as to the enemy's position, other than the tracer rounds *'coming from all three sides of our perimeter.'*

In contrast to Unwins, night time combat experiences, 1st Sergeant Cole said he had fought the enemy during the full light of day. Cole's Iraqi enemy resorted to deception that violates the rules of war

A US Marine inspects a sea mine after it has been pulled from the sea.

A paratrooper from the US Army 173rd Airborne Brigade mans a defensive position in Northern Iraq after 1,000 paratroopers from the brigade conducted an airborne operation to seize an airfield in Northern Iraq.

under the Geneva Conventions.

On the morning of 27 March, Cole said his battalion was headed north on Iraqi Highway 1 as the main attacking element. *'It was a bright morning,'* the sergeant recalled. Berms and ditches had been established along both sides of the highway, which seemed to both channel and restrict the several-hundred-vehicle strong convoy as it continued up the road.

Cole recalled the high mobility, multipurpose wheeled vehicle he was in was in the lead of a column of trucks just behind the heavy armour. Many Iraqi civilians were observing the convoy, seemed friendly and were waving to the Marines. Shortly after this, he noted, the US troops were under attack, first with firing heard at the column's front where the tanks were. Then, more firing was evident, emanating from the rear. *'There were engagements north of us; there were engagements south of us,* the sergeant recalled. *'Some Iraqi civilians had moved toward the Marines',* he said, *'as close as maybe 50 meters off the road, standing on top of the berms. It was difficult to determine where the firing was coming from,'* Cole said, noting that bullets were pinging off the Marines vehicles and ricocheting off the berms. Not all of the civilian garbed Iraqis were attacking the Marines, the sergeant emphasised, noting some seemed as surprised and *'just as afraid as anyone else from the look of fear on their faces.'*

In the middle of all this bedlam, *'the difficult part was trying to return fire and figure out who to shoot at'* Cole asserted. He said the bright sky against the berms helped to mask the enemy's positions. He turned in his seat, and began to return fire out of the vehicle's window.

Then he was hit in the arm.

'A bullet entered my forearm and exited through the back of my tri-ceps, knocking the rifle out of my hand,' Cole recalled.

The attack ended.

Cole attributed his and the convoy's survival of the ambush *'to everybody's clear head, good thinking and the training'.*

THURSDAY, 27 MARCH

Baghdad is rocked by huge explosions as giant 'Bunker Buster' bombs are used for the first time in the war, following the easing up of the sandstorms that have been prevailing in the area. At the same time, air operations intensify against the Republican Guard units around the city, as coalition aircraft mount a maximum effort to break them.

Outside Baghdad, an Iraqi convoy heading south to reinforce Najaf is pulverized by B-52 bombers, operating out of RAF Fairford in the UK.

Meanwhile, in the south of Iraq, a missile launcher that has been targeting Kuwait, is discovered and destroyed just outside of Basra, while nearby, British forces find a large cache of chemical warfare suits, fueling speculation that

Saddam is about to launch a chemical, biological or gas attack.

In Baghdad, the Iraqi Information Minister announces that over 350 civilians have been killed as a result of the coalition air campaign.News also comes through, that between 02.00 and 04.00 hours, two mines were discovered by ships clearing the way into Umm Qasr, causing a twenty-four hour delay for the RFA logistics ship Sir Galahad, which has 300 tonnes of humanitarian aid on board.

And 'Comical Ali's' thoughts for the day were:

'Rumsfeld, he needs to be hit on the head.

Yesterday we heard this villain called Rumsfeld. He,

of course, is a war criminal.

Who is this dog Franks in Qatar?'

FRIDAY 28 MARCH

Kuwait is hit by a modified anti-shipping missile that skipped across the sea and then exploded close to a popular upmarket shopping mall, causing great damage, but thankfully no serious casualties, as the attack took place in the middle of the night.

Central Command, in response, confirms that intensive operations are being mounted to track and destroy the launch sites, but these are proving illusive to find. It also announced that air strikes had reduced Saddam's crack Medina Division of the Republican Guard by one-third. It is reported that Iraqi civilians fleeing the embattled city of Basra are being fired upon by Iraqi forces.

News also comes through of more US troop deployments, following an announcement that up to 120,000 more service personnel are to be sent into Iraq, to join the 250,000 already deployed in the region, of which 90,000 are ground troops. It is also confirmed that some 60,000 troops are serving on ships in the region, following Turkey's decision to deny US forces access to its territory. During the day, US Marines and other troops were involved in a five hour long battle with around 1,500 Iraqi's near Najaf proving that the Iraqis were still a viable force.

Around noon, the RFA logistics landing ship Sir *Galahad* docked in Umm Qasr with 300 tonnes of humanitarian aid, including food and fresh water. The arrival of the ship was warmly welcomed by the Iraqi civilians of Umm Qasr, as it marked the first tangible proof that the coalition really was here to help them.

Whilst navigating itself through the swept channel to the port, the ship was escorted by large and small mine countermeasures vessels and specially trained US mine hunting dolphins.

A soldier watches over Kuwaiti firefighters as they attempt to extinguish an oil fire at the Rumaila Oilfield, 27 March.

SATURDAY 29 MARCH

The day starts badly for US forces, after four soldiers were killed at a checkpoint in Najaf, by a suicide bomber in a taxi. The incident occured after the soldiers had walked towards the taxi, following the driver's request for assistance. It was later revealed that the suicide bomber was an Iraqi Army Officer and not a Fedayeen Saddam member as was first thought.

Later that day, the Iraqi military ominously announced that such tactics are now 'routine' military policy and will be prosecuted at every opportunity available.

Relentless air attacks on Baghdad, are now beginning to take their toll on the Iraqi military and government officials, as they are being targeted both in their official offices and in their residences.

Back in the UK, the human cost of the war starts to sink in, after members of the British public witness on their televisions, the arrival at RAF Brize Norton of the first ten bodies of British servicemen killed in the war.

An Al Kut vehicle sits destroyed beside the road the morning after 1st Bn., 64th AR cleared the Rams objective area, 5 kilometers south of An Najaf, Iraq. US Army photo by Spc. Mason T. Lowery

A Soldier from the 7th Infantry Regiment, provides perimeter security for the transport of three Iraqis. The men were apprehended from the white car in the background, which, upon search, had 13 AK-47 assault rifles in the trunk. US Army photo by Sgt. Craig Zentkovich

Smoke and flames engulf an Iraqi anti-tank aircraft gun and vehicle following a strike from an AH-64 **Apache.** US Army photo by Sgt. Craig Zentkovich

It was also reported that US forces, including Marines of the 1st Marines Expeditionary Force, were now less than fifty miles from Baghdad, and were meeting strong resistance.

Other significant actions that day, involved Apache helicopters from the 101st Airborne Division, mounting intensive massed attacks against well-defended Iraqi positions, while other elements of the Coalition forces attacked the headquarters of the ruling Ba'ath party in nine separate locations.

And 'Comical Ali's' thoughts for the day were:

A 214th Field Artillery Brigade Command Vehicle moves out from a firing position at objective RAMS in Central Iraq on 28 March.

'Bush doesn't even know if Spain is a republic or a kingdom.

Bush, Blair and Rumsfeld. They are the funny trio.

We're going to drag the drunken junkie nose of Bush through Iraq's deserts with his follower dog Blair...

There are 26 million Saddams in Iraq.'

Task Force Tarawa tank supporting units stop for a replen in the Iraqi desert on 28 March.

SUNDAY 30 MARCH

Baghdad burned, following a night of intensive bombing that was aimed primarily at Republican Guard units to the south of the city. During the night of 29-30 March, Royal Marines supported by other troops, artillery and tanks, fight their way into Abu al Khasib, a suburb south-west of Basra.

This attack was the biggest of the war so far, for the British and continued until around midday, by which time all Iraqi resistance had ceased. In further actions, an Iraqi general and five of his officers were captured following another engagement with the Royal Marines leading to the discovery of a significant amount of weapons. As the day progressed, the cordon around Basra was tightened yet further, with British infantry units now deployed to the north, south and west of Basra, while the Royal Marines occupied the south-west. The day, however, was not without its losses, as one Royal Marine was killed and three others injured following an ambush on their patrol craft during a recce mission along the River Zubayr on the Al-Faw peninsula.

Further north of Basra, coalition troops captured the Hadithah Dam on the River Euphrates, located some 200 miles north-west of Baghdad. This operation was highly important as it prevented the Iraqi's from deliberately flooding the area.

Meanwhile, as General Tommy Franks announced that the war was on schedule, word came in that three US servicemen had been killed, and one wounded following a non combat related helicopter crash.

Elsewhere in the region, an Egyptian electrician drives his pick-up truck into US soldiers as they lined up outside a PX store in Kuwait, injuring fifteen of them.

Within days of the commencement of the invasion phase of Operation 'Iraqi Freedom', an old enemy resurfaced to cast its evil dimension on the war. It was, of course, the curse of Friendly Fire.

The war saw many such incidents and included the loss of an RAF Tornado, which was brought down by a US Patriot SAM, while returning from a mission; an incident between two British Challenger 2 tanks near Basra; the loss of a British light tank destroyed by an A-10 Thunderbolt; a blue-on-blue contact between Royal Marines during a river patrol; the shooting down of a US Navy F-18 Hornet by US forces near Baghdad, and an attack on US Special Forces supporting the Kurds in northern Iraq- carried out by US Navy F-14 Tomcats. All of these incidents, and indeed many others like them, are currently under investigation at present by both British and American forces, and will, no doubt, be the subject of much heated debate as to who was to blame. Friendly fire is a perennial nightmare for any military force operating as part of a coalition, as it is likely to damage both the morale and confidence of the forces involved. As such, it makes a good propaganda tool for an adversary to exploit. Friendly fire is virtually always the result of a mistake or failure of some kind, and usually attracts considerable media attention-often to the detriment of the subsequent investigation that always follows such incidents.

There is also the matter of coalition population's opinions to consider, as they may use fratricide as evidence of incompetence in their partner nation, which may result in the perception that the other nation's armed forces are letting the side down through poor training, being too gung-ho, or sheer stupidity.

In military parlance, friendly fire is often described as being regrettable but inevitable. It is generally a consequence of the 'fog of war', a term that is defined as uncertainty and confusion generated in wartime by a combination of limited, incomplete, inaccurate and contradictory information, deliberate deception, and the mayhem and stress caused by combat.

In modern warfare, people must make fast decisions, often with violent consequences- that are based on either partial or unreliable information. They face the quandary that if they wait too long to verify the intelligence, they run the risk of the enemy exploiting it to their advantage but if they act too fast and get it wrong, the consequences can often be fatal.

There are broadly two categories of friendly fire. There are those that genuinely relate to 'fog of war', ie one tank crosses the path of another during a sandstorm just as it is about to open fire on enemy forces. Such an incident is possible, as tanks do not have an IFF capability at present, although most coalition tanks and vehicles did carry a louvred device on their vehicles that enabled them to show up as a cold spot on a friendly vehicles thermal imager.

During an engagement with enemy forces, quick decisions have to be made by young service personnel who have little or no combat experience. Often nervous and frightened, they tend to shoot first and ask questions later, with death being a possible consequence for them if they get it wrong, and the enemy gets a first round hit on them.

Modern manoeuvre type warfare can exacerbrate this problem considerably, as the concept of mission orders that both British and American forces observe, gives very junior commanders a job to do in the form of a mission that can be freely interpreted by them as to how best to accomplish the task in hand. Although using one's initiative and imagination is greatly encouraged within the military, there is a downside; that being the unpredictability of their fellow commanders as to what their take will be on the mission interpretation aspect. Although the advent of the digitized battlespace will greatly help in mission awareness and battle appreciation for both ground and air based assets, its best feature is the fact that it will create a common operational picture for everyone to see. This will enable forces to know where all their assets are, as well as those of friendly forces thus minimizing the risk of a friendly fire incident.

The second category of friendly fire incident, is that caused by technical failure or procedural error.

Within any military force, there will be a procedure or method of operating both for peacetime and combat related operations,which is specifically designed to prevent fratricide.

A British patrol maintains all around defence as it slowly advances forward in enemy held territory.

However, if the procedures are not followed or obeyed through either a lack of training or understanding, there is a risk of friendly fire. There are also cultural and behavioural dimensions to consider. For instance, in some countries there may well be a gun culture where people carry and use weapons as a matter of routine, whereas in another country a gun may be an alien sight and not part of that culture, making a person from a non-violent country more likely to be the victim of a friendly fire incident if the other person is from that of an unrestrained country.

Right: British soldier makes safe captured Iraqi weapons.

British trucks travel in convoy, moving supplies and troops to the front.

Firing on friendly troops is always a possibility in the 'fog of war'. Confusion, fear, weather and night operations can all be responsible for a 'blue on blue' incident.

These cultural and behavioural differences are most likely to manifest themselves within the military as there tends to be a more permissive environment for such incidents to occur. It will often be the case that a friendly nation will train with that of another on a regular basis during peacetime and will have every confidence in each other's abilities and doctrines. However, it is only during time of conflict when subjective risk and glory take their full effect that the cultural and behavioural differences become apparent.

MONDAY 31 MARCH

Baghdad was hit again, by aircraft and Cruise missiles in what was the biggest raid of the war so far, and involved USAF B-1, B-2 and B-52 bombers in a combined bombing package, that features all three aircraft types, hitting the same target at the same time, the result, devastation on mass. Targets included, presidential palaces, the Ministry of Information building, an intelligence centre and a barracks.

Outside Baghdad, the Republican Guard received another thrashing from the bombers, and sustain heavy casualties. South of Baghdad, there was fierce fighting around Nasiriyah, involving coalition special forces and US Marines, resulting in great destruction, both of buildings and enemy vehicles. During the numerous attacks that followed, Marines found gas masks and anti-nerve gas doses which gave cause for great concern.

In Hindiyah, south-east of Karbala, US forces engaged Iraqi troops in fierce fighting over an important bridge that crosses the River Euphrates. US Central Command (USCC) later stated that their troops saw lorry loads of children mixed with Fedayeen fighters fleeing the scene- but were unable to engage them for fear of hitting the children.

In the south-east, US troops including elements of the 101st Airborne (Air Assault), reach the town of Hillah, while other units engaged enemy forces in the town of Samawa. During these attacks, an Iraqi general was captured as was an airfield and a training camp- for 'regime death squads'.

In another action, US Marines supported by aircraft and helicopter gunships capture the town of Shatra, some twenty miles north of Nasiriyah. The Marines had earlier bypassed the town, but were forced to return there after several supply convoys came under attack.

Later in the day, information came through that a force of some 100 tribal men had sided with coalition forces during their attacks on Shatra and Diwaniyahin, resulting in the capture of prisoners and equipment, as well as the removal of explosives from a bridge.

The day, also saw several ground engagements against the Republican Guard, namely the Medina Division at Karbala, who came under intense artillery bombardment from the US V Corps.

In the north of Iraq, US aircraft bombed Iraqi positions near Kalak, while in the south, Britain's 16 Air Assault Brigade, along with artillery and air support, engaged Iraqi forces north of the Ramaila oilfields. The battle was a fierce one, and resulted in the destruction of seventeen T-55 tanks and five artillery pieces as well as other equipment. Elsewhere in the south, the Black Watch battle group rescued two Kenyan civilians who had been working for the British, and had been taken prisoner by Iraqi forces at Al Zubayr.

New details of operations were also released that confirmed that since the war began, RAF aircraft had flown more than 1,200 sorties, while Royal Navy submarines and US surface ships/submarines had fired more than 700 TLAMs.

Central Command also confirmed that more than 8,000 precision bombs have been dropped in Iraq to date, and that US Navy Tomcats had mounted air strikes against Iraq forces dug in twenty-five miles east of the city of Mosul.

COMBAT REPORT
LOCATION: SOUTHERN IRAQ
Account from: Iraqi POW

'I never wanted to fight the Americans or the British, but I had no choice as my family were being threatened by some of Saddam's secret police. I am a Shia so I had little chance of survival if I stayed at home. For me being captured it was a relief- I cannot tell you how happy I am to be out of this war, thanks be to God.

'Before my capture I was put in a trench along with some others and told to stay there until further orders were issued. During the day we saw many aircraft flying over us but they never attacked, they seemed to be heading further north. On one occasion some helicopters flew near us but again they did not attack, we also did not fire at them.

After a couple of days we were moved up towards Nasiriyah and told to attack any vehicles that passed us by on the main highway. There were barely twenty of us in number, and all we had for weapons were assault rifles and a couple of small rockets (possibly RPGs?)

'*As we watched the road from behind some date palms a large group of American soldiers with their tanks moved towards the main bridge and stopped. They seemed to be just waiting. After a time another group of vehicles approached from further down the road and moved towards the bridge, but they could not see each other because of the vegetation and date palm plantation. There was no way that we could attack such a force and live as there were many of them and few of us. The soldier leading us had much experience in warfare and divided us into two groups, but did not explain why. We were in an irrigation ditch which offered good protection and cover from the Americans on the bridge. One soldier asked what was going to happen next as we were all scared to death, but he received no answer. After what seemed like a life-time of waiting he ordered my group to fire at the Americans on the bridge, while the others were ordered to fire at the convoy on the other side of the vegetation. As God is my witness, when I fired I hit nothing as my hand was shaking too much to aim correctly. I think that my friends also had the same problem as me.*

'*After we fired, there was a pause before the Americans fired back, but when they did fire it sounded like hell; I have never been so scared in my life. As the Americans fired in our direction the palms above us began falling on top of us like rain. We dropped down into the ditch once again and began to move away towards a group of buildings that were in the distance.*

'*As we moved away quickly along the ditch we realized that the Americans were not firing at us, but at each other, on account of the plantation blocking their view. Their shooting seemed to be wild and uncontrolled, but who were we to complain, we were alive because of this.*

'*After about five minutes of firing, two helicopters (believed to be Cobras) flew over the plantation and I assume spotted that their fellow countrymen were firing at each other and not us. After a few minutes, the firing began to stop-and we all knew that our time was up if we did not surrender. As we approached the buildings ahead of us, we put our weapons down and stood by the side of a large building so that we could easily be seen from the nearby road. A group of Americans eventually spotted us and accepted our surrender. We were lucky to have been spared by them; they were honourable and generous men.*'

Corpsman Christopher Pavicek provides aid to a wounded Iraqi soldier after a fire-fight with 1st LAR outside the town of An Nu'maniyah.

TUESDAY 1 APRIL

Acting on information from an Iraqi civilian, coalition forces conduct a daring rescue operation to save captured POW, Army Private First Class Jessica Lynch from an Iraqi hospital in Nasiriyah.

Around Baghdad, there are a series of large explosions – following a number of air assaults against the city, that last for more than thirty minutes. As these attacks are taking place, Republican Guard units to the south of Baghdad, come under intense US artillery bombardment – indicating that ground forces are moving ever closer.

In other operations elsewhere in Iraq, the Baghdad Division of the Republican Guard are destroyed in fierce fighting with the US Marines around Kut, while the Medina and Nebuchadnezzar divisions of the Republican Guard are engaged by the US 3rd Infantry Division in fierce fighting around Karbala. US Marines also encountered fierce resistance in the town of Diwaniyah where they discovered a large ammunition dump.

Meanwhile in the south of Iraq, around Basra, British troops destroyed Iraqi artillery and missiles prior to an air strike by aircraft from the USS *Kitty Hawk* who again targeted Saddam's presidential yacht, the *Al Mansur*.

And 'Comical Ali's' thought for the day:

'Our initial assessment is that they will all die'.

162

Aboard USS *Kitty Hawk*, 2 April. An F/A-18C
Hornet launches past on looking shooters
located on the bow.

WEDNESDAY 2 APRIL

US Central Command announces that the 3rd Infantry Division, supported by aircraft and tanks has now completely destroyed the Medina Division of the Republican Guard at Karbala, and is poised to march on Baghdad.

From their position on the outskirts of Baghdad, they also confirmed securing another crossing over the River Euphrates, but this news is tempered by the loss of a Black Hawk helicopter to small-arms fire, resulting in seven killed and four injured.

In another unrelated incident, the crew of an F-14 Tomcat had to be rescued by a CSAR (Combat Search and Rescue) helicopter after it developed mechanical problems over Iraq-culminating with the crew being forced to eject over enemy held territory.

A Pararescueman from the 301st Rescue
Squadron, gets out of his HH60 helicopter
after completing a mission.

Elsewhere in Iraq, the 101st Airborne Division (Air Assault) took over a bridge spanning the Tigris River in Najaf, after Iraqi forces fled to the other bank and dug in around a sacred site, known as the Dome of Ali. While this action was taking place, elements of the 82nd Airborne Division attacked Iraqi forces at Samawah.

And 'Comical Ali's' thoughts for the day were:

'They are trapped in Umm Qasr. They are trapped near Basra, They are trapped near Nasiriyah. They are trapped near Najaf. They are trapped everywhere. Let the American infidels bask in their illusion'

THURSDAY 3 APRIL

Saddam International Airport was captured during the night by the 3rd Infantry Division, following a fierce battle with the Special Republican Guard that involved both USAF F-15E Strike Eagle fighters and US Navy F-18 Hornets. Within hours of the victory, which cost over 300 Iraqi lives, the airport was renamed Baghdad International Airport. This important development also means that US forces are now less than ten miles from Baghdad City.

During the day, in a desparate bid to drive the Americans back, the Iraqis mounted a series of counterattacks but these are thwarted by both air and ground assets.

Near the south of Baghdad, in the Latifiya industrial estate, US Forces found thousands of boxes containing phials of an unidentified liquid and powder as well as chemical warfare mauals – the powder however, was later identified as a nerve gas antidote. West of Baghdad, US Special Forces entered a presidential palace during the night and seized documents of immense value as they searched for information on the whereabouts of Saddam and his henchmen.

A satellite photograph showing the location of Baghdad International Airport, once named Saddam International Airport.

In Nejaf, something of a Mexican stand-off takes place between Iraqi forces and the 101st Airborne as they consolidate their position. Elsewhere on the Euphrates River, over 500 Iraqi troops are killed trying to recapture a bridge – as it is of key importance to the American advance on Baghdad.

In the south of Iraq, British forces battled with Iraqi irregulars on two fronts outside of Basra and Zubayr where they came under fire from rocket-propelled grenades and machine guns as well as a tank. In the subsequent firefights that took place, the tank was destroyed and twelve Iraqis taken prisoner. Later in the day, the British mounted forays into Basra – both to gauge resistance and to identify possible break-in points for assault troops.

During the day it was announced that in the previous twenty-four hours, coalition aircraft had flown more than 1,000 sorties over Iraq, and had expended more than 725 Tomahawk cruise missiles and 12,000 precision-guided weapons since the war began.

And 'Comical Ali's' thoughts for the day.

> **'At Saddam Airport? Now that's just silly!!!**
> **Today we slaughtered them in the airport. They**
> **are out of Saddam International Airport. The force**
> **that was in the airport, this force was**
> **destroyed.'**

WORLDS APART

While Iraq's people lived in squalor, their leader Saddam Hussein lived in absolute luxury, having squandered the country's wealth on lavish palaces and good living. Of all the images that shocked British and American forces most, as they advanced through Iraq, nothing stunned them more than the sight of Saddam's palaces, all seventy-eight of them.

Having seen how most Iraqis lived, it was nothing short of outrageous to see how one man had robbed his country of all its wealth and given absolutely nothing back in return. Each palace featured an abundance of gold, crystal and marble, set in rich fertile grounds, while just outside poverty reigned supreme.

The British and Americans made good use of the palaces, both as temporary sleeping quarters and operational headquarters. After being subjected to numerous sandstorms and rough living conditions, the palaces made great bolt-holes for the coalition forces. As General Tommy Franks said '*This was an oil-for-palace program*', a reference to the UN oil for food programme.

Saddam Hussein, denied himself nothing when it came to his palaces, and was even known to have diverted water flows in order to fill his lakes, often to the detriment of the local people. When the Royal Marines first entered the Basra palace, they were dumbfounded when they saw miles of Italian marble and gold-plated toilet brushes, causing one officer Major Kevin Oliver to say:

US Army Sgt. Mark Phiffer stands guard near a burning oil well in the Rumaylah Oil fields in southern Iraq, 2 April.

Courtesy Joint Combat Camera Center

'Comparing the palace to villages farther south, here you have mansions bedecked in gold. There they have absolutely nothing. 'Forget all the marble. What strikes me most about this place is the sheer degree of utter waste. It disgusts me.'

Concluded Royal Marine Maj. Jeff Moulton:

'I don't know what will happen to this place now. It will go back to the local people sooner or later. It was built with their blood and money, so I would say it belongs to them.'

British soldiers carry out a search and clear mission in one of Saddam's former Palaces.

A dead Iraqi soldier lies by the side of a road as members of Naval Mobile Construction Battalion Seventy Four, pass by on 3 April. He was a member of a small force killed by Marines defending a nearby bridge.

FRIDAY 4 APRIL

Iraqi television broadcast images of what it claims is Saddam Hussein on walkabout in Baghdad – however, most accept that the image seen is that of a double and not the man himself.

Meanwhile, outside Baghdad itself, US Marines began moving on the city, following the mass surrender of 2,500 members of the Republican Guard to them, as they advanced from Kut towards Baghdad. Ironically, US Colonel Joe Dowdy, commander of Regimental Combat Team 1, 1st Marines Expeditionary Force, was relieved of his command with no reasons given.

He had led the team to within 130 miles of Baghdad, before this decision was taken. Throughout the day, British forces engaged Iraqi irregulars around Basra, and captured a ballistic missile battery near Al Zubayr that had been threatening Kuwait, while further south in Umm Qasr, humanitarian aid continued to pour

British forces discover an Iraqi anti-shipping missile in a well hidden location close to Basra. Although never used directly against Coalition warships, they were targeted at ground forces deployed in Kuwait, with many close calls reported.

in, making for great PR.

In the air campaign, coalition aircraft attacked buildings in the centre of Baghdad, including several presidential palaces-however, they were beginning to run out of targets.

It was also announced that in western Iraq, a car bomb had killed three coalition troops and injured a further two. Word also came through that Washington Post columnist Michael Kelly had been tragically killed in a Humvee accident. He was the first American journalist to die in Operation 'Iraqi Freedom'.

And 'Comical Ali's' thought for the day:

'Lying is forbidden in Iraq. President Saddam Hussein will tolerate nothing but truthfulness as he is a man of great honour and integrity. Everyone is encouraged to speak freely of the truths evidenced in their eyes and hearts.'

SATURDAY 5 APRIL

With pedal to the metal, a US force of some twenty Abrams tanks and ten Bradley fighting vehicles enter Baghdad for the first time on a probing mission, but do not cross the Tigris River into the centre of the city as it is deemed too dangerous. They entered the City from the main southern road and headed through the Dawra suburb before linking up with other US troops at Baghdad International Airport. During the incursion, the troops met with resistance on several occasions, and sustained four casualties. During the mission, one tank developed a mechanical problem that resulted in a fire – causing the crew to bale out. The crew however had the presence of mind to destroy it before being rescued.

In preparation for the full assault phase, coalition aircraft began round-the-clock bombing of possible defensive positions as there still remained a great threat.

At Karbala, the 101st Airborne Division, supported by tanks and Apache helicopter gunships launched an all out assault on the city after coalition aircraft had bombed a Republican Guard barracks, an ammunition dump and the headquarters of the ruling Ba'ath party.

In the south of Iraq, members of the 3rd Regiment Royal Artillery spent the night at the Iraqi Army's 51st Division headquarters located between Basra and Al Zubayr. While undertaking a thorough search of the barracks, troops came across the remains of more than 200 people, some in wooden coffins and others in plastic bags.

A forensics team was immediately sent in to examine the grim remains, which were almost entirely bones. Many of the dead had been shot in the head, leading to the conclusion that they had been executed – but not in the most recent war. The general concensus of opinion being that they had been killed in the Iran-Iraq war of the 1980s, and that they were Iranian, rather than Iraqi.

In the south, British forces continued to extend their area of control northwards from the main southern oilfields near Basra, while in the north, US Special Forces took control of the road north from Baghdad to Tikrit – the birthplace of Saddam Hussein. In addition to this operation, US forces also began moving towards Iraqi forces defending the city of Mosul.

And 'Comical Ali's' thoughts for the day.

> **'Be assured. Baghdad is safe, protected. We have destroyed two tanks, fighter planes, two helicopters and their shovels-we have driven them back.'**

101ST AIRBORNE DIVISION (AIR ASSAULT)

The 101st Airborne Division is the biggest air cavalry unit in the world today, and played a key role in Operation Iraqi Freedom. This is their story.

From the time the 101st Airborne Division (Air Assault) first left its forward operating base in the Kuwaiti desert, right up until its arrival in the northern Iraqi city of Mosul-a distance of some 1,200km, it was in the thick of the action. Firing an amazing 3,500 rounds of artillery along the way. During a briefing given by the Divisions commander, Major General David H. Petraeus, in which he described their drive north, he stated:

'Our soldiers had a number of very tough fights in southern Iraq, liberating An Najaf, Karbala and Al Hillah, and then clearing Al Mamadia, Escondaria and south Baghdad, as well as Hadithah in the western desert.

'We then air assaulted 500km. further north to secure and clear Mosul, Tall Afar, Qaiyara and other cities in Nineveh Province. Three of the division's soldiers were killed in combat and some seventy-nine were wounded.

'Mosul had been the scene of some stiff firefights. We came in with a tank battalion, an Apache battalion, a Kiowa squadron, and several battalions of infantry, a brigade, and a lot of other combat multipliers, artillery and so forth.

'We immediately secured the city, establishing a civil military oper-ation centre in the former governance building in the centre of the city, with its leaders, and so forth, to ensure that there weren't repeated instances. We did have several firefights our first week here but we

Black Hawk helicopters from the 2nd Brigade, 101st Airborne Division (Air Assault) move into an Iraqi city during an operation.
US Army photo by Sgt. Luis Lazzara

took no casualties.'

As an example of the sheer intensity of the combat in which his units were involved, he stated that they had fired some 3,500 rounds of artillery, nearly 1,000 2.75-inch rockets and Hellfire missiles, 114 tactical missiles and over 40,000 rounds of machine-gun ammunition from Apache and Kiowa attack helicopters. They also used some 150 sorties of close air support, and 'tons of everything else in our inventory' he said.

'Our Apaches did a great job for us,' said General Petraeus.

'We did in fact change our tactics from night-long deep attack operations, for two reasons. After a successful deep attack, but one in which we crashed a helicopter in a night dust landing on return, and also had problems on take-off, so we had two problems.

'The other problem frankly, was that the Iraqis dispersed very early on and moved their tanks and fighting vehicles and artillery away from

US soldiers secure a military compound outside the town of An Nu' maniyah, 5 April. Photo courtesy JCCC

the avenues of approach that the 3rd division, in particular, was going to use. And so they weren't massed in the way that we want usually for Apache operations. We did , as I say, have one quite successful deep attack operation, had reasonable battle damage assessment (BDA). But it was not the kind that we had hoped to see with the 100-plus tanks, tracks, artillery and air defense systems.

'Following that, when we could not get the target definition that we needed, we went to daylight, deep armed reconnaissance operations and conducted a number of very successful operations of that type. 'We packaged these operations with ATACMS missiles, and we called for 114 of these. Each of these clears an entire grid square. They're massive munitions. We had those in a direct line between the shooters and the Apaches. We also had JSTARS supporting them, to direct them; AWACS, EA-6 jammers, and close air support all packaged together with HARM shooters. And that package went down range; we could identify the target at up to eight kilometers.

A soldier from the Civil Affairs Battalion speaks with a boy, while bags of rice and wheat are delivered to his village near the city of Najaf in central Iraq.

'And then, depending on how much fuel the Apache had, if he had a lot of fuel, would bring in close air support, ATACMS, and save his missiles and rockets for later. And then, as he got toward the end of his time on station, find a target, use his munitions, be relieved in place by another platoon or company of Apaches, and do the same thing again and again and again.'

The General said they also had considerable success with attack helicopters operating in close support of infantry soldiers.

'The one operation in which we actually ran into a substantial fight with the Republican Guards, and one of the few cases that I,m aware of where the Republican Guards employed combined arm operations was the morning that the V Corps attacked with an armed recon by our Apaches to the north-west of Karbala, the lake.'

'The 3rd Infantry Division attacked into the Karbala Gap, both in the west and the east of the city; and then, of course, really never

stopped from there. We attacked into south Al Hillah, where we encountered a dug-in Republican Guard battalion with a tank company, with artillery and with air defense, and it fought very, very effectively. We had a very heavy fight there, lost our first soldier.'

'The Apache company in that operation fought very, very hard, and took some degree of fire.'

All of them made it safely back, another sign that the Apache can get hit and just keep on flying, as it showed in Afghanistan as well, in close combat.

'In that fight, we destroyed that Republican Guards battalion; we destroyed the tank company. We destroyed two artillery battalions, destroyed an artillery battery and a number of other systems. We never again saw a Republican Guard unit stand and fight and employ combined arms like that.

General Petraeus, also went on to mention that the division often employed its Kiowa Warrior cavalry squadron attack helicopters directly over cities.

'The Kiowas were hard targets to hit generally and could take the doors off and look directly down through the palm trees and into the city streets where the regular army and militia and Fedayeen were hiding their systems, and then using the Apaches around the edge of the city and occasionally bringing them in for really robust attacks. That worked quite successfully.

SUNDAY 6 APRIL

British forces advance into the centre of Basra in a two pronged attack, and experience light resistance – as most of the Iraqi forces – both regular and irregular have fled the city. The attack followed a number of probing actions that tested the level of opposition, and was only made once the element of risk to the British troops had been substantially reduced. This was also done to minimise the level of casualties – both to friendly civilians and enemy forces alike.

The assault on Basra, began under the protective umbrella of US Marine Cobra gunships and British Army Air Corps Lynx helicopters, when Challenger tanks of the Royal Scots Dragoon Guards alongside troops of the 1st Battalion Black Watch in Warrior armoured fighting vehicles, moved into the south and west of Basra to test the strength of enemy opposition. 'They found only limited resistance' said Air Marshal Brian Burridge, UK National Contingent Commander.

'Commanders on the ground – Major General Robin Brims, officer commanding 1 Armoured Division, and Brigadier Graham Binns, of the 7th Armoured Brigade – decided to exploit this opportunity and began the liberation.'

The Challegers and Warriors from the Royal Scotts Dragoon Guards and the Black Watch, supported by elements of the 1st Battalion Irish Guards, pressed further into the city from the west, and were greeted with cheers from the local Iraqi's who welcomed them as liberators, and not as conquerors. As the British forces continued to advance, the 2nd Royal Tank Regiment battlegroup moved rapidly into the centre of the city and took up all round defensive positions – so as to prevent an Iraqi counterattack – while the Royal Regiment of Fusiliers battlegroup in their Challengers and Warriors deployed to the north of the city and the dock area.

Later in the afternoon, 40 Commando Royal Marines moved deep into the south of the city, focusing their forces primarily around the palace area, while Britains elite Airborne force, the 3rd Battalion, Parachute Regiment began sweep and clear operations around the old town of Basra – later described by the Air Marshal as a *'myriad of narrow, winding streets and alleyways so has to be done on foot.'*

Although most locals were clearly pleased to see the British forces in the flesh, some sinister elements lurking in the shadows of the city were not. The operation to take Basra, was both well planned and executed, and was achieved for the loss of only two British soldiers – in itself a remarkable feat.

As the operation progressed, word came through that Saddam's cousin Ali Hassad al-Majid – AKA Chemical Ali – had been killed during an air strike on the city – following a tip-off by special forces as to where he was hiding. Al Majid, was infamous throughout Iraq for ordering a gas attack that killed thousands of Kurds – his passing will not be mourned.

Further north on the western outskirts of Baghdad, US troops of the 3rd Infantry Division engage in a fierce firefight with Iraqi forces equipped with tanks and armoured vehicles – many of which were later destroyed by artillery and air strikes. US forces now control most of the main roads into the city – but the situation is still fluid in a number of places-on account of the level of Iraqi resistance. Elsewhere around the City, the divisions 1st Brigade Combat Team seized a palace that was thought to be a Special Republican Guard headquarters, while in other areas, US forces consolidated their positions prior to the main assault phase. During the fighting, over sixty Iraqi vehicles were destroyed, along with three T-72 tanks and three armoured personnel cariers.

US Forces had now almost encircled the city, apart from a gap leading north. Meanwhile in Karbala, troops of the 101st Airborne Division have reached the centre of the city after just one day of fierce fighting, while in Najaf, to the south of Karbala, elements of the division continued their isolation strategy against the occupying Iraqi forces.

In Samawah, north-west of Nasiriyah, the 82nd Airborne Division carried out humanitarian assistance by restoring water and electricity to the town- as the situation there was now deemed benign. As the day went on, news came through that the US 5th Corp, including the 3rd Infantry Division were now in

A British NCO barks out orders to his men prior to going over the top.

control of the corridor that runs from Karbala to Baghdad in the west, while in the east, the 1st Marines Expeditionary Force controll the corridor from north of Kut to Baghdad.

During the night, US Marines carried out a raid against a camp near Samanpak, which was being used for training foreign nationals in terror tactics and guerilla warfare. After a ferocious firefight, in which some nationals from Syria and Egypt were either killed or captured the camp was destroyed – thereby preventing its use again.

A tired but alert British patrol carrying out a routine 'feet on the beat' mission.

A USMC Cobra attack helicopter rides shot gun for a British Challenger tank as it moves through a plantation. Note the louvred IR device on the tanks turret designed to prevent friendly fire incidents by means of creating a cold spot on a targeting sight.

In the north of Iraq, Special Forces directed air attacks against regime forces near Kirkut, and set up ambushes along several roads leading to the west and to the north – their purpose being to prevent ballistic missile movement and to deny regime leaders an escape route to Syria.

During the day, coalition aircraft undertook some 850 sorties-of which 600 were strike missions – while the rest were in support of ground forces.

And 'Comical Ali's' thoughts for the day.

'We have surrounded them in their tanks. We will kill them all... most of them.'

MONDAY 7 APRIL

Acting on intelligence gleened from Coalition personnel operating covertly in Baghdad, Central Command orders a B-1 bomber to drop four 2,000-pound JDAM (Joint Direct Attack Munitions) 'Bunker-buster' bombs on a restaurant in the Al-Mansour district of Baghdad where Saddam Hussein has reportably been spotted.

As this mission was taking place, some sixty-five US Abrams tanks and forty Bradley armoured fighting vehicles, supported by A-10 Warthog ground attack aircraft and helicopter gunships forced their way into downtown Baghdad, while US Marines engaged Special Republican Guard units defending the eastern suburbs of the city. During the fighting, two of Saddam's presidential palaces fell to the Americans – one of which he regularly used for regime meetings. As the attacks were taking place, Iraqi forces blew up a number of bridges over the Tigris River but their efforts were in vain as the US forces were now able to overcome almost anything at this stage of the assault on the City. Overall, the situation was now deemed tactically permissive – which meant that the Americans could now exploit virtually every military opportunity that presented itself – very much in the same way as the British had done in Basra.

Within Baghdad itself, a statue of Saddam on horseback was destroyed by US artillery, as a means of demonstrating that Saddams regime was now over.

Meanwhile in the south-east of the city, the 1st US Marines Expeditionary Force and the US 5th Corps crossed the Diala River by means of mobile pontoon bridge units as the two bridges that crossed the tributary had been destroyed by Iraqi forces.

Once over the mobile bridge, the Marines swept into the City from the south-east and secured the Rashid military airport as well as a number of other key objectives-capturing or destroying a large number of armoured personnel carriers and T-72 tanks in the process. In the south of Iraq, the Royal Fleet Auxiliary landing ship Sir Percivale docked at Umm Qasr with a cargo of 300 tonnes of humanitarian aid, while in the town itself, clean water was now being pumped in from Kuwait at a rate of 2 million litres per day – courtesy of the

British Army's Royal Engineers.

During a press briefing given on 7 April, the Air Marshal stated:

'In the first seven days of this month, we have delivered over 1 million litres of bottled water and over 100,000 humanitarian daily rations by lorry from Kuwait.'

As the day progressed, word came in of a spectacular rescue mission – mounted to recover two seriously injured special forces operatives from a location just five miles south of Baghdad.

The operation began, when, in severe weather conditions, a US CSAR (Combat Search and Rescue) helicopter force was directed by the Special Operations Command Rescue Coordination centre via the Joint Search and Rescue Centre to perform an urgent Medevac.

Aware of the immense risks that they were about to undertake, the USAF HH-60G Pave Hawk helicopter crews departed from their remote desert airbase and flew directly to an extraction zone as designated.

In all, the rescue package consisted of two helicopters plus two A-10 Thunderbolt II close support aircraft – their job being to ride shotgun during the mission. As a back-up to the main force, a duplicate package was put together as a reserve – in case of further combat losses or technical failures.

When made aware of the soldiers' injuries, the helicopter crews requested a Special Operations MC-130E Combat Talon aircraft, complete with a flight surgeon and two medical technicians on board to RV with them at Najaf – as this would save flight time and maximise their chances of survival. In addition to this specialist aircraft, an HC-130P King refuelling aircraft was also deployed to the region – but from another airbase – its mission, to refuel the rescue helicopters if need be.

Battling blowing sandstorms that cut visibility at times to half a mile, right up to an altitude of 3,500 ft, the Pave Hawks came in under cover of the storm and safely evacuated the two men to the MC-130E which was waiting for them about seventy-five miles south of Baghdad-where they were picked up and flown to Kuwait for intensive medical care.

Meanwhile at the Pentagon, General Richard B. Meyers, chairman Joint Chiefs of Staff, stated that there were now more than 340,000 Coalition forces in the region, of which more than 125,000 were inside Iraq.

He went on to say that most of the major roads into and out of Baghdad were secure, and that;

'Republican Guard divisions have only been able to conduct sporadic attacks on our forces. Of the 800-plus tanks they began with, all but a couple of dozen have been destroyed or abandoned. We have more than 7,000 prisoners of war.'

In the north of Iraq, Special Operations forces called up close air support, which destroyed a force of several armoured personnel carriers, tanks and infantry

Members of the 363rd Expeditionary Security Forces Squadron, stand guard at an entry control point during a sand storm on 7 April. The 363rd ESFS members worked around the clock performing force protection measures, air base defence and protecting personnel.

near Ibrill, while in another similar engagement at Kirkut, tanks, armoured personnel carriers and trucks were also destroyed-marking the end of what was a very busy day.

And 'Comical Ali's' thoughts for the day.

'They're not even (within) 100 miles (of Baghdad). They are not in any place. They hold no place in Iraq. This is an illusion... they are trying to sell to the others an illusion. Their infidels are committing suicide by the hundreds on the gates of Baghdad. Baghdad is safe, protected.'

TUESDAY 8 APRIL

US Forces drive their armoured stake further into the heart of the Iraqi Regime as they fight for the city of Baghdad – street by street.

Central Command also confirms that Coalition forces are now in total

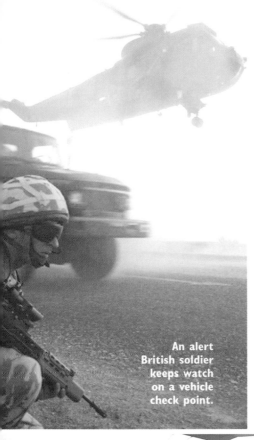

control of the skies above Iraq – as their is now little or no effective incoming anti-aircraft fire.

Overnight, the 5th Corps consolidated their position within Baghdad and engaged Iraqi forces on a number of occasions – destroying both armoured personnl carriers and T-72 tanks alike. By day-break, US forces within the City of Baghdad were probing the streets in great strength – as large- scale Iraqi resistance had virtually collapsed. Instead, the troops were now being engaged by die-hard Ba'ath Party members and Saddam Fedayeen militia - as they had everything to lose- especially as Saddam's demise was now staring them in the face.

US forces were now looking victory in the mouth, and could sense it as they advanced ever more closely to the centre of Baghdad, while outside the city, heavy resistance was still being encountered in Najaf, Karbala and Samawa-despite significant US opeations to quell it.

Meanwhile in Basra, looters or Ali Baba's as they are called in Iraq, took to

An alert British soldier keeps watch on a vehicle check point.

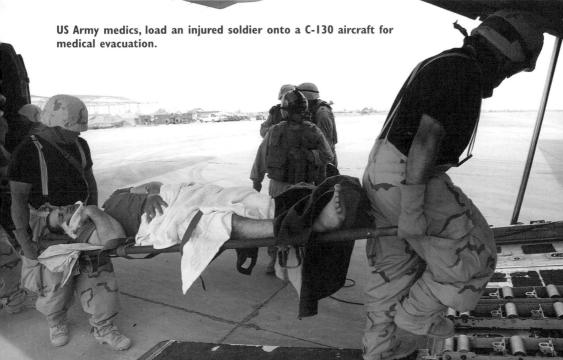

US Army medics, load an injured soldier onto a C-130 aircraft for medical evacuation.

the streets and stripped shops, buildings and hospitals bare of their furniture and equipment – while British soldiers stood by and let them. It was to be a foretaste of things to come.

During the day, it was announced that two journalists – one a Ukranian, the other a Spaniard – were killed and at least four others injured after an American Abrams tank opened fire on the Palestine hotel in central Baghdad – after spotting what they believed were Iraqi snipers about to engage them.

Meanwhile in the north of Iraq, US forces launched a search and rescue mission after an F-15 Strike Eagle fighter crashed in Tikrit – the status of its two aircrew unknown.

And 'Comical Ali's' many thoughts for the day were.

'These images are not the suburbs of Baghdad. From what I glimpsed, the rows of palm trees on the side, which you saw in the images, are located in Ghreib, where we have surrounded the American and British infidels.'

'The situation is excellent, they are going to try to approach Baghdad... and their grave will be there.

Their forces committed suicide by the hundreds...The battle is fierce and God made us victorious. The fighting continues.

They think we are retarded – they are retarded.

God will roast their stomachs in hell at the hands of Iraqis.

No I am not scared, and neither should you be!

I triple guarantee you, there are no American soldiers in Baghdad.

There are only two American tanks in the city.

We are Winning!

Saddams statues are not being torn down, they are merely being removed for cleaning...yes, cleaning and maintenance!'

WEDNESDAY 9 APRIL

Baghdad finally falls to US forces, as Iraqi soldiers and Saddams sinister security services flee the city's streets as the death knell finally sounds for Saddam Hussein's evil regime.

The day is dominated by images of a gigantic statue of Saddam Hussein being toppled by the people of Baghdad – with just a little assistance from the US

Marines – who kindly obliged the Iraqi people with the use of their tracked combat engineering vehicle.

The day was an emotional one for the Iraqi people – as it marked the removal of the self imposed strait-jacket that was Saddam's rule. Some rejoiced at the news of his demise, while others considered their futures. It was a mixed day emotionally for many.

The downside of the day however, was the outbreak of sporadic looting and ransacking of government buidings, museums and hospitals – which left many decent Iraqis feeling angry and frustrated – as the US forces simply turned a blind eye to it. In part this was understandable, as the people of Baghdad had been ruled with a rod of iron for decades – and needed to blow off some steam to release their years of understandable pent-up frustration and anger. The view being taken by the Americans was – better the frustration be poured out against Saddam's legacy, rather than the Coalitions inheritance.

Word of Saddam's downfall, soon spread like an epidemic – with the liberated residents taking to the streets in their thousands. But for some, the news sounded too good to be true. Although pockets of resistance continued throughout the city and the countryside – the word was out, that Saddam's twenty-four years of oppression were now over – and that change was in the air – be it for better or worse.

And 'Comical Ali's' thought for the day. Er, there wasn't any – as he is now on indefinite administrative leave until further notice. Shame, as he did tell a good story, did our Mohammed Saeed al-Sahaf – AKA Baghdad Bob or 'Comical Ali' as he was better known.

A haggered looking 'Comical Ali' as seen on news footage. The true events of the war appeared to have aged him twenty years.

THURSDAY 10 APRIL

As word spreads of Saddam's demise, Iraq's 5th Corps surrenders to Coalition and Kurdish forces near Mosul, while nearby the fight for Saddam's hometown of Tikrit continues. Meanwhile in Baghdad, a suicide bomber blew himself up at a military checkpoint – injuring four US Marines.

Elsewhere in Iraq, in the town of Ramadi, an air strike is launched against Saddam's half-brother, Barzan, Ibrahim Hasan al Tikriti, while in the south, operations continue to round up Saddam's former henchmen.

In the north of Iraq, there are fears of a Turkish invasion following an announcement that Turkish Kurds intend to occupy a number of contentious towns – leading to a possible uprising against Turkish authority.

The four Aces in the deck of cards issued to US forces.

FRIDAY 11 APRIL

Iraq's Adnan Mechanized Division of the Republican Guard abandons Kirkuk, and heads for Tikrit, to make a last stand against Coalition forces. As this redeployment is taking place, fighting ends in the stronghold of Mosul – but for all concerned, it is an uneasy peace.

In a bid to pacify Turkish concerns over northern Iraq, US forces move in and secure the oil wells located in and around Kirkut.

Meanwhile in Baghdad, looting continues unabated, while US forces make an effort to get the City's police and firemen back to work – so as to create an impression of normality. In an interesting development, US forces are issued with a deck of cards featuring the faces of the fifty-two most – wanted regime members – with Saddam's face pictured on the ace of spades.

SATURDAY 12 APRIL

Only days into US occupation, and already chaos rules in Baghdad – following days and nights of looting in which some of Iraq's most priceless antiquities are stolen from the national museum.

During raids carried out throughout the City against Saddams henchmen, American forces arrest Lieutenant General Amir al-Saadi – one of Iraq's top scientists. In interviews that follow, he categorically states that Iraq has no

A Special Operations Force HUMVEE, moves through western Baghdad, 12 April.

A Royal Marine Commando, mans a .50 calibre machine-gun in Basra

British troops, begin to maintain law and order with the help of local Militia men.

British troops patrol past a monument of Saddam on the streets of Basra, a picture that signals the end of his twenty-four years of terror and the downfall of his evil regime.

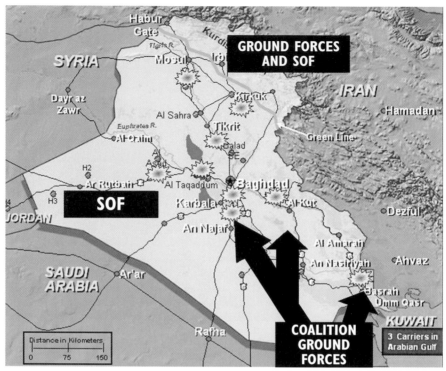

Deployment of Coalition Forces during Operation Iraqi Freedom.

weapons of mass destruction – the main justification for the war meanwhile, following a number of searches of a mosque and the homes of Ba'ath Party officials, thirteen surface – to air missiles are found.

However, on the good news front, former POW Private First Class Jessica Lynch arrives back in the United States to a hero's welcome.

SUNDAY 13 APRIL

As the battle for Tikrit rages, US Marines with F-18 fighters and Cobra gunships engage in fierce firefights with 2,500 Iraqi troops committed to the bitter end to defend Saddam's last remaining stronghold.

During a briefing given by General Tommy Franks, it was revealed that Iraq's army had been for all intents and purposes destroyed, and that one of Saddam Hussein's half-brothers had been captured while trying to flee into Syria. One other interesting piece of information revealed today, concerned the fate of seven US soldiers previously listed as missing in action, but now known to be safe on account of being rescued by US forces in an unrelated operation.

MONDAY 14 APRIL

Finally, after fierce fighting, US Marines rolled into the City of Tikrit –

signifying the final nail in Saddam's political coffin.

Meanwhile, the Pentagon confirms that Operation 'Iraqi Freedom' is a complete military success – having gained control of the country in less than thirty days – a remarkable acheivement in modern warfare.

The Bush administration also gives Syria a stern warning about its support of former regime members – as many have now fled Iraq for Syria. The British however remain tight lipped about Syria – as it gave two members of the British special forces sanctuary, after they were forced to escape from Iraq – following their mission being compromised near Mosul.

In an interesting development, eleven mobile labs that could be used for chemical and biological research are found during a series of weapons of mass destruction searches that have taken place – although a good find, they are however not the so called 'smoking gun' that the Coalition has been looking for.

TUESDAY 15 APRIL

The US Army's V Corps move into the centre of Baghdad to relieve US Marines guarding the capital, while special forces capture convicted Palestinian terrorist Abu Abbass just outside of Baghdad – an important find as he was the mastermind behind the Achille Lauro ship hijacking.

During a press briefing, Army Brigadier General Vincent Brooks of Central Command announces the discovery of a massive stash of weapons including ninety-one cases of TNT, several cases of home-made bombs as well as nearly two dozen crates of rocket-propelled grenades.

Today was also significant, as it marked the first conference between Sunni, Shiite and Kurd leaders who called for a multi-ethnic democratic regime.

WEDNESDAY 16 APRIL

Fighting broke out in Mosul, after US troops raised their flag, Old Glory, over an Iraqi government building. As tensions mounted, US soldiers took to the streets in a bid to both defuse the situation and maintain civil order.

In Ramadi, the Iraqi 12th Armour Brigade surrendered after realizing that their situation was militarily untenable, while in Baghdad, US tanks are deployed in the courtyard of Iraq's national museum in a desparate bid to stop the looting of priceless historical treasures.

With the threat of large-scale fighting now substantially reduced, coalition forces start to head back for home – but for some, their work is only just beginning.

THURSDAY 17 APRIL

With the war effectively over, the search for former regime members could now intensify as there were far more troops available in theatre for such operations.

An Iraqi tank smoulders after being destroyed by US Army Special Forces and 26th Marine Expeditionary Unit personnel in Mosul, 16 April.

Today, US special forces captured former Iraqi intelligence chief, Barzan Ibrahim Hasan al Tikriti, during a surprise raid in Baghdad. He was yet another of Saddam's half-brothers.

Elsewhere in Baghdad, elements of Task Force 20, a newly formed special forces unit comprising members of Delta Force, carried out search operations in Saddam's former bunker complexes, but found nothing significant relating to the man himself.

US soldiers keep a careful eye out for trouble as local villagers collect water from tanker trucks supplied by the US Army outside the municipal stadium in Kirkuk, 17 April.

Up until today, 126 Coalition personnel have been killed and 495 wounded, while one American is still posted as missing in action. These figures were provided by Central Command.

Poignantly, as these figures were being released, news came through that the seven former US POWs rescued recently during military operations were now receiving medical attention and therapy at the Landstuhl Regional Medical Centre in Germany.

CHAPTER SEVEN

THE VICTORY SPEECH

GIVEN BY PRESIDENT G. W. BUSH ON 16 APRIL 2003 WHILE ADDRESSING EMPLOYEES OF THE BOEING PLANT IN ST LOUIS:

Thanks to the courage and the might of our military, the American people are more secure. Thanks to the courage and might of our military, the Iraqi people are now free.

You and I and all the world are witnessing historic days in the cause of freedom. One month ago-just one month ago - the forces of our coalition stood at the borders of Iraq, with orders to advance hundreds of miles through hostile territory, against a ruthless enemy. Today, organized military resistance is virtually ended; the major cities of Iraq have been liberated.

Two weeks ago, the Iraqi regime operated a gulag of dissidents, and increadibly enough, a prison for young children. Now the gates to that prison have been thrown wide open, and we are putting the dictators, political prisons and torture chambers out of business.

One week ago, Baghdad was filled with statues and giant pictures of the dictator. They're kind of hard to find today. The fall of that statue in Baghdad marked the end of a nightmare for the Iraqi people, and it marked the start of a new day of freedom.

Four days ago, seven American soldiers, six men and one woman, were held captive by forces still loyal to the fallen regime. Today, those brave Americans are with their fellow comrades, and are headed home to their loved ones.

On 11 September 2001, America found that we are not immune to the threats that gather for years across the ocean; threats that can arrive in sudden tragedy. Since September the 11th, we've been engaged in a global war against terror, a war being waged on many fronts. That war continues, and we are winning.

In any conflict, however, this nation's greatest single asset is the kind of men and women who put on the uniform of the United States. The methods of war have changed, but the need for courage has not. And we,ve seen, once again, the courage of the men and women who wear the uniform of the United States of America. These are young Americans who engaged in furious battles - then carried wounded enemy to medical treatment. These are young Americans willing to accept any danger to rescue one of their own. These are the kind of people who, when they are wounded themselves, ask to rejoin their comrades in battle. Some of our soldiers and Marines will never be returning to their families. And these are the men and women who our nation will honor forever.

This past month has been a time of testing and uncertainty for our country. The American people have responded with resolve and with optimism. Whatever challenges may come, we can be confident.

Our nation is strong, our purpose is firm, and our cause is just.

God bless you all.

CHAPTER EIGHT

THE CONCLUSIONS

As Operation 'Iraqi Freedom' reached its predictable conclusion - that of victory - a perception began to circulate within Britain and America that the military campaign had not gone to plan and that its execution had been clumsy and disjointed. In part this view was understandable, as the war appeared to have got off to something of a false start - on account of the fact that after the first initial salvo of Cruise missiles hit Baghdad, there appeared to be little or no significant overt military activity for several days- leading to the conclusion that they, also, were unaware of any plan for such an attack at this time. The critics of course were correct in their assumption about the initial attack being unplanned as that was indeed the case. The effect of the first night's attack was to throw the military schedule out by a couple of days-but to the credit of the military planners, they rapidly improvised, adapted and overcame any problems that were created by the change in the initial Operational Plan (OPLAN) for Operation 'Iraqi Freedom'.

It transpired that President Bush had felt compelled to take the opportunity to strike at Saddam Hussein and his regime when he believed that they were vulnerable to attack - as his forty-eight hour ultimatum to get out of town or else was still within the deadline set, -fueling speculation that Saddam had been set up. Whatever the real reason behind the attack, it had no adverse effect on the military campaign overall and was probably, if anything, a blessing in disguise - as it also caught the Iraqis off- guard.

If Operation 'Iraqi Freedom' is to be judged in any way, it should be on the basis of how well it achieved its military objectives and nothing more. The reasons behind the war, and even the case built to justify it, are questions for the politicians to answer and not the miltary. As the old saying goes: 'Ours is not to

reason why, ours is but to do or die.' And from that point of view, Operation 'Iraqi Freedom' was a remarkable success. The only negative aspect being, that of failing to keep law and order in the towns and cities of Iraq, once the regime of Saddam Hussein had fallen. Yes, there are lessons to be learned - there always are - but these relate mainly to troop numbers deployed in theatre and not to their performance, which was nothing short of superb.

From the air campaign point of view, everything generally seemed to go to plan, with high sortie rates being achieved on a daily basis in support of the ground forces. However, unlike the first Gulf War where the air campaign dominated from the start and the ground campaign was a side-line activity, this time it was to be the other way around, as the ground forces were the main event, and the air forces the side show.

Yeager Airport, Maj. Kyle Adams, 130th Airlift Wing, returns home to his wife after spending five months supporting Operation 'Iraqi Freedom'. US Airforce photo by Senior Airman Bryan G. Stevens

What is remarkable about the air campaign fought over the skies of Iraq is this - for every three bombs dropped- two targets were destroyed, and the fact that over twenty-five per cent of all precision guided attacks were designated by only a handful of special forces operating covertly near the target areas- a remarkable feat.

However, surely the most fascinating aspect of this war must be that of target assignment methods- which were so slick that a tactical air planner could

Saddam's Airforce. A Russian built Foxbat fighter jet is unearthed in the Iraqi desert.

An Iraqi MIG-25 Foxbat is towed away for further inspection after being unearthed during an unsuccessful search for weapons of mass destruction.

> **'Ours is not to reason why, ours is but to do or die.'**

identify an enemy target, select a weapon suitable for its destruction, and then designate the nearest aircraft to it that had this type of weapon - and all within thirty seconds. Before it could take as long as eight hours to accomplish such a task- that's nothing short of amazing.

Offshore, the coalition warships did a sterling job protecting the supply ships and carriers as they went about their business of supporting the ground forces - a job they did extremely well.

However, one group of individuals who did much to make Operation 'Iraqi Freedom' a success- were those of the special forces, who accomplished so much with so little; their story has yet to be told.

Operation 'Iraqi Freedom' will be remembered for many things in years to come, but I hope that there is one thing that is never forgotten and that is the bravery and determination of the men and women of the coalition forces who did so much to give the Iraqi people back their freedom. Their part in this campaign must never be forgotten.

CHAPTER NINE

THE DIFFERENCE BETWEEN THE TWO GULF WARS

One of the most extraordinary military campaigns ever conducted, was how US Vice President Richard Cheney described Operation Iraqi Freedom when giving brief details of what led to success in Iraq.

The campaign that US and coalition forces launched on 19 March followed 'a carefully drawn plan with fixed objectives and the flexibility to meet them,' he said in a speech to the US Heritage Foundation in Washington. Vice-President Cheney noted that Operation 'Iraqi Freedom' displayed vastly improved capabilities over the first US led war in the Persian Gulf in 1991. In Operation Desert Storm, twenty per cent of the nation's air-to-ground fighters employed laser-guided bombs. In Operation 'Iraqi Freedom', all US air-to-ground fighters were capable of employing laser-guided bombs.

'As a result,' Mr Cheney said, *'with only two-thirds of the attack air-craft deployed in 'Desert Storm', we could strike twice as many targets.'*

Ground forces also employed improved combat power, he said. In Operation 'Desert Storm', US Marines had M-60 tanks. In Operation 'Iraqi Freedom', they had the Abrams M-1, equipped with a thermal sight and a 122-mm gun that *'increased their range by 50 per cent and enabled them to engage the enemy before they could even fire a single round.'*

He said that in Operation 'Desert Storm', Bradley armoured vehicle crews estimated the range of their targets, often missing on the first round. In Operation 'Iraqi Freedom', improved laser range finders enabled the crews to hit their targets with their first round. Only one type of unmanned aerial vehicle was available to locate enemy targets in the early 1990s, Mr Cheney continued. In 2003, there are ten types,

'ranging from a tactical system that would allow our soldiers to look over the next hill, to strategic systems that operate at 65,000 feet and

could provide images the size of Illinois.'

US forces have also dramatically improved their ability to use targeting photos, he continued, and command and control systems have become more flexible and effective. Where in the past only air component commanders had a near real-time picture of the air campaign, in Operation 'Iraq Freedom', all US component commanders shared a real-time computer display of coalition air, land and sea forces.

> *'These advances in command and control allowed us to integrate joint operations much more effectively than ever before, thereby enabling commanders to make decisions more rapidly, to target strikes more precisely, to minimize civilian casualties and to accomplish missions more successfully'.*

Operation 'Iraqi Freedom' was also conducted differently from 'Desert Storm', he noted, highlighting the expanded role of special operations forces. The 1991 war began with a thirty-eight-day air campaign, followed by a brief ground attack. This time, the ground war began before the air war. Unlike in 1991, when Saddam Hussein had time to set Kuwait's oilfields on fire, special

Satellite images such as these were vital to Coalition commanders in determining targets to be hit by both aircraft and cruise missiles. Once struck, the area would be revisited for post-strike battle damage assessment (BDA).

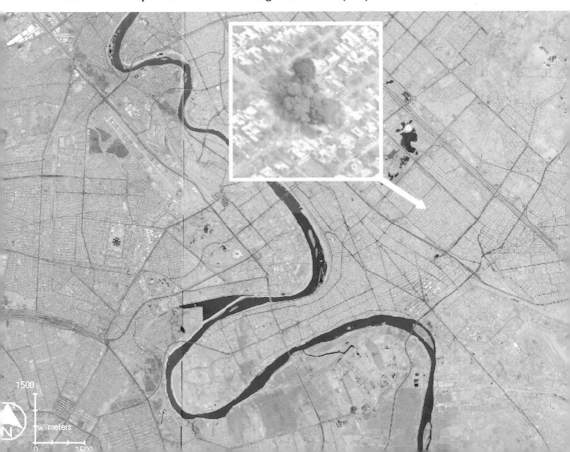

The result of Saddams scorched earth policy at the height of Operation 'Desert Storm'. Thanks to the efforts of Coalition Special Forces, there was no repeat of such instances in Operation 'Iraqi Freedom'.

Despite the best of efforts of the Patriot missile operators, some of Saddam's deadly arsenal of Surface to Surface missile, did penetrate the Coalition Air Defence Systems. Thankfully there was no serious casualties.

A member of the Australian SAS, poses for a night vision camera shot. Elite soldiers such as these, played a greater role in this war, than they did in 'Desert Storm', twelve years earlier.

operations forces went in early to protect 600 oil wells, to protect the environment and safeguard a vital resource for the Iraqi people. In Operation 'Desert Storm', Saddam's forces fired Scud missiles at Israel and Saudi Arabia. This time, special operations forces seized control and prevented missile launches.

'US, British, Australian and Polish special ops forces played a much more central role in the success of Operation 'Iraqi Freedom' than they did 12 years ago,' the vice President said. 'With less than half of the ground forces, and two-thirds of the air assets used 12 years ago in Operation 'Desert Storm', we have achieved a far more difficult objective in less time and with fewer casualties.'

CHAPTER TEN

FALLEN HEROES

On 14 April 2003, President Bush thanked the men and women of America's armed services for their sacrifices and patriotism during Operation Iraqi Freedom.

This is what he had to say:

'My fellow citizens: When freedom needs defending, America turns to our military. I want to thank those who wear our uniform. Thank you for your sacrifice. This nation has made another pledge: We will never forget the men and women who have fallen in service to America. We owe them our freedom. And we pray that their loved ones will receive God,s comfort and God's grace.

May God bless our country and all who defend her.'

Dedicated to the memory of those that fell during Operation 'Iraqi Freedom'.

The helmets, weapons and boots of the fallen soldierss of the 2nd Brigade Combat Team, 3rd Infantry Division. They stand in memory of the brave men who wore them in combat.

UNITED STATES

Army Capt. James F. Adamouski, 29
Navy Lt. Thomas Mullen Adams, 27
Army Spc. Jamaal R. Addison, 22
Army Capt. Tristan N. Aiken, 31
Marine Lance Cpl. Brian E. Anderson, 26
Marine Maj. Jay Thomas Aubin, 36
Marine Lance Cpl. Andrew Julian Aviles, 18
Marine Pfc. Chad E. Bales, 20
Marine Capt. Ryan Anthony Beaupre, 30
Army Pfc. Wilfred D. Bellard, 20
Marine Sgt. Michael E. Bitz, 31
Marine Lance Cpl. Thomas Blair, 24
Marine Gunnery Sgt. Jeffrey E. Bohr, 39
Army Staff Sgt. Stevon A. Booker, 34
Army Spc. Matthew G. Boule, 22
Army Cpl. Henry L. Brown, 22
Army Pvt. John E. Brown, 21
Army Spc. Larry K. Brown, 22
Marine Lance Cpl. Brian Rory Buesing, 20
Army Sgt. George Edward Buggs, 31
Marine Pfc. Tamario D. Bukett, 21
Army Sgt. Jacob L. Butler, 24
Marine Staff Sgt. James W. Cawley, 41
Marine Cpl. Kemaphoom A. Chanawongse, 22
Marine 2nd Lt. Therrel S. Childers, 30
Marine Lance Cpl. Donald J. Cline, Jr, 21
Marine Capt. Aaron J. Contreras, 31
Army Spc. Daniel Francis J. Cunningham, 33
Army Cpl. Michael Edward Curtin, 23
Air Force Capt. Eric B. Das, 30
Army Staff Sgt. Wilbert Davis, 40
Army 1st Sgt. Robert J. Dowdy, 38
Army Pvt. Ruben Estrella-Soto, 18
Marine Cpl. Mark A. Evnin, 21
Army Master Sgt. George A. Fernandez, 36
Army Spc. Thomas A. Foley III, 23
Marine Capt. Travis A. Ford, 30
Marine Lance Cpl. David K.Fribley, 26
Marine Cpl. Jose A. Garibay, 21
Marine Pfc. Juan Guadalupe Garza Jr, 20
Marine Pvt. Jonathan L. Gifford, 30

Marine Cpl. Armando Ariel Gonzalez, 25
Marine Cpl. Jesus A. Gonzalez, 22
Marine Cpl. Jorge A. Gonzalez, 20
Marine Cpl. Bernard G. Gooden, 22
Army Spc. Richard A. Goward, 32
Marine Pfc. Christian Daniel Gurtner, 19
Marine Lance Cpl. Jose Gutierrez, 28
Army Chief Warrant Officer Erik A. Halvorsen, 40
Army Staff Sgt. Terry W. Hemingway, 39
Marine Sgt. Nicolas M. Hodson, 22
Army Staff Sgt. Lincoln Hollinsaid, 27
Marine Pvt. Nolen R. Hutchings, 19
Army Pfc. Gregory P. Huxley Jr, 19
Army Chief Warrant Officer Scott Jamar, 22
Marine Cpl. Evan James, 20
Army Spc. William A. Jeffries, 39
Army Pfc. Howard Johnson II, 21
Navy Hospital Corpsman Third Class Michael Vann Johnson, 25
Army Pfc. Devon D. Jones, 19
Marine Staff Sgt. Phillip A. Jordan, 42
Army 2nd Lieutenant Jeffrey J. Kaylor, 24
Marine Cpl. Brian Matthew Kennedy, 25
Army Spc.James M. Kiehl, 22
Army Cpt. Edward J. Korn, 31
Marine Sgt. Bradley S. Korthaus, 28
Marine Sgt. Michael V. Lalush, 23
Army Staff Sgt. Nino D. Licaudais, 23
Army Spc. Ryan P. Long, 21
Marine Lance Cpl. Joseph B. Maglione, 22
Army Sgt. 1st Class John W. Marshall, 50
Marine Pfc. Francisco A. Martinez Flores, 21
Army CWO Johnny Villareal Mata, 35
Marine Staff Sgt. Donald C. May Jr, 31
Army Pfc. Joseph P. Mayek, 20
Marine Sgt. Brian D. McGinnia, 23
Marine 1st Lieutenant. Brian M. McPhillips, 25
Marine Cpl. Jesus Martin Antonio Medellin, 21
Marine Gunnery Sgt. Joseph, Menusa, 33
Army Spc. Gil Mercado, 25
Army Pfc.Jason M. Meyer, 23
Marine Cpl. Jason M. David Mileo, 20
Army Pfc. Anthony S. Miller, 19
Army Spc. George A. Mitchell, 35

Three captains assigned to 1st Brigade, 101st Airborne Division, comfort each other during the memorial service for Captain Christopher Seifert, Brigade S2 assistant, who was killed by a grenade, thrown during an incident involving a fellow member of the Division. US Army photo by Pfc James Matise

Marine Maj. Kevin G.Nave, 36
Marine Lance Cpl. Patricia R.Nixon, 21
Marine Lance Cpl. Patrick T.O'Day, 20
Donald Samuel Oaks Jr, 20
Marine Lance Cpl. Eric J. Orlowski, 26
Marine Lance Cpl. David Edward Owens Jr, 20
Marine Sgt. Fernando Padilla-Ramirez, 26
Army Sgt. Michael F. Pedersen, 26
Army Pfc. Lori Ann Piestewa, 23
Marine 2nd Lt. Frederick E.Pokorney Jr, 31
Army Pvt. Kelly S. Prewitt, 24
Army Sgt.1st Class Randall S.Rehn, 36
Marine Sgt. Brendon C.Reiss, 23
Army Pfc. Diego Fernando Rincon, 19
Marine Sgt. Duane R.Rios, 25
Army Cpt. Russell B. Rippetoe, 27

Army Cpl. John T.Rivero, 23
Army Sgt. Todd J.Robbins, 33
Marine Cpl. Robert M. Rodriguez, 21
Marine Cpl. Randal Kent Rosacker, 21
Army Spc. Brandon Rowe, 20
Marine Cpt. Benjamin Sammis, 21
Army Spc. Gregory P.Sanders, 19
Air Force Staff Sgt. Scott D.Sather, 29
Army Cpt. Christopher Scott Seifert, 27
Marine Cpl. Erik H.Silva, 22
Army Pvt. Brandon Ulysses Sloan, 19
Marine Lance Cpl.Thomas J.Slocum, 22
Army Chief Warrant Officer. Eric A. Smith, 42
Army Sgt. 1st Class Paul R.Smith, 33
Marine 1st Sgt. Edward Smith, 38
Army Sgt. Roderic A.Solomon, 32
Army Staff Sgt. Robert A.Stever, 36
Air Nationl Guard Maj. Gregory Stone, 40
Marine Lance Cpl. Jesus A. Suarez Del Solar, 20
Marine Staff Sgt. Riayan A. Tejeda, 26
Army Spc. Brandon S. Tobler, 19
Army Sgt. Donald Ralph Walters, 33

A US Air Force Honor Guard at Arlington National Cemetery, provides an escort for the casket of Major Gregory Stone, the first Air Force casualty during Operation 'Iraqi Freedom'.

Marine Staff Sgt. Kendall Damon Waters-Bey, 29
Army Pfc. Michael Russell Creighton Weldon, 20
Navy Lieutenant Nathan D. White, 30
Marine Lance Cpl. William W. White, 24
Army Sgt. Eugene Williams, 24
Marine Lance Cpl. Michael J.Williams, 31

MISSING IN ACTION

Sgt. Edward J. Anguiano, 24

GREAT BRITAIN

Cpl. Stephen Allbutt, 35
Sapper Luke Allsop, 24
Lance Cpl. Shaun Andrew Brierley, 29
Colour Sgt. John Cecil
Trooper David Clarke, 19
Staff Sgt. Simon Cullingworth, 36
Lance Bombardier Llewelyn Evans
Lt. Philip Green, 31
Capt. Philip Stuart Guy, 29
Marine Sholto Hedenskog
Sgt. Les Hehir, 34
Lance Cpl. Matty Hull, 25
Lt. Anthony King, 35
Lt. Marc Lawrence, 25
Marine Christopher Maddison
Flight Lt. Kevin Barry Main
Lance Cpl. Ian Malone, 28
Staff Sgt. Chris Muir, 32
Piper Christopher Muzvuru, 21
Sgt. Steven Mark Roberts, 33
Flight Lt. David Rhys Williams
Mechanic 2nd Class Ian Seymour
Lance Cpl. Karl Shearer, 24
Lance Cpl. Barry Stephen, 31
Warrant Officer 2nd Class Mark Stratford, 39
Fusilier Kelan John Turrington, 18
Maj.Jason Ward, 34
Lt. Philip West, 32
Lt.James williams, 28
Lt.Andrew Wilson, 36

JOURNALISTS WHO LOST THEIR LIVES DURING OPERATION IRAQI FREEDOM

David Bloom, 39
Michael Kelly, 46
Kaveh Golestan, 52
Paul Moran, 39
Terry Lloyd, 50
Tariq Ayoub, 34
Christian Liebeg, 35
Julio Anuita Parrado, 32
Mario Podesta, 51
Veronica Cabrera, 28
Taras Protsyuk
Jose Couso, 37
Kamaran Abdurazak Muhamed, 25
Gaby Rado, 48

PRAISE FROM THE PRESIDENT

Major combat operations in Iraq are over, and America and her allies have prevailed, President Bush announced on the evening of 1 May 2003.

'In this battle we have fought for the cause of liberty and for the peace of the world. Our nation and our coalition are proud of this accomplishment,'

President Bush said this aboard the aircraft carrier USS *Abraham Lincoln* as she neared her homeport of San Diego-having spent ten months at sea. She arrived the following day to a hero's welcome.

'Yet it is you, the members of the United States military, who achieved it. Your courage, your willingness to face danger for your country and for each other made this day possible' said President Bush.

He also thanked coalition countries, particularly Britain, Australia and Poland, who all contributed military forces-and the Iraqi people who welcomed American troops.

The President then compared the current conflict to the terrible battles of the Second World War that destroyed entire cities, while leaving the tyrants who started the fighting unharmed.

'Today we have the greater power to free a nation by breaking a dangerous and aggressive regime. With new tactics and precision weapons, we can achieve military objectives without directing violence against civilians.'

President Bush linked the battle of Iraq to the broader war on terrorism, calling it part of a larger war that had begun on 11 September 2001.

President George W. Bush walks across the tarmac with NFO Lieutenant Ryan Phillips to Navy One, an S-3B Viking jet, at Naval Air Station North Island in San Diego 1 May. The President was soon to address the nation, aboard the USS *Abraham Lincoln*.

The President poses with flight deck crew of the USS *Abraham Lincoln*.

'That terrible morning, nineteen evil men, the shock troops of a hateful ideology, gave America and the civilized world a glimpse of their ambitions,' President Bush said, 'By seeking to turn our cities into killing fields, terrorists and their allies believed they could destroy this nation's resolve and force our retreat from the world. They have failed,' he stated.

The President did not forget the many service members who died in Iraq. 'Every name, every life is a loss to our military, to our nation, and to our loved ones who grieve. There's no homecoming for these families,' President Bush said.

POST WAR IRAQ

It would be a wonderful thing if I could write about a new Iraq that is peaceful, prosperous and united, but sadly that is not the case.

Since Saddam's demise, there has been widespread looting, civil disorder and anarchy on a scale never before seen in Iraq, prompting some to demand the return of Saddam. Nobody ever said that it was going to be an easy task to govern Iraq after decades of tyrannical dictatorship, but nobody ever said that it was going to be this hard either.

There are people in Iraq who are, indeed, glad to see both British and American soldiers on their streets, but conversely, there are also many who are not. What has not been understood by many in the West, is the fact that just because an Iraqi hates Saddam, it does not always follow that he will welcome outsiders who appear to be taking his place. Iraq has many different tribes and ethnic groups, who find it hard enough to live with each other, let alone a foreign stranger. As an Iraqi friend of mine said recently, after returning from Baghdad, following thirty-one years of absence.

'How can we expect the West to understand us, when we now no longer understand ourselves. We have become a nation of nomads.'

Under Saddam, Iraq lived within a political strait-jacket that kept order by means of fear, violence and death. But now that it's been removed, all the latent ethnic and tribal rivalries that have been subdued for so long, are now free to surface, and the results are not pretty. At the time of writing this book, and only two months after Operation 'Iraqi Freedom' officially ended, twenty-five American soldiers have been killed, and a further 182 wounded trying to keep the peace in northern Iraq, while in the south, six British soldiers have been killed and nine wounded, indicating that it is clearly going to be a long and costly peace keeping operation for all concerned.

There have been many pessimists in the United States, that have already compared Iraq with Vietnam, but that is an unfair comparison, as Iraq was invaded by America, while in Vietnam they were invited in by the official government of the day.

A better comparison would be Northern Ireland, as it too has ethnic divisions and a long history of problems associated with them. Further more, both the Irish and the Iraqis now view their liberators as an occupying force, and yet in both cases, the intentions of the troops concerned and indeed those of their respective governments, were completely honourable.

However, perception is everything, as it only takes a small minority with a grudge to convince the majority that all is not well, and once that happens, you have one hell of a job turning the clock back.

Before the war started, we were all told that the Iraqis would welcome our troops in the streets as their liberators, if not their saviours, but that was wishful thinking and simply did not happen in most towns and cities, as there was just too much distrust and apprehension amongst the Iraqi people. In the case of the British, who have vastly more peacekeeping experience than their American allies, particularly in urban operations, their tactic was to adopt a soft approach during foot patrols, by way of wearing berets instead of helmets and making lots of eye contact with the locals, while that of the Americans was to adopt a detached drive-by approach where there is little or no direct contact with the locals. To be fair to the American forces, they have the harder job by far, as their area of responsibility is infinitely more difficult to police on account of heavy resistance from former members of Saddam's regime still active in the area.

For the both the British and the Americans, life is not going to get any easier in the short term either, considering the fact that in Northern Ireland, Britain, with all its overwhelming military superiority, and the support of the vast majority of the people, could only achieve a stalemate against the IRA terrorists, whereas in Iraq, the situation is considerably worse, and is deteriorating further by the day. What certainly does not help is this. There is no government in Iraq, save for an American-led administration that seems to lurch from crisis to crisis on a daily basis, as the first American viceroy, who was a retired general, simply could not cope and was withdrawn just after one week in office.

With the promise of democracy now slipping away, the best that can be hoped for is that local religious and community leaders band together to help the coalition forces, as the other alternatives just don't bear thinking about.

Also not helping matters, is the fact that most people in Iraq believe that Saddam is still alive, and that he will return to power one day. This perception is fully understandable, as many of us in the West also believe that he is still alive, and that peace and stability will only be possible in Iraq, when he is found, be it dead or alive, with the former option being the more preferable of the two.

Meanwhile, the lives of ordinary Iraqi people are being torn apart by fear and insecurity, and lack of social amenities such as electricity, education, medical care and work, creating a fertile environment for insurection.

The original plan for post-war Iraq, involved the use of the Iraqi army as a proxy force, but when the Americans disbanded the army without pay, they simply went home with their weapons and, of course, much resentment at how they had been treated by the Americans. The irony is that many of them rejoiced at Saddam's demise, but now may well take up arms against their liberators. It is also ominous, that the Shi'ites, who once hated Saddam so much that they tried to overthrow him after the last Gulf War, are now turning on the very people that have just freed them from decades of oppression.

Peacekeeping and nation-building are difficult jobs at the best of times, as we have witnessed in both Northern Ireland and Afghanistan, but yet we must prevail. As Donald Rumsfeld, the American Defence Secretary said of nation-building: *'It is like setting bones, if you get it wrong, the result will be crooked.'*

In a desperate bid to bring about peace in Iraq, America has offered a reward of $25,000,000 for information leading to the capture of Saddam Hussein, with $15,000,000 each for his two sons. Although a welcome step in the right direction, much more work needs to be done in respect of winning the hearts and minds of the Iraqi people, as they need to be convinced that America is in their country for their benefit and not its own. Also, there may well be a role to play for the United Nations in Iraq, as they could act as an honest and impartial broker for peace, if only given the opportunity. Either way, something needs to change in Iraq and soon, as America's sons and daughters will be shedding their blood, for the sins of their fathers, for decades to come.

Airborne Infantrymen clear a small farmhouse in Baghdad. The paratroopers were working with local police to locate rocket-propelled grenades suspected of being on the property. Photo by Spc. Jason B. Baker

Ex-Iraqi army officers demand pay in a peaceful demonstration outside a government building occupied by the US Army. Photo by Army Pfc. Mary Rose Xenikakis

A British Army MP along with an Iraqi police man, seen here wearing a red arm band, patrol a market place as part of a hearts and minds operation mounted to reassure the local population.

A member of the 870th Military Police Company from Pittsburgh, Calif, mans his Squad Automatic Weapon on top of an armoured Hummvee, damaged by a mob in Karbala, Iraq.

THE POST-WAR TOLL

During Operation 'Iraqi Freedom', 140 US and thirty-two British service personnel were killed in the course of their duties. However, since 1 May, when President Bush proclaimed victory, the following losses have been sustained: Fifty-two American's killed; twenty-four as a result of hostile action. Ten British fatalities, six of which were the result of hostile fire.

They occured as follows:

4 May: A US soldier is shot dead while directing traffic.

26 May: One US soldier is killed and three wounded by a landmine in one incident, while one US soldier is killed and another wounded during a convoy ambush in northern Iraq.

27 May: Two US soldiers are killed, and nine wounded, following a rocket-propelled grenade (RPG) attack on a Bradley fighting vehicle.

5 June: One US soldier is killed, and five wounded in Fallujah, following an RPG attack.

7 June: One US soldier is killed, and four wounded near Tikrit, following an attack that involved both RPGs and small arms fire.

9 June: One US soldier is killed at a checkpoint in al-Qaim, after being asked to help a 'sick' person in a car.

10 June: One US paratrooper is killed, and one other wounded following an RPG attack.

19 June: One US soldier is killed, and two others are injured, following an RPG attack on an American military ambulance.

24 June: Six British military police are murdered in an Iraqi police station in Majar al-Kabir in one incident, while eight other British soldiers are wounded during another incident in the same town, while performing a rescue mission.

26 June: Two US soldiers are abducted in Baghdad,and later found dead-while in other separate incidents in the city, two US soldiers are killed and eight others wounded.

27 June: One US soldier is shot in the neck, and three others are injured, following two separate vehicle attacks.

28 June: One US soldier is killed, and four others are wounded, following a grenade attack on their convoy in Baghdad.

At present, US forces operating in Iraq are being attacked on average seventeen times per day, with a casualty rate of one soldier per day. However, the Pentagon dismisses these attacks as being nothing more than 'mere flea bites'. We shall no doubt see in due course, how the American public views these attacks.

FINAL THOUGHTS FROM THE AUTHOR

Warfare poses a dilema for us. On the one hand we abhor it, but on the other we are fascinated by it. In a world where modern warfare can be beamed into our living rooms via the television, we can literally see battles take place in front of our eyes as they are happening, and for those with a strong appetite for war and all of its associated horrors, there are the twenty-four hour news networks across the world to satisfy their needs.

Is it such a good thing to see naked warfare infront of our eyes? I will leave that decision to you. I, however, take the view that we should see it, and we should be horrified by it, so that we do everything conceivably possible to avoid it, as war should always be the last option, and not the first.

In our modern day world, we face numerous threats, and they are serious ones. They are, however, not the same as before. In the old days of the Cold War, life for the military strategist was relatively easy as his potential adversary was well-known and well planned for.

Today's enemy wears a different face, and fights a different type of war. There is no set template, and there is no set method of fighting, as no two wars are alike. The enemy today is primarily terrorism, be it from individual groups, regimes or, in some cases, even state sponsored.

Our world today is built on shifting sands, and we need to have armed forces that are trained and equipped to fight anywhere in the world at very short notice. They must be flexible enough to adapt to the very high demands of modern asymetric warfare and yet be equally as good at the role of peacekeeping, never forgetting that a soldier is trained first and foremost to kill.

As new miliary tactics, techniques and procedures are developed for the battlefield of the future, others are consigned to the pages of history, some forever. The days of linear warfare may long be gone, but certain legacies of this period have made a come-back, albeit temporarily. Who would have thought that in this day and age of high-tech warfare we would see a good old fashioned siege, but it happened in Basra, and Baghdad during the Second Gulf War. The military. however, hate the word siege, as it implies an exhaustion of tactical options. Instead they prefer the term, containment, as it sounds softer and less dramatic.

It is fair to say that of all the realms of human activity, warfare is probably the most likely to confound the promises and predictions of the armchair generals, and their cronies. In the old days, tactical planners and generals tended to plan their next campaign with the tactics and techniques from the previous conflict. However in today's world we use super-sophisticated computer modelling to plan our operations, but often neglect or overlook the lessons of the past.

Wars tend to work in cycles, with no two being the same. However, occasionally, an echo from the past can be seen again, with the feeling that we have been here before but in another time and place. The lesson is that military plans seldom proceed in a straight line, and indeed rarely survive first contact with the enemy. Although, history never repeats itself, there are however interesting and curious loops, in which patterns and trends appear to revert back to a bygone age.

There are many paradoxes in warfare. After the end of the First Gulf War in 1991, they declared the tank, the king of land warfare. Yet barely nine years later in Kosovo, they declared it obsolete on account of its inability to cross many of the country's small rural bridges which were never designed in the first place to take the weight of a motor vehicle, let alone a tank.

Then amazingly, during the Second Gulf War, our television screens were filled with the impressive sight of massive US Abram tank formations charging through the deserts of Iraq on their way to Baghdad. As if to reinforce this point even further, the British fought their biggest tank battle since the Second World War, just outside the Iraqi city of Basra, where in this single action, they defeated a much larger force of armour by means of their impressive Challenger 2 Tanks, which performed superbly. Of interest is the fact that despite the success of the tank in this conflict, neither the British or the Americans have any current plans for a new Main Battle Tank (MBT). This is somewhat surprising since the British Challenger 2 tank proved to be virtually indestructable during this war, with only one documented loss, that being as a consequence of a friendly fire incident involving ironically, another Challenger.

The king of land warfare. An M1A1 Abrams tank, dwarfs it's crew members with it's immense size.

The tank played a vital role in winning the war in Iraq. Here a convoy of Abrams move carefully through the streets of Baghdad.

A US infantry soldier along with a Bradley Fighting Vehicle, provide security around Yarmuk Hospital. Patrolling in urban areas is a very dangerous business which has claimed the lives of many Coalition soldiers.

In the air, things were even more bizarre. Take the mighty B-52 for instance, a product born and bred during the Cold War, yet still going strong. It fought as well as any modern bomber during the Second Gulf War, which is a remarkable feat considering the fact that in most cases the B-52 is older than its pilots, some even believe that it will be the first military platform to celebrate a centenary of operational service, that is impressive.

Man has never been content with anything for long, and in the world of modern warfare that is still the case. However, does it really make sense to have highly intelligent computer whizz- kids designing high-tech equipment for infantry soldiers whose average mental age is only that of a fourteen year old, when most of them have never seen combat or indeed military service. I mention this point because on a number of occasions during this conflict incidents occured where high-tech equipment went horribly wrong, be it through operator error or malfunction, leaving many people dead as a consequence. The lesson clearly needs to be learned.

We are also becoming ever more dependent on intelligence for the planning of military operations, often placing our fate and indeed of our countrymen in the lap of computers, sensors and satellites. As good as they are, they cannot beat the MK 1 eyeball on the ground, as that is still the best, and most reliable, way of gaining intelligence; hence the extensive use of special forces during Operation Iraqi Freedom. In the old days of the British Empire for example, intelligence was given to the military by means of local agents, who fed their masters with rumours, facts and local gossip about current affairs within their region. Although it was a crude system, it worked and it got results as nothing was ever ignored. Today, however, the paucity of human intelligence (Humint) constitutes a dangerous defect as the emphasis is now on satellite intelligence (Satint) and Signals intelligence (Sigint) from intercepted radio, and mobile phones. Today the problem is that we have too much intelligence. So much so, in fact, that we simply cannot process it quick enough, and when we do, by the time that information is acted on it is often too late, as the enemy has fled or even worse still has inflicted damage to our own forces.

The ending of the Cold War brought about an initial euphoria within the military, as they felt that they could now reorganize for a new world order that they perceived would be more calm and peaceful following the collapse of the Soviet Union. However, they were wrong as very few people appreciated the fact that in essence the Cold War served as something of a global straitjacket, and once removed it allowed old ethnic and tribal differences to resurface; hence the source of most of our present day troubles, including those of Iraq, as Saddam effectively kept Iraq under control by means of fear, intimidation, violence and death.

In our new politically correct world, we are now trying to fight politically correct wars. These entail no civilian casualties, no collateral damage, no friendly forces casualties and minimum enemy casualties. It sounds wonderful in theory, but the reality of such warfare is still some way off, as witnessed in Iraq, during Operation 'Iraqi Freedom'. Politically correct warfare does not sit well with the military as they like to do things their own way, for better or worse. Things however do change within the military, albeit at a slower pace. You only have to look at the issue of women in the armed forces to see how things are changing for the better.

In terms of military equipment, the soldier of today is better trained and equipped than ever before. The days of dragging a soldier off the street, giving him two weeks training and then sending him off to war have long gone, at least in the West that is. Today's soldier requires months of intensive training, and that's just to reach a basic level of military competence. Military training is becoming more and more realistic, and although it gives a soldier a good practical preparation for what is to come, it cannot give combat experience, only war can do that and, for many, Iraq was their first blood.

We live in a society where we expect all the bad guys to become casualties in an action , yet we should sustain little or none. This is totally unrealistic, yet we expect it. There is no doubt that the level of casualties sustained in modern warfare is dropping, and that can only be good news, but the days of a bloodless war are frankly a long, long way off.

In Operation 'Iraqi Freedom', we saw a marked increase in the use of unmanned aircraft, namely those of reconnaissance UAV's (Unmanned Air Vehicles), but the case for manned aircraft is still as valid as ever, as you cannot at present beat having a man in the loop.

One tragic aspect of this war, and indeed one of many fought before, is the curse of friendly fire. A painful reminder of our vulnerability in combat if ever there was one, made only worse by the fact that the loss of a friend is hard enough to bear when it is from that of an enemy, but is impossible to bear when it is caused by a friend.

It should be remembered, that America went to war with Iraq, as part of a global strategy to eradicate terrorism around the world-with Iraq being just one of many countries on the so-called axis of evil list, a register of regimes, dictators and despots that has been compiled by President Bush's neo-conservatives, and one through which America is slowly working its way through.

However, there is a fundamental problem with this strategy, and it is this: Operation 'Iraqi Freedom' may be over, but the war with Iraq is far from over, and we open another front elsewhere at our peril, as we may not be able to put the next genie of evil back into its bottle.

FINAL THOUGHTS FROM 'COMICAL ALI.'

And, whatever became of our friend 'Comical Ali' I hear you say? Well, just after he went on his unplanned stint of indefinite administrative leave, rumours started to circulate within Iraq, that he had hanged himself under a bridge near the Iranian border. Thankfully that rumour was untrue.

As speculation among his many fans and admirers around the world began to mount as to his current whereabouts; news came through from US Intelligence that he had been found living in his cousin's house in Baghdad, and was currently helping the USA with its enquiries. Days later he appeared in a television interview, having undergone his interrogation, but a shock awaited everybody as he was now totally grey and had visibly aged by some twenty years. He was also now very thin, and spoke with a quiet hoarse voice. It was hard to believe looking at him, that he once held the world's attention on a daily basis, as he enlightened us with his interesting, but somewhat bizarre thoughts on the war, and indeed the way in which he perceived it was going. It transpired, that he totally believed in everything that he said, and that all his information was based upon daily intelligence reports received from the Iraqi army. His last classic thought was this:

'The information that I received from the Iraqi army on a daily basis was correct. However my interpretation of it was not.'

This has to be the under-statement of the century.

To his credit, he was the last Iraqi minister to leave his post, fleeing his position only as US tanks arrived in front of his podium. However, he may well have the last laugh on us, as he has since become a global celebrity, with his own web-site, merchandizing and now, it seems, his own television programme, which is aired in the Middle East. But most interesting of all, he is currently writing a book about his life and his experiences, a best seller no doubt!

ABBREVIATIONS

AAA Anti-aircraft artillery
ABG Armoured Battle Group
ADV Air Defence Variant
AFV Armoured Fighting Vehicle
APC Armoured Personnel Carrier
AWACS Airborne Warning and Control System
C2 Command and Control
C4I Command, Control, Communications, Computers and Intelligence
CAS Close Air Support
CALCM Conventionally Armed Air Launched Cruise Missiles
CIA Central Intelligence Agency
CSAR Combat Search and Rescue
CV(F) Carrier Vessel Fleet
DoD Department of Defense
FCS Future Combat System
IR Infrared
LCAC Landing Craft Air Cushion
LPH Landing Platform Helicopter
MBT Main Battle Tank
MLRS Multiple Launch Rocket System
MOD Ministry of Defence
NATO North Atlantic Treaty Organization
SAR Synthetic Aperature Radar
SAS Special Air Service
SAM Surface-to Air-Missile
SBS Special Boat Service
SEAD Suppression of Enemy Air Defences
SF Special Forces
SOCOM Special Operations Command
SOG Special Operations Group
STOVL Short Take-Off and Vertical Landing
UAV Unmanned Air Vehicle
UCAV Unmanned Combat Air Vehicle
UN United Nations
WMD Weapons Mass Destruction
UN United Nations
WMD Weapons of Mass Destruction

INDEX